# PRAISE FOR RICK BRAGG:

———

"It is hard to think of a writer who reminds us more forcefully and wonderfully of what people and families are all about."

### –THE NEW YORK TIMES

"As toothsome as a catfish supper. [Bragg] is every bit the equal of . . . Harper Lee and Truman Capote."

### –PEOPLE

"Earthy, mischievous, yet gorgeous . . . [Bragg's] tales . . . would not be out of place if they were told around a campfire."

### –SAN FRANCISCO CHRONICLE

"Bragg captures the rhythms of small-town life with grace and pathos."

### –CHICAGO TRIBUNE

"[Bragg has] a true gift for great storytelling, the kind . . . that makes you think it's just a plain old story, until he gets to the end and you're either weeping or covered with goosebumps."

### –NEW ORLEANS TIMES-PICAYUNE

"Bragg tells about the South with such power and bone-naked love . . . he will make you cry."

### –ATLANTA JOURNAL-CONSTITUTION

# MY SOUTHERN JOURNEY

## TRUE STORIES FROM THE HEART OF THE SOUTH

### WITH A NEW INTRODUCTION

## RICK BRAGG

Oxmoor House®

©2018 Time Inc. Books

Published by Oxmoor House,
an imprint of Time Inc. Books,
a division of Meredith Corporation
225 Liberty Street
New York, NY 10281

ISBN-13: 978-0-8487-5746-5
Library of Congress Control Number:
2015936802

Printed in the United States of America
First Edition 2018
10 9 8 7 6 5 4 3 2 1

Executive Editor: Katherine Cobbs
Senior Editor: Erica Sanders
Project Editors: Lacie Pinyan,
 Sarah Waller
Design Director: Melissa Clark
Designer: Maribeth Jones
Assistant Production Director:
 Sue Chodakiewicz
Assistant Production Manager:
 Diane Rose Keener
Cut Paper Artist: Annie Howe
Copy Editor: Susan Alison
Proofreader: Julie Gillis
Indexers: Mary Ann Laurens,
 *Marra*thon Production Services
Fellows: Nicole Fisher, Anna Moe

We welcome your comments and
suggestions about Time Inc. Books.
Time Inc. Books
Attention: Book Editors
P.O. Box 62310
Tampa, Florida 33662-2310

Time Inc. Books products may be
purchased for business or promotional
use. For information on bulk purchases,
please contact Christi Crowley in
the Special Sales Department at
(845) 895-9858.

**Essay Credits:**
· pg. 54: *GQ*, May 2002, "For a Vegetable,
 I'll Have White Gravy"
· pg. 60: *Bon Appetit*, November 2004,
 "Back to the Bayou"
· pg. 70: *Garden & Gun*, February/March 2010,
 "Your First Oyster"—© 2010 Rick Bragg, as first
 published in *Garden & Gun*
· pg. 84: *Louisiana Kitchen*, June 2012,
 "Magic on the Plate"
· pg. 96: *Garden & Gun*, August/September, 2014,
 "Requiem for a Fish Sandwich"—© 2014 Rick
 Bragg, as first published in *Garden & Gun*
· pg. 138: *Smithsonian*, June 2009, "My Kind of
 Town, Fairhope, Alabama"—From SMITHSONIAN
 Magazine, June 2009
· pg. 142: *Garden & Gun*, August/September, 2010,
 "The Lost Gulf"—© 2010 Rick Bragg, as first
 published in *Garden & Gun*

· pg. 164: *Long Leaf Style*, Summer 2008,
 "Why I Write About Home"
· pg. 178: *GQ*, June 2002, "Wood, Paint, Nails,
 and Soul"
· pg. 198: *ESPN The Magazine*, August 2012, "Down
 Here"—© 2012, *ESPN The Magazine*. Reprinted
 courtesy of ESPN
· pg. 224: *Best Life*, September 2005,
 "A Cast of Characters"
· pg. 230: *Sports Illustrated*, August 2007 "Nick of
 Time"—© *Sports Illustrated*, August 2007
· pg. 242: *ESPN The Magazine*, January 2014,
 "Last Weekend"—© 2014, *ESPN The
 Magazine*. Reprinted courtesy of ESPN
· pg. 246: *Sports Ilustrated*, April 2004 "Long Time
 Coming"—© *Sports Illustrated*, April 2004

*\* Disclaimer: Some essays have been edited slightly by the author since their original publication.*

*For my Aunt Juanita and my Aunt Jo*
*and*
*to the memory of my Aunt Edna and my Aunt Sue*

# CONTENTS

# II. TABLE / 53

# III. PLACE / 103

# IV. CRAFT / 163

# V. SPIRIT / 197

# CONTENTS

# INTRODUCTION

The first time I really thought much about who I was—who I was as a Southerner, I mean—I was high up in a snowy place, on the warm side of a cold, grimy window, and as homesick as I had ever been. What had come over me, to make me lug my one suitcase through LaGuardia only to queue up, shivering, in a taxi line without a discernable end, with not one scarf, wool hat, or pair of long johns to my name? But I was a young man then, and young men from Alabama will jump off a barn roof—or move to New York City in the middle of January without so much as a topcoat—just to see what happens next.

Down below, under a billion watts of flashing bulbs, red-faced people thronged the Theater District, some out for a night in the big city, others, real New Yorkers, hurried on their way to the subway tunnels, and home. It seems like I could see the Winter Garden Theatre down there, somewhere, but it may have been something else. I find it hard to remember some things from that time clearly, in the same way it is hard to walk down Broadway in a straight line.

I do recall it was the winter of 1994, the most forlorn in years. It seemed like mountains of smutty snow were shoved into vacant lots, to melt. But nothing melts at 23 degrees. The worst of it was the unnatural way the neon—ten thousand miles of it—lit the cold. Cold should be dark, not shining and flashing and glowing, like the light was still on inside the closed refrigerator door.

From where I stood, the city seemed to disregard winter altogether. The yellow cabs slid by on streets slick with a glittering glaze of dirty white, and the throngs on the sidewalks just trudged onward, slipping but not falling, as if holding each other up by their very belligerence. The truth is, if one of them had slipped, I am not sure there was room for them to fall altogether down; they would have just been carried along, all the way to 52nd Street. It was different back home; there was space around the cold. I remember skating across a parking lot in Atlanta after an ice storm, and had no trouble whatsoever finding a place to fall ... twice.

I had been cold before. The previous year, in an unreasonable, unnecessary winter in Cambridge, Massachusetts, the snow plows covered the cars parked at the side of the streets. The cold seemed to have a steel edge to it. Normal people, I remember thinking, were not intended for such as this. Woolly mammoths, maybe, or Minnesotans.

But there was something about New York cold, a Manhattan winter, that seemed to stab a little deeper into the Southern soul ... or maybe the romantic in me just wanted that to be true; maybe I just needed thicker socks.

––––––––

I blame California. I had been living in Los Angeles just a month or so before—not for long, but long enough to get good and warm. Now I was just one more nitwit in earmuffs, necktie flapping in the north wind, purporting to be a writer on the island of Manhattan, but really just one more poor fool staring from the meager warmth of a Gray's Papaya, more pitiful than picturesque. There was much to admire here, and it would change my life. But that night, it kind of broke my heart.

There was no room or time to mosey, to dawdle. No one came up here to piddle, or loafer. Even the drunks, it seemed, had somewhere to be. People said that about the place; no one came up here unless they wanted something from it. But what I would have given, right then, for one old man leaning on a street lamp or sitting on a bench, digging in his coat pocket for a Case knife, or a Zippo lighter, or a stick of Juicy Fruit. What I would have given for one old woman, saltshaker in her apron pocket, in the middle of a backyard garden, or an ancient iron streetcar clanking down St. Charles Avenue, or one more dinner on the ground, fried chicken sweating in Tupperware, deviled eggs under wax paper, and pineapple pudding under glass.

Still, I had always believed I was a tough man, tough enough to be a damn writer in the big city anyway, and not to be knocked down by something as silly as puny nostalgia. So I went to heal myself. I put on enough clothes to smother myself and teetered and staggered bravely to the curb, where a yellow cab mercifully crunched to a stop. It took two full minutes to wedge myself into the back seat, which had the legroom of a Hot Wheels car. Slush melted and pooled in the floorboard.

"Uptown," I said. "Harlem."

"I don't go that far," the driver said.

I waved a twenty. In New York, this is like showing someone a shiny new penny.

But I refused to get out, and we went to a place the cold could not reach.

I remember the rush of warm air as I walked in the door of the restaurant, a famous old place, the opposite of cool, of avant-garde. There was a row of thick, heavy glass domes on the front counter, sheltering a line of cake plates. There was red velvet cake, and a caramel. The air smelled of baking cornbread, and sage. I had a plate of stewed turkey wing, cornbread dressing, green beans, and baked macaroni and cheese. The fatty meat of the wing, so tender it slipped off the bone, looked like it had come from the biggest turkey in the world. I did not have any caramel cake, but as I walked out I almost—almost— asked the nice lady at the counter if she would lift the glass dome off the cake plate for just a second or two, so I could smell it. It cost a lot more than I would have paid in Montgomery, or Macon, but it cost a lot less than it was worth then. The place was called Sylvia's; I ate there three days a week.

Earlier that day, in a Times Square deli, I had paid $20 for a chicken salad sandwich, and a pickle. I would have eaten in Harlem every day if I had not had to threaten the cab drivers.

I took a livery cab back, where the doorman greeted me warmly. He always smiled at my accent, and always said everything very slowly so I would be able to understand. I rode the elevator with a woman who would not make eye contact, and a bony, wormy, twitchy dog.

I closed the door, and put Hank Williams, His Greatest Hits on the $20 CD player I had paid $200 for in Times Square, and listened to him sing about little boys who called another man Daddy, and wooden Indians, and hot rod Fords, and distant trains. And I slouched there, in that cramped and dingy Midtown Manhattan apartment, and I let Hank do what Hank has always done for my people: He spread out the pain and loneliness of this world wide and thin enough so that we could stand it, so that, instead of pressing down on one poor fool so much, it covered us all, as one.

> *A woman will give you the blues*
> *She'll have you pullin' out your hair, and wearin' out your walkin' shoes*

It would be nice to say I dreamed of home, or that the ghost of Thomas Wolfe came to me in the night and whispered drunkenly in my ear, and I wrote great words on my old Underwood until my soul was smooth. The truth is I cannot recall what I dreamed, only that when I awakened in the middle of the night it was warm, and maybe a little humid, as if it were the Gulf of Mexico out there, or the pine barrens, as if the clogged streets had run into some red dirt pulpwood road, as if, outside, the outside, the street vendors were hawking not soft pretzels and hotdogs from their carts but boiled peanuts, fat watermelon, and cantaloupe from the tailgate of some battered truck. But I am a Southerner, and it is our prerogative, being us, to remember things the way we damn well please.

---

I am sometimes asked, especially when I am north of the Ohio River, what the word Southern really implies. The well-meaning Northerners, often fresh from fishing in a hole augered through the ice of some Great Lake, are not asking about geography, about where the South begins, which is in itself increasingly hard to say. They want to know what being Southern is.

They have heard far too many pointy-headed little fellows in bow ties and seersucker suits, fresh from a Faulkner convention at Ole Miss, tell them that the word Southern is merely a state of mind. That might be a little too cryptic for the more literal-minded people of the North, though I guess it all amounts to the same thing, in the end.

I think it's stewed turkey wing, north of 125th Street. I think it's slow brown rivers that move a hundred miles without a sound. I think it's steel guitar, and old men, their voices tortured by Camels and cheap whiskey, singing "Rollin' in my sweet baby's arms..." I think it's a patch of red dirt, freshly turned, behind every single house on every single street in town, and trays of tomato plants reaching for the sun through the back window of a Pontiac that will never run again, but makes an excellent greenhouse just the same.

The one thing I know is that being Southern is not being warm. It is in knowing how to get that way.

———

This book, cover to cover, is perhaps a romantic rendition of a place and a people and the things we hold dear; it is a book about the best of us, our food and music and traditions, about the softer side of who we are. Its stories were written, many of them, from pure nostalgia, which is, I have been told, not pure and perfect memory but what memory would have been, if it had been remembered right.

I have always loved the way a writer for a Southern newspaper described a venerable old reporter who began his career in the days when a manual typewriter was considered a marvel of technology: "He might not be able to tell you how things are, but he can tell you how they used to be." It may be I am getting to that age. It may be I cannot recall having already arrived there and, unaware, doddered on.

I love my South, but to do that, sometimes, you have to love the way it used to be ... or you have to remember it the way it ought to have been. This is a dangerous thing, I guess, unless of course you are talking about potato salad and pocketknives. I was born in '59, and am old enough to know the South as a meaner place, and that a memory can cut you in two. I am old enough, barely, to remember bad, bad days, when my people discarded their finer nature altogether and—for the sake of belonging—vanished into clichés of cruelty that were not written into history so much as burned. And I am old enough to see that South not only linger on and on but rise again, in many places, offending, threatening anew. I have said, in print, what I think about that threat, and what it means to us as a people. Some people would discard us, all of us, for that offense, by association. We can't help that. But when our baser nature reappears, like an ugly hat that should have never come back into style, we need to own up to it, and not pretend it is not there.

Mostly, my recent writings on my South have been kinder, gentler, softer. It is hard to do much harm writing about old women and roses, or how the sand feels running through your toes on the Gulf of Mexico, or the unfortunate day, pretending to be a carpenter, you glued yourself to the wall.

This book is, mostly, the part of us that endures, that shines through. It is, I hope, the best of us, and it may have to do, till we find our finer nature again.

It seemed like, once, we even knew how to make something sweeter out of snow. My grandmother scraped it off the car hoods, and mixed it—working quickly—with sweetened condensed milk and sugar and vanilla flavoring, and spooned it into bowls. It was one of the things I thought about, marooned in Midtown, in the winter of '94.

———

That morning, in the predawn glow of Times Square, is where my writing life began its turn from writing other people's stories to thinking and writing my own. I had received some interest from editors and agents about doing a book, but I really had no working idea, at least not one that I believed anyone would want to read. I scratched a few meaningless lines in a reporter's notebook, and finally, a little dejected, I knew that after almost two decades of writing for a living, I was an expert, an authority, on not one thing.

The only thing I knew, really knew, was home.

I knew the pines, and the low mountains, and ditches full of poke salad and Johnson grass and scraps of dirty cotton. I knew, from a thousand stories or more, who my people were and where they came from and how they survived in the deep green of the Southern highlands. I knew, staring at that skinny scrap of paper, that I was not better than them, or worse than them, or smarter or dumber. I was just of them, and so, of the South. It has always struck me appropriate, somehow, how red dirt is so similar in color to blood.

I knew what made life worth living here, and I tried not so much to write about those great, grand things but to write about a hundred or a thousand or so very small ones, and would be greatly surprised, one day, to discover that all those little things had added up to something more. At least that is what people tell me. People are kind that way.

———

I am a tourist now, when I go north to visit the big city. Likely, I always have been. I try not to visit in the winter, but sometimes winter will sneak up on you, up there. I like to walk the place a little, now, after the crowds have thinned, and after the snow has been mostly pushed away. I never walk very far, because I gave my heavy coat away a long time ago, believing, foolishly, I would never need it again.

# PART I
# HOME

# THE ROSES OF FAIRHOPE

*Southern Living,* Southern Journal: March 2011

———

I made the trip with three old women, in a good time for roses. We had threatened to do it for years. We would pack a car with cold chicken and flip-flops and drive south like we used to, till the Alabama foothills faded into souvenir shops, shrimp shacks, and that first ragged palm. They had taken me there, when men still whistled at them and WALLACE stickers papered the bumpers of cars. How could I not take them now?

But we never got out of the driveway, somehow. My Aunt Edna's heart was failing, Aunt Juanita had to care for my homebound uncle, and my mother, Margaret, did not leave home unless blown from it by tornadoes or TNT. So I was stunned, two years ago, when my 72-year-old mother told me to come get them. I found the three oldest sisters in the yard, suitcases in their hands. Aunt Jo, the youngest sister, stayed home to watch the livestock.

Edna barbecued 250 some-odd chicken thighs and made two gallons of potato salad, for the two-day trip. They packed pork and beans, raw onions, cornbread, a jar of iced tea, a hard-frozen Clorox jug of water, and not one cell phone.

As we drove they talked of childhood, dirt roads where the dark closed in like a lid on a box, and a daddy who chased the bad things away the second he walked in. By the time we hit Montgomery, they had ridden a horse named Bob, poked a dead chicken named Mrs. Rearden, and fished beside a little man named Jessie Clines. They were remembering their mama, and a groundhog who lived under the floorboards, as we drove across Mobile Bay.

I wanted them to see the sunset from the Fairhope pier, and as we rolled down the bluff, I heard them go quiet. But the sunset was just a light to see by. It was the roses. They were blooming in a circle the size of a baseball infield, more than 2,000 of them, with names like Derby horses or unrealized dreams—Mr. Lincoln, Strike It Rich, Touch of Class, Crimson Glory, Lasting Love. My mother, who never even liked roses much, said, "Oh, Lord." Juanita, tough and tiny, made of whalebone and hell, looked about to cry.

Their big sister stepped from the car as if in a trance. I had not known how sick Edna was. Her steps were unsure, halting, as she moved into the garden. The sisters moved close, in case she fell.

Aunt Edna had sewed soldiers' clothes at the Army base, raised five girls, buried a husband, worked a red-clay garden, pieced a thousand quilts, loved on great-grandchildren, and caught more crappie than any man I have ever known. I believed she was eternal, like the red-clay bank where she built her solid, redbrick house.

"So purty," she said, again and again. She lingered in the rose garden a long time, till the sun vanished over the western shore. She saw the Fairhope roses six times on this trip. The last time, because she was tired, we sat in the car.

A year later, I spoke at her funeral. I surprised myself, blubbered like an old fool. For the first time in a long time it mattered what came out of my head, but the words crashed together inside my skull and I lost the fine things I wanted to say, and stood stupidly in front of people who loved her.

Her daughters just hugged me, one by one, and thanked me for the roses.

# MAMA ALWAYS SAID...
# CHOOSE YOUR WORDS CAREFULLY

*Southern Living*, May 2012

---

W hen I cut my own hair, as a child, she did not castigate me, though I looked like I had done it with a Weedwhacker and my bangs made it seem like one of my eyes had dropped 2 inches down my face. "Maybe," she told me, "you shouldn't be pointing sharp things at your eyes," allowing caution, not criticism, to stick in my mind. When I cut it again, as a grown man, she told me it looked nice and neat, when in fact it looked like I was on a chain gang in the Depression. I went to get it fixed, and the stylist said, "Oh, Lord," then combed some hair over the gapped places, charged me $20, and sent me home. My point is, that stylist did not love me like my mother does, and so did not even try to spare me from myself.

When I write a book, my mother reads it first. Your first critic should be one in your pocket.

"That," she always says, "is a fine book."

She points out the typos—she is good at that—and nonsensical things with a gentle, "Now, hon', you need to look at this..."

I guess I should not be surprised. Mothers, as a group, tend to know the thing to say. They know, when you come home from seventh grade with a red C- on your science project, it is only because ol' Mrs. So-and-So is a good friend of Mrs. So-and-So, so little Elrod got an A because he has better connections in the high-stakes world of Alabama public education.

It is why, when I have done good in my life, I have given her the trophies. They sit in dust on her shelves. From time to time I fail, and she says the right thing then, too.

"Son," she says, "I don't need a plaque to know what kind of man you are."

And that is why I love her.

# MY BROTHER'S GARDEN

Southern Living, Southern Journal: May 2012

---

My little brother's beard has turned gray, and his clothes hang on him like a scarecrow's hang on crossed broom handles. From a distance, there in the rising dust of the garden, he looks like he stepped out of an old family photograph, like my uncles, like my grandfather, men who knew the secrets of the dirt. He reaches down and pinches a false bloom off a squash. I do not know how he knows it is false. When I ask him these things, he just looks at me, puzzled, and says, "I've always knowed." Today, every day, his rows are straight as a needle, immaculate. You could roll a marble across his ground. I watch him stoop to pull a single, solitary weed, and then I ease away, thinking: If you know, how come I don't?

The South, like chiggers and divinity candy, is everlasting. It will always be, though it will not always be as we remember. The South of our childhoods rusts, peels, and goes away. Brush arbors have left no trace on it. Preachers who thrust ragged Bibles at bare rafters now shout politics from the pulpit. Civility, toward even those with whom we do not agree, is an heirloom. Quilts, the kind made for warmth instead of cash, are a thing of antiquity, their patterns a mystery slowly fading in an old woman's eyes. Young men can play 5,000 video games but cannot sharpen a pocket knife; lost are the men who tested their truck's electrical system by holding to a coil wire. I listen for the past, but I cannot hear it. The juke joints fall silent, cotton mills wind down to a final, solitary thread, and a last buck dancer shuffles off into the mountain mist. Then I see my brother Mark in his garden, and know that not everything must fade away.

I can still see my maternal grandmother, Ava, go at a copperhead with a hoe held together with black electrical tape; it never had a chance. My paternal grandfather, Bobby, worked 12 hours milling cotton, six more with his hands in red dirt. My uncle John wore out 15 straw hats and worked three tractors to death. Now it is Mark's turn, to curse the drought, and the late frost, and the rocks in the earth.

Five years ago, he hacked and burned clean an acre of hedge- and weed-infested land, mixed the ashes with a prodigious amount of manure, and created an oasis in a rock-strewn mountain pasture. Now, season after season, he walks down the hill with an old, white German shepherd by his side—he named her Pretty Girl—and does battle with the things that would take it all away: a blight that appears overnight like a bad dream; and hungry insects, some he cannot even name. The old dog watches from a cool place in the dirt, and when thunder sounds in the distance she steps in front of my brother's tractor and will not move, to tell him it is time to go in before the lightning gets there. A good dog will do that.

Because, you see, there is more than science at work here. He knows the science, the nature of the soil, how to plant—how far apart, how deep—and the hybrids and histories of seeds. But there is also magic—what some folks call folklore—that must be considered, like the singing of frogs, the stages of the moon. Most, I will never understand. For some reason, he named his tractors after family. The one called Ricky is slow to start, has a bad running gear, and its seat has no padding.

People here say they have never seen a more beautiful garden, of peppers, onions, potatoes, squash. His tomatoes line our mama's windowsills. The canning process takes all summer and much of the fall, her house thick with the smell of vinegar and dill. I forget how pretty a jar of hot peppers can be.

But I guess everyone here has a Mark. Look behind the redbrick ranchers or frame houses or mobile homes and you will see a patch of turned dirt. In it, staring down as if they can divine the future, will be a Southern woman or man. When all else is torn down, or new, this is how I'll know where I am.

# PRETTY GIRL

*Southern Living*, Southern Journal: May 2014

———

Her name was perfect.

She came to them in the dead of night, in the cold. She was more than half dead, starved down to bones, her hair completely eaten away by mange. She had been run off from more than one yard when she finally crept into an empty doghouse in the trees beyond my mother's yard. At least she was out of the wind.

They found her, my mother and brother, in the daylight of the next day. They could not even tell, at first, she was a dog.

"And it broke my heart," my mother said.

They did not call the vet because she knew what the vet would do. She was too far gone to save; any fool could see that. My mama lives in the country and has to run off two wandering dogs a week, but this time, "I just couldn't. She couldn't even get up." How do you run off a dog that cannot stand?

The broke-down dog had stumbled on two people who hate to give up on anything, even a month-old newspaper. They save batteries that have not had a spark of anything in them for a long, long time. My mother keeps pens that stopped writing in 1974. My point is, there is always a little use, a little good, a little life left in anything, and who are they to decide when something is done for good.

My brother Mark looked at her, at her tragic face, and named her. "Hey, Pretty Girl," he said.

It was like he could see beyond the ruin, or maybe into it. I don't know.

Her hips were bad, which was probably why she was discarded in the first place, and her teeth were worn down. Her eyes were clouded. But they fed her, and gave her water, and bathed her in burnt motor oil, the way my people have been curing the mange for generations. They got her looking less atrocious, and then they called the vet.

The vet found she had heartworms. She was walking dead, anyway, at her age. It was then I saw her, still a sack of bones. It would be a kindness, I told my mother, to put her down. She nodded her head.

A month later I pulled into the driveway to see a beautiful white German shepherd standing watch at the front of the house. It was not a miracle; her ailments did not magically cease. But together, my mother and brother had tended her, and even let her live in the house. She ate people food, and drank buttermilk out of an aluminum pie tin. She was supposed to last, at most, a few weeks or months. She lived three more years—decades, in dog years—following my brother to the garden to watch for snakes and listen for thunder.

"I prayed for her," my mother said. "Some people say you ain't supposed to pray for a dog, but..." And then after the gift of years, Pretty Girl began to fail, and died. She is buried in the mountain pasture.

The hot weather will be on us soon. The garden is already planted. Some things were planted according to science, according to soil and weather. And some things were planted according to lore, the shape of the moon, and more. That is fine with me. There are things we cannot explain, things beyond science, like how a man could name a ravaged and dying dog, and have her rise inside that, somehow, to make it true.

# CRAZY CAT LADY

*Southern Living,* Southern Journal: September 2014

————

I know my mother was saddened when she recently lost her dog.

That is no reason to fill the hole in her heart with 13 cats.

"I am ashamed of myself," she admitted.

It is not her fault; this evil was visited upon her. A friend, well-meaning but ill-reasoned, brought her a cat that had not been fixed. Let the hilarity commence.

They named the smoke gray cat Stinky, because it was.

"We thought it was a boy," said my brother Mark.

But along came a raggedy stray tomcat my mother named Will.

"He was a travelin' man," Mark said.

Will begot, with Stinky, four kittens: Little Will, Shorty, Little Stinky, and Elvira. "Elvira?" I asked. "I liked the song," Mark said.

Will, his work done, hit the highway. Another stray, Big Spooky, moved in. Before Stinky—who was now referred to as Big Stinky—could be caught and fixed, Big Stinky delivered into this world a second litter: Little Spooky, Vincent Price, and Stephen King.

"I been watchin' spooky movies," Mark said.

A fourth kitten had Siamese markings.

"Possum Willy," my mother said, "because he looks like a..."

"I got it," I said.

Shorty, who was also believed to be a boy, produced a litter.

"Haven't named them yet," Mark said.

The problem in this narrative—well, one of them—is that Little Stinky soon eclipsed Big Stinky in size, making Little Stinky Big Stinky and Big Stinky Little Stinky, so that I can no longer adequately follow what is happening.

I so miss that dog. Don't worry—a veterinarian will soon be involved, lest there be any mean letters. (If there are any, send them to the Editor in Chief.) I told my mother we will try to cut her cat population off at 13 by first spaying the females. But the cats are half wild, and most of them will let only her touch them, and she is too old for cat wrangling. Mark, who I suspect enjoys naming them way too much, will probably not step forward. My older brother, Sam, is too deliberate. A deliberate man cannot catch a cat. There are just some things a steady man cannot do.

I wonder who that leaves.

But I fear it is already too late. My mother is now the crazy cat lady. Cats hang on the screened doors, mewling for food, which she buys in big bags. The cats share it with the raccoons and possums, a kind of modern-day Noah's Ark there on her 40 acres of mountain pasture.

Her driveway is about a quarter-mile long. She walks to the mailbox, for her health.

"Now they all follow her in a straight line, all of them, there and back," my brother told me.

"I am ashamed of myself," my mother reiterated.

"You've just got a soft heart," I said.

"They swirl and swirl 'round my feet," she said.

I patted her.

"I didn't even like cats," she said.

There ain't enough pats in the world.

We cannot give away even one cat. People promise to take one, and we watch the driveway.

They never come. But another stray did, a kitten.

"Sylvester Highstockings," Mark said.

I told him I did not want to know.

# THE PORCH

*Southern Living,* Southern Journal: August 2012

———

The old house has started to fade inside my mind. I try to remember it but the walls are mostly blank, the hallways filled with shadow. The fights, hugs, prayers, and curses that occurred there still linger in my memory, but the wooden boxes that held those things, the rooms my paternal grandparents once shared with their great extended family, have lost form. I think it was painted white, that house. It seems like it was white.

But the porch, now...I still see the porch. The last time I stood upon it I was 6 years old, but I still see the nail heads in the weathered pine, still hear the squeal of the rocker pressing the planks, still see tiny comets arc across the air when somebody flicked the glowing nub of a Pall Mall over the rail and into the night.

I remember that it was wide and deep, as high off the ground as a man is tall. The planks, once painted, were worn down to a bare, ancient gray by rain and sun, and by a few billion brogans, black wingtips, and scandalous high-heeled shoes. But it was built to stand until the Rapture, and maybe a little while beyond.

They say a kitchen is the heart of a house, but I believe the porch is its soul. From the very steps, you knew if you were welcome or not, knew everything you needed to know about the people inside. My grandmother Velma welcomed the whole world there on those boards, except for a few insurance men and anyone with a pamphlet.

Usually, she welcomed them with a saucer of blackberry cobbler, or banana pudding, or a plate of the best meatloaf this world has ever known. My grandfather Bobby, if it was a weekend and the world had not run out of whiskey, sometimes welcomed visitors with something more, but that is another story.

The porch was always cool, as if summer stopped at that first step. The house was like a furnace in the hot months, and the porch, perched in the foothills of the Alabama highland, was a cool oasis in the heat. There was no electric light on the porch, no bright bulb to draw insects or add to the heat. Porches were for talking, and rocking babies, and cutting okra and snapping beans and telling lies. A body did not need a lot of light for that, and— if the lying got out of hand—the darker the better.

I remember its scent, an ambrosia of black coffee mixing in the wind with the sweet smell of canned milk, and honeysuckle, and snuff. It made the babies sneeze. In the evening, the children would retreat beneath the porch to be away from their mamas and daddies but still not quite away, to be with them and yet not right with them, which is a delicious thing that only a child really understands. We convened there to whisper, pinch, fuss, eavesdrop, and enjoy the dark, our heads filled with ghost stories and our fists wrapped around our broken-bladed pocket knives. But then a screech owl would split the night, or a cousin would mutter, "I wonder if there's snakes down here," and we would come pouring from around the pylons and up the steps.

I don't see people on porches much anymore. For a while they even stopped building them after air-conditioning, and television. I see people sitting around on patios, but it is not the same. But people seem to like them. As the late writer Lewis Grizzard once wrote, it is hard to get drunk and fall off a backyard.

Like most people, I have a dream house under construction in my head. The plans shift and reform and sometimes I even scratch out a few lines with pencil on a legal pad, but I always tear it up and start over. I have been building it all my life, slow evening after slow evening. If I had worked with bricks and lumber instead of dreams and paper, I would be sitting about 19 stories high by now. Maybe I should find a good architect. Or maybe I should just get one last, clean sheet of paper, and start with a porch. I already have one in mind.

# TAKE YOUR MEDICINE, BOY

*Southern Living,* Southern Journal: February 2015

———

T he boy was trouble. You could see that as he pushed through
the door, then came stomping past the booths in the Huddle
House in his toddler-size cowboy boots. He was wearing a
strawberry-jelly scowl, his shirt had ridden up his belly, and his
hands, which I am sure were sticky, were touching everything. His
tired mother noticed, too late, that he was on the lam, and caught
up with him just about the time he made it to our booth. His
round cheeks were red—it was clear he had a cold—and he sneezed
and then coughed a good-bye as he was dragged away.

"Reminds me of you," my brother Sam said over his ham-and-
cheese omelet.

My mother nodded.

"You was bad to get colds," she said, and watched as the boy
went, protesting, up the aisle. She loves boys.

Well let's hope, I thought to myself, they don't treat his ailment
the same way my people treated mine. If they do, the poor child
will be as tight as Dick's hatband by time for beddy-bye.

They called it, oddly, a "toddy." Their homemade remedies
for the cold, flu, and croup varied a little, depending on which
grandparents were mixing the concoctions, but the active
ingredient was always the same. It required, to start, a few
tablespoons of corn whiskey, which some people—but nobody

I know who'd ever had any—called moonshine. Hooch was more like it. Busthead. Popskull. There wasn't anything nice about it.

Into the glass the old women of the family squeezed a lemon, if they had one; lemons were dear in the foothills of the Appalachians in those days, for mill workers and pulpwooders and roofers. Then, they stirred in a tablespoon of golden honey.

If there was no honey, they took a hammer and broke off a big chunk of peppermint candy and let it melt in the glass. Sometimes, if the child coughed loud enough and their hearts broke and their fear rose, they would place the chunk of peppermint in the toe of a white sock and bash it with the hammer, or just swing it against a post on the porch. It melted quicker that way, beat to dust.

I remember once they gave this medicine to my brother Sam.

He said he did not remember it.

"I reckon so," I said.

He does remember he went to sleep.

My mother recalls there was giggling.

I do remember the first time they gave it to me. I am not sure how old I was, but I was in school, so had to have been at least 6. The peppermint did not do the job, and the corn whiskey burned a hole from my lips to my lower intestine, but, oh, what a wonderful feeling it was when the fire went out. The world went soft. The world turned gold. I floated. I flew into the dark. Moonshine. I get it now.

I know they would not have hurt us for anything in the world. Nothing was more precious, to these people who worked so hard with their hands for so little, than their babies. They simply used what they had.

I am glad that little boy in the Huddle House lives in a more enlightened time, but maybe just a little sorry, too.

# TIME FOR THE
# YEAR'S BEST NAP

*Southern Living*, Southern Journal: November 2012

_____

The turkey carcass is down to bones. The mashed potatoes are nothing more than a sad, hopeful, metallic scraping—some people just can't accept that gone is gone. The pinto beans and ham are in Tupperware, divided 14 ways. The last biscuit is a memory. (Or so it seems. My mama always hides one or two away for my boy, Jake.) Over the last crumbs of dressing, old women say, "Don't know what happened...it just wasn't fit to eat."

It is time for my people to gather in the living room and unburden themselves of all the fine gossip they have been holding onto since September, like money. I will be there, with them, sometimes with a half-eaten piece of chocolate cake balanced dangerously on one knee, but I will hear almost none of it.

I would rather be awake, to find out whose garden did well and whose didn't, and whose foreign car isn't running good—because you know they should have known better—and whose children have misbehaved. I would like to know what is happening to our kin across the state line—my Aunt Juanita calls them "the Georgia people," like they are a new species—and who last killed a snake. They will say that the snakes seem to have stayed out longer this year, and no one will say it any more but we're pretty sure it's because those men walked on the moon. I want to hear it all, swirling around me, assuring me that no matter what happens in this uncertain world the things that truly matter, things here, are all right.

But the same peace of mind that settles on me as that talk drifts around the room is the same peace and comfort that tugs me into the calm darkness. My mama will look at me from across the wood floor and say, quickly, "Let him sleep." I know this because sometimes I am not quite out, and it is the last thing I hear.

It would be all right with me if it was the last thing I ever hear.

I will blame the chair. I bought it out of a catalog a quarter-century ago, what the catalog called a British club chair, but it just looks like a leather chair to me. It is firm and soft at the same time, and there is some kind of drug in it, I swear, that makes my chin droop and makes me begin to snore softly. The talk continues around me, and I would like to tell you what it is all about but of course I do not know. I just know I love the idea of it, of the stories being told with me and yet without me, at the same time. The old white dog sleeps, too, across the room. In human years she is... well, a miracle.

I am not a napper, and do not even sleep well at night. But here, in this chair on Thanksgiving Day, it is automatic, certain. Maybe I should steal the chair from my mama's and take it to live with me all the time. Then, at least, I could hear all the news at home.

But I do not believe I will. They tell me sometimes I am out for only a few minutes, but that cannot be. I wake feeling restored, feeling alive and happy to be. It is almost enough to make a person believe in magic, because I know there are hours and hours worth of good things happening as I shut my eyes.

# MY TIME MACHINE

*Southern Living*, Southern Journal: April 2013

———

They say we Southerners live in the past. That, they say, is our problem; the past is dead, Faulkner or no Faulkner.

I guess I could try to explain, to tell them that for us memory is not an inventory, not a catalog of events, but a time machine. It lifts us off the dull treadmill of grown-up responsibilities to a time of adventure and wonder. The past is not dead, and so the dead are never really gone. We resurrect them, daily, for one more story, one more buck dance or ball game, or one more cast into the cool water. I could try to explain this, but instead I think I'll take a boat ride.

I recently suffered through two weeks of agony from a kidney stone, cursing the air around me. Prescription drugs finally dulled the pain, and I drifted. I could have gone anywhere in that pleasant fog, but found myself on a floating house in the middle of the vast, brown Coosa River near the Alabama-Georgia line, waiting as my Aunt Edna tied an orange life jacket around my chest. I was 7 or 8 years old, and if she did not hurry my girl cousins would catch every crappie on the Alabama side.

"I got to go," I pleaded.

"What you got to do," she said, "is stand still."

It was a homemade boat. A great, towering box of a thing that Aunt Edna and Uncle Charlie and other kin built in the yard. They worked their shifts at the army base in Anniston, and then worked another shift on this, drills whirring, welding rods arcing blue flame into the night. Back then, every man welded, every man could run a wire, and Aunt Edna could outwork most of them.

"What is it?" I asked, between pulls on a Nehi orange.

"It's a houseboat, dummy," said my cousin Linda, who was prone to say what she thought.

When it was finally done, the vessel had an enclosed main cabin with chairs, a table, and a gas stove. It had a second deck up high, where you could see the entire world, but I was deemed too mentally unsound to go up there once they dragged the boat off dry land. Once in the water, we discovered one structural flaw. It was so tall it was bad to hang up under bridges. I sometimes wondered if they asked me along just so it would ride a little lower in the water. But I have had less noble purposes in this life than ballast.

We fished all day and sometimes all night on the backwater, always for crappie. Aunt Edna would fry them in iron skillets and save the hot grease for the best hush puppies I have ever had, not a daub of plain meal but a hoecake-like disk redolent with green onion, white onion, and Cheddar cheese. Once, I came into the main cabin to see her standing over a skillet of frying quail. We ate it with biscuits and gravy, right in the middle of a river.

But the best of it was the ride. I would find a place in the sun and just watch the banks glide by. Now and then, Uncle Charlie would shout to the old men fishing from the banks.

"Got the time?"

"Alabamer time?" the old men would ask. "Or Georgie time?"

They have passed on, of course—Charlie, Edna, even Linda. The houseboat is in ruin.

But they are not gone.

Nobody is, on Alabama time.

# ALL-NIGHT GOSPEL

*Southern Living,* Southern Journal: March 2014

———

I have reached a place in life where I do not think clearly about the present, or the future. What I do, mostly, is remember, my thoughts triggered by some flyer flapping on a telephone pole, or a scrap of a song.

I was on a Tennessee interstate in the spitting rain, with two states behind me and a thousand miles to go, scanning a radio thick with yammering bullies whose mamas did not love them enough. Between bullies I landed on a preacher, a gentle man who sounded like my childhood, who said to love my brother. Then came a song I cannot precisely recall, but in a mile or so it erased the wet, gray asphalt and the miles ahead. The signal soon died, but not before—in my mind—I was home.

I was a little boy in Boutwell Auditorium, on a night without wrestling, munching on a hot dog that was the best I ever had, because we were in *Birmingham.* In my other fist was a can of Coke so cold it burned my hand. On stage, men in suits sang of clouds of victory. Next to me, my mother, her face alight, tapped her shoes, flapped a fan donated by a funeral home, and sang along. I recall this one song, about a wall around heaven, so high you can't get over it, so low you can't get under it ...

*... so wide, you can't get around it*
*You got to come in at the door*

It was an all-night gospel singing, common in the Deep South of the 1960s and 1970s, though for Congregational Holiness "all-night" wrapped up about 11:45. I still remember the headliners: The Florida Boys, the Dixie Echoes, Happy Goodman Family, J.D. Sumner and the Stamps Quartet, Blackwood Brothers Quartet, The Inspirations, Hovie Lister and the Statesmen, The Chuck Wagon Gang...

Faith was less political then. It had a beat you could dance to, if dancing had been allowed. We went every few months, to places like Sylacauga, where they sang in the football stadium and I ate a Wet-Nap—but that is another story—and Gadsden, where the Dixie Echoes had them praising and weeping in Convention Hall. I went mostly for the concessions, and because any time a car turned out of our driveway I flung myself inside. I do not recall listening closely to the music. But when I hear the songs on the radio, I find myself singing along.

My mother, after a 40-year absence, went to a singing not long ago at Young's Chapel on Alabama Highway 278, in the hills between Piedmont and Gadsden. "It was The Chuck Wagon Gang," she said, "but, you know, the younger ones. They still had their name on the bus. I know one thing. They sure did some awful pretty singing." They did "The Church in the Wildwood," one of her favorites.

*Oh, come, come, come, come,*
*Come to the church in the wildwood*
*Oh, come to the church in the vale*

It made her happy. I hope they read this, and know. She has never liked recorded music, she said, but I got her a CD player anyway. My sister-in-law, Teresa, got her some gospel music, and when my mother heard the songs she stood there and sang along.

I would have liked to have seen that.

But I guess I already have.

# SAVING FACE

*Southern Living*, Southern Journal: April 2014

---

I will always remember the first time it happened. I was signing books in a deserted hotel ballroom, deserted except for me, a few nice people handing me volumes, and two thousand pictures of my mother's face, the elegant cover of a 300-page story I had written about her and my people. The most important thing I will ever write, and closest to my heart.

It was a beautiful book—not the inside, I mean, but the outside. The cover, which had the feel of old parchment, showed a photograph of my young mother, taken about the time I was born in '59. Her face was serene, peaceful, and lovely. I believe my mother was, and is, the most beautiful woman on this planet. I always will. But the photograph on the cover of this book had an almost otherworldly quality about it. I have seen people stop what they were doing and walk all the way across a bookstore to pick it up and look at it, closer. (That is what authors do for fun. They hang out in bookstores and stalk people through the aisles, trying to turn them, by mind control, to the memoir aisle.)

Anyway, that day in the ballroom, I had already worn out two fine-point Sharpies and was a few hundred books into the stack when I noticed, on every single beautiful cover, my mother had been defaced.

They put stickers on books when they are signed, that say, in case anyone is confused, SIGNED BY AUTHOR. I do not know who else would have signed it, although, once or twice, when someone mistook me for another writer, I signed one of their books for meanness. I have also taken several sweet compliments intended for Rick Bass.

It was the placement that was unfortunate. On some books, they had covered up her left eye, making her look, vaguely, like a pirate. On others, it was on the right eye, which made her look no less the buccaneer. Some, and this was unfortunate, were plastered over her mouth, making her resemble the "Speak No Evil" monkey in that trilogy. The ones on her cheek made her look like an accident victim. The ones on her forehead made her look like Zelda Fitzgerald (use your imagination) or, if they happened to be round in shape, a coal miner. They have a lamp strapped to their... never mind.

I started to peel them off, then looked at the boxes and boxes of books and just sighed.

It got worse over time. I would walk into a store and see, stuck to my mother's lovely face, 20 PERCENT OFF. The most unpleasant were the stickers that said nothing, just blue or red or yellow dots, which I'm sure meant something in secret bookstore code but made my mama look like she had measles, or a bad case of pinkeye. I cannot always peel them all off. But most of the time, I try.

My mother told me, once, that the cover sometimes makes her a little sad because, "I don't look like that no more." I think she does. But at least she does not walk around the house with REMAINDERED stamped across her head.

Happy Birthday, Mama. I love you.

# ENDLESS SUMMER

*Southern Living*, Southern Journal: August 2013

———

I t was a magnificent mud hole.

It was an inland sea, as much like any other mud hole as the Erie Canal is to a ditch. It was hip deep on a small boy, 40 feet long, and spanned the entire dirt road that linked the blacktop of the Roy Webb Road to the creeks, forests, and fields behind our house in Calhoun County, Alabama.

I spent a whole summer contemplating that mud hole. I waded in it, threw rocks at it, caught snakes in it, threw rocks at snakes in it, and, as the hot days crawled by, studied the entire life cycle of frogs. I built a great vessel and sailed across it (well, mostly I just sank into the muck while trying to balance on an old sheet of plywood) and forever ruined the resale value of my G.I. Joe. There may be nothing more forlorn in this world than a G.I. Joe with no pants and one plastic shoe.

My brothers thought I was wasting time, and—not for the first time—wondered if perhaps we had different daddies. But time was different then, as I have said before. Time came in big buckets. It was not only summer, in a time before jobs locked us in chains and girls robbed us of our sense, but it was August, the most endless month of those forever summers, and August just never ran out.

It stewed and simmered in that nearly liquid air, and lasted.

It should have flown, for when it ended came that hateful season of shoes. And school, where the air always smelled like floor polish and chalk dust and the second-grade teacher was rumored to have cooked and eaten at least two boys, that we knew of.

But it didn't fly. It lolled.

I caught a million fish, and survived a million red wasps, doctored with a truckload of wet snuff, one daub at a time. I hit a million home runs, till the baseball, socked so many times it was only round in a metaphorical sense, finally vanished into a blackberry bush rumored to be inhabited by a 4-foot-long eastern diamondback. We just waited him out. There was time.

So how did it all change?

When did the summers grow short, truncated? When did the endless month of August become not even a month at all but a jumping-off place for the season to come? They sell Halloween candy in the drugstore, in summer.

The children start school now in August. They say it has to do with air-conditioning, but I know sadism when I see it. I think a bunch of people who were not allowed to stomp in a mud hole when they were young—who were never allowed to hold translucent tadpoles in their hands and watch their hearts move—decided to make sure that no child would ever have the necessary time to contemplate a grand mud hole ever again.

Well, I hope they're satisfied. People ask all the time, what's wrong with kids today? I have long held that they have been brain-mushed by too much screen time, but as summer races past me now I think it is something else. I think they do not know how sweet it is to feel the mud mush between their toes.

# HAPPY AS A PIG

*Southern Living*, Southern Journal: April 2015

---

For a woman who grew up in the mountain landscape of the Great Depression, my mother is irritatingly hard to please.

I got her a big, soft, leather easy chair. She said it cost too much, and it made her uneasy to sit in it.

I bought a big-screen television with a thousand channels, so she could watch every TV preacher who ever wept for a love offering. She said the old set was fine and she only watched two channels anyway.

I purchased a new washing machine. She claimed it was harder to operate than a rocket ship and said, "I reckon I could learn to use it, but I'd have to go back to school.

"Wadn't nothin' wrong with the other one," she added. "You just have to bang the lid down three or four hard times to get it to click on."

"Is there anything," I asked, "you do want?"

"Well," she said, "I need some grease."

What she meant was lard, and not store-bought lard, which has not been made right since the Johnson Administration; you might as well try to fry an egg in Dippity-Do.

She needed what she calls cracklin' meat, slabs of fatback with a sliver of lean, something that can be rendered into delicious, crispy nuggets. The cracklin's could be used to flavor cornbread or greens, or be eaten at the side of a plate of peas or beans or, well, anything, yet they are just a by-product.

It was the grease she needed, an essential. But the fresh, pure, white fat is harder and harder to find. She can usually only find it in tiny blocks in the cooler, never of a quality to satisfy her.

My mother is the best cook who ever lived; I will fight you over that. One of the reasons her food has flavor, she explained, is that most of her greens, beans, and other vegetables and all gravy and all egg dishes take on the flavor of that fat. I have seen her throw out dishes, not spoiled, merely bland.

I try not to repeat Southern clichés. No one, for instance, should eat a hamburger in a bun made from Krispy Kreme Doughnuts. But grease is good. It has shortened many lives, probably my own, but is a life of rice cakes really life, or just passing time?

So, we went on a quest. Finally, at a country butcher shop in Alexandria, Alabama, we found it, but too late. A gentleman at the counter was buying what appeared to be 50 pounds of perfect cracklin' meat, an hour or two off the hog. My mother just stared, with avarice.

"I never have wanted what someone else had," she said.

She asked if there was more, but the butcher said no, it was a rare thing, and I thought she was going to cry. The butcher, wondering how he would live with breaking an old woman's heart, went to the back to check and returned saying he had found some. We walked out with $20 worth of pork fat.

My mother was giddy—she would have skipped, if she could. For two days, as she rendered it, the house smelled like what I like to think heaven is like, and she was happy, which is all a boy really needs, as her birthday nears. I think I'll take her out to eat, just so she can tell me she isn't hungry.

# RED DIRT

The trains may seem longer in the city, as the traffic piles up at the crossings and the freight cars squeal and clatter but barely crawl, and all there is to do is sit, and sit, and maybe try and decipher the graffiti on the endless iron boxes from broad-shouldered places like Pittsburgh, and Cleveland, places that make you think of rust and trains. But I think they might be longer, truly, in the country, in those crossings where the train intrudes like a drunk uncle on the otherwise quiet landscape. Or at least, that is what I will choose to believe. When I was a boy I would sneak away from the watchful women in my family and walk the mile or more to the track that cut across the Roy Webb Road, and count those passing cars. There seemed to be a thousand, or more, but I was very small and arithmetic has never been my blessing, and I always knew I had to get back before I was missed, before the women piled in the Biscayne and came looking for me with hands twisting at their aprons and blood in their eye.

The trains hauled coal, and pig iron, and even people. And sometimes, in car after lumbering car, came whole mountains of the red earth. There was so much of it, it seemed to me then, that they would surely dig the very ground from beneath our feet, and we would just float away.

"Why do they want our dirt?" I asked, and the grown-ups just told me there was money in it, son, and dismissed me to talk about important things, like how it was a bad year for feed corn, and whether Wallace would run again, and why they would rather push a Chevy than drive a Ford.

I would learn that it was valuable to outsiders for the same reason it was valuable to us. It held things up.

I knew they baked bricks from it; there was a brickyard on Highway 21. But my uncles and big brother would explain how the builders used it as foundations for houses in places with mealy, mushy, crumbly, inferior dirt. Why, even under the great buildings of this world, beneath the great edifices, lay our dirt.

We got good dirt, they told me.

It would be decades before I would hear the poets go on and on about it, about how they were sons of the clay and all that, like a poet ever held a shovel handle in his life.

────────

I believe there are three establishments a Southern man should not be caught dead in, or four if you are a member of the Church of Christ caught doing the rumba at an Arthur Murray. A Southern man should not get turned around while searching for the fishing licenses counter at Walmart and wind up anywhere in proximity of the ladies unmentionables. He should not go in a bridal boutique, which should involve no explanation. And he has no business, ever, in one of those delicate stores wherein ladies with big purses lean over souvenirs of the Old South, sigh, and mumble, "Well, ain't that just *precious.*"

I have stumbled into such places by mistake, and sometimes cannot get out before my blood sugar is permanently escalated by all that cloying sweetness wafting from the merchandise. There are little-bitty cotton bales, and soaps with a hint of honeysuckle, and incense sticks that smell like somebody has burned the peach cobbler. It happened again, not too long ago, but before I could retreat I was mesmerized by the T-shirt rack, not because of the usual clichés printed on them but the colors themselves. They were, according to the tags on them, dyed from the natural pigments of the Southern land. There was one dyed with iced tea—I swear I am not making this up—and one that appeared to be kudzu green. But the one that stopped me cold was a dull, rusty red. The tag proclaimed it to be colored by the honest-to-God Georgia clay.

The superior look on my face, the armor a Southern man must wear into such a place to keep his dignity, slipped clean away, and I began to laugh, to laugh until parts of me not particularly well-toned began to shake. I am not prone to belly laughs, mostly because when I start I cannot stop and have been told I look ridiculous; there are many things a big man cannot do that a smaller man can, and apparently one of them is prolonged laughter in a public place. I have been told I alarm the children.

But I could not help myself.

I thought of Alabama, 1965, and a ground the color of dried blood.

I imagined my mother as a young woman, standing over me, aghast at my condition. I imagined a little-bitty me, covered from the soles of my once-white socks to my blond eyebrows, in red mud, that of the Alabama variety. It had rained, and I danced and flopped and backstroked through every mud hole I could find across five square acres, including the vast mud hole that stretched just beyond my Aunt Juanita's house. I had begun this celebration in a clean white T-shirt, a brand-new pair of Dollar Store jeans, and a pair of hand-me-down Converse tennis shoes. Now I was of one color, with two blue eyes peering out.

"Where are your shoes?" she asked.

"The mud hole got 'em," I answered, and it was God's truth.

I had heard stories of monsters that lurked in deep pools.

Surely there was one in a mud hole 14 feet across.

She could not decide whether to smile or cry. We lived in that place together, her and me.

Her head shook from side to side.

Finally she just sat down, quiet, with a death grip on my skinny wrist. Not that we had a lot of nice things in our little house, but I could have begrimed them all if she had let me loose in there.

You hate it, when your mama is quiet. Better she hollers. Better she raves.

I waited.

Finally, she spoke briefly to God, and reached for the Clorox.

I can still see her standing over a dented, wringer-washing machine on the tiny back porch of the little red house, running those clothes through wash after wash, uselessly, hopelessly, because the red dirt is permanent, the stains it leaves on us, in us, are forever.

And now, like everything else in the modern-day South, someone had gone and turned it into fashion, right there beside an $18 box of Goo Goo Clusters.

So I had my good laugh, a long and wobbly laugh, and put that $20 T-shirt back on the rack. I knew where to find something more original and a good bit cheaper than that, cheaper, and priceless all at the same time. The mud hole is still there, just on the other side of my Aunt Juanita's house. At $20 a pop, there must be a billion dollars or more waiting for us down there, after a hard rain. And if it ever went dry, we would just pray for a good downpour; God could always make more mud. The T-shirts themselves, we would have to buy. It does no good to pray to Walmart.

---

The red dirt covered the land. It was the land, the one resource we would never run out of, down here. It was a thing you fought with, that you turned and dug and moved from place to place, a thing that colored everything and everyone, from the knees of our jeans to our very skin, a pervasive thing, like the heat itself. In the wet, it was a slick, dangerous thing that could suck down a man or even a whole mule, and we were hearing of men who went down into the red earth for some construction or something as simple as a water or sewer line, and the red earth swallowed them whole.

It was slick as butter on a linoleum floor, when it was wet. Pulpwood trucks slid sideways and pinned men against trees. When I was a teenager hired on to cut pulpwood, a rumbling chain saw in hand, I slipped on a downed, mud-slicked tree and almost cut off my own head. Another time, I slipped in that red mush and came within the width of a sheet of paper of badly hurting, maybe killing, another boy; in time, in the wet, the other boys worked safely away from me. For a long time, I hated the red mud; it was hard enough, that dangerous and dirty work, when the earth stood still beneath your boots.

How could such a thing be good to build on, then? The smarter men explained that it set up firm and solid, deep underground, and even wet it was still firmer and harder and more waterproof than inferior soil, such as sand. All I knew was, if you let it set up around the axles of a '69 Mustang mired in a ditch, you might as well plant flowers in it because you could not dig it out with an army of coal miners.

In the drought, it took to the very air. I used to see great dust storms in the movies, in the great Sahara or the Old West, and make a tsk-tsk noise in my throat. We lived ringed by red-earth cotton fields, and the hot winds sent whole fields into the blue sky. It coated the cars in a red film, and broke my mother's heart anew, when she put the damp, white sheets on the line, to be turned red in an unpredictable wind.

I thought about it more because we were, as I grew older, in the business of dirt. My Uncle Ed owned great, yellow machines to do battle with the red dirt, bulldozers and front-end loaders and big dump trucks. We were the muscle, my brothers and me. We cut roads, dug lakes, fashioned neat, flat lawns from the ragged ground.

We moved into a place, those great machines rumbling, growling, and tore away the green, uncovering the red earth in great scars, so that other men could build things in it, and when they were done we would come back and sew the green across it again, with grass seed. I came home, every day, looking almost as bad as that boy who fell in the mud hole. I had the red dirt in the pockets of my jeans, in my shirt pockets, even in the folds of money—$1 bills, mostly—I carried there. My hair was so full of it I could shake a cloud from it, and it rode in the creases of my neck, what the old people called sweat beads.

But even when I was small, there was a beauty in it. In the spring, when the farmers turned the earth before planting, you could almost divine the future in it, in the smell of it, a smell I could describe if I was only better at what I do. I guess you could just say it smelled like promise, like the beginning of things. It was not that decayed smell of old bottomland, not that loamy smell of the Black Belt, where the dirt had the color of burnt trees. The red dirt of the Upper South was inferior, maybe, as a place for crops, a soil that lacked the richness of other places in the South, but it smelled clean.

You never get away from it, even when you are. You will pull out an old pair of jeans or a raggedy sock, and there it is, the telltale trace.

Once, when I was good and grown, I gave a talk about writing to a gathering of people from mostly someplace else. It was a good, impassioned talk, and it seemed like, in my fervor, I had carried the people with me, the way any good preacher will do. It seemed as if they were dang-near aglow with the fire of the written word, and when the sermon was at its zenith, I asked if there were questions. A Yankee woman raised her hand, to ask me a question, I was sure, about the beauty of language.

"Mr. Bragg," she asked, "is it true that Southerners eat dirt?"

I thought that she was making fun of me but she had read that it was so.

The truth is that I have never eaten any dirt, not as much as a spoonful.

But it is in me, ground in, from the outside.

# PART 2
# TABLE

# FOR A VEGETABLE,
# I'LL HAVE WHITE GRAVY

*GQ*, May 2002

I always wanted some washboard abs. But I also always seem to want some baby back ribs.

Washboard abs are hard to get. Baby back ribs are $6.99.

Washboard abs come with size 32 jeans, good overall cardiovascular health, and, if you believe the infomercials, beautiful women. Baby back ribs come with coleslaw and a Wet-Nap.

Washboard abs come with... to heck with it. I am a man, what I like to believe is a real man, a Southern man.

If God meant for me to have washboard abs, he would have left me in the hay fields of Calhoun County, slinging 50-pound bales up on the flatbed. He would have left me standing in the middle of a field of rocks, making—as the song goes—little uns outta big uns in the red-hot sun.

That was when I was 19, the last time I had anything close to washboard abs, half a lifetime ago, when the sweat and the pain of making a dollar were brutal enough to fight off the ravages of the diet of my youth, a diet of cornbread and sweet tea and fried pork chops and pinto beans with ham and mashed potatoes and creamed corn and fried okra and fried squash and fried green tomatoes and my mama's favorite dessert, a plate of home-canned blackberries with a tablespoon of sugar dumped on top, like snow on top of a purple mountain.

No, I ain't never gonna have me no washboard abs. One, I am a man, and men eat.

Two, I am a Southern man, and Southern men, the real ones, eat badly.

It's not like I'm lying around the house eating Golden Flake Cheese Curls by the double handful until the orange dust obscures my vision of a better life. I am, in fact, in remarkably good shape for a man who thinks white gravy is a vegetable. I can see my toes. I can take long, long walks, even up stairs, without having to rest.

I would like to do better. I would like to look like a model. I would like to walk through life with supermodels on my arm. And if I really thought I would be covered in supermodels, I would diet until my friends were scratching their heads.

"Hey, you seen ol' Rick?"

"Hell yeah; he's looking absolutely waiflike."

"Never thought I'd see the day when that boy was shopping for Armani."

"Yup. But his butt is fetching."

OK, my friends don't talk like that. But they might if I ever got waiflike.

Another reason I won't diet is that then I might actually be tempted to buy the clothes in this magazine. I live in jeans and white Oxford shirts and scuffed cowboy boots, and I like it that way. I remember leafing through a magazine once and seeing a man in a leather jacket with what seemed to be a feather boa. It might have been a mink stole. I just remember marveling.

That sunken-cheeked, rail-thin little fellow will probably live to be 100. He will probably be eating sushi and drinking dirty martinis when my biscuit-eating behind is feeding the worms. I can live with that. I can live with the fact he may be drinking dirty martinis with supermodels. I could not live with pointy shoes and pants that fall down off my butt. I am at the age where your pants just naturally start to fall down.

I have friends who are in real good shape, and every damn one of them shops more than my girl cousins. I have one friend who actually goes out and gets his hair cut to look like the people in those magazines. One of these days, he is going to show up with a pageboy and I am just going to have to slap him.

No, it is too big a risk to take.

Thank God, I have—quite literally—bacon grease in my veins.

The very first smell I can remember is the warm, rich, thick aroma of pork cracklings—we call them cracklin's—being rendered down in big black pots over hissing, crackling outdoor fires.

After the hog killing, after the old men disappeared into the killing pen with a .22 rifle and a curved butcher knife, the cubes of pork fat were dumped into the pots and cooked down, to make the lard.

I remember the sound of the wicked blade as an old man scraped it across his whetstone, remember how it was so sharp that we were not even allowed to hold it for fear we would cut our own throats by accident. I remember the sound of the single bullet—a flat crack, like a dead branch breaking—and the sight of the gutted hog as it was hoisted up by its hind legs and bled with that knife, then scalded and scraped till it was naked. I guess I should have been horrified by all that. I just thought it was interesting.

But mostly I remember the smell. Like a million mamas had got up early and fried a million skillets of bacon. The chunks of fat boiled in their own grease, and eventually little nuggets of cracklin's, the world's most savory by-product, floated to the top. The old men would pass them around and munch on them as they worked, and the children would hover around, begging.

Later, my mama would take the cracklin's and mix them in a skillet of cornmeal and then bake it. As the meal cooked, the essence of the cracklin's would melt through the pone of bread, and when it was done she would cut it into triangles and serve it with pinto beans and stewed squash and sliced Spanish onions and pickled pepper so hot it would blind a baby if he rubbed it on his eyes.

No, it wasn't good for us, at least not for our bodies. I don't even really know if it was good for our souls. But it was, by God, interesting.

It was Southern.

I guess, in the dieting world, we don't stand a chance.

Our mamas put sweet tea in our baby bottles and gave us Coca-Cola to settle our stomachs. They made us candy by pouring corn syrup into a hot skillet and letting it get hard. They sent us to school with bacon and biscuits wrapped in waxed paper.

They made us sheet cakes with peanut butter icing. They fried so much damn chicken that it is a wonder there is a chicken left in this world.

One time, I went to visit my mama and she told me how

sorry she was that there was nothing cooked and that all she had was some fried okra and some fresh creamed corn and some cornbread that was still sweating under a dinner plate on the stove.

Another woman tried to save me, once.

She had me eating bagels. A bagel is a fine thing, for some people, but it is a biscuit without sin or indulgence. It is a biscuit that has been saved.

I wondered, once, how a bagel would stand up under cream gravy. It was not a thing I want to think about very much.

The woman also tried to save me at lunchtime. We ate salads and fruit and whole-wheat everything, and I was not happy, but I did it for love. I lost a pound.

She tried to save me at dinner. She tried and tried.

It may be that it is a genetic thing, like sandy hair and blue eyes. I may not be able to diet for the same reason that some people are redheaded or can play the piano.

More likely, it was just that being Southern, I have spent most of my life in places where sin lurks behind every tree, on every stoop.

In the country outside Jacksonville, Alabama, it was my aunts who made it impossible to diet. My Aunt Gracie Juanita fried chicken in an iron skillet and told me it was buzzard. I was 8 years old before I realized she was having a lot of fun at my expense.

My Aunt Jo made cornbread dressing in a pan the size of a Ford F-150. My Aunt Edna always had an entire meal sitting on her stove, even at 3 a.m.

At my first newspaper job, I ate spareribs from God at Dreamland on the way to Tuscaloosa and peanut butter pie at Betty's Bar-B-Q in Anniston. In Birmingham there was a place called Friar Tuck's Fried Chicken that summoned me every day at lunchtime. I used to eat the four-wing special, telling myself the wing could not possibly have as many calories as the rest of the bird, being little and all.

I felt like crying when it closed.

In Florida I discovered the grouper sandwich and the bacon-wrapped stuffed shrimp. Then, in Miami, it was roast pork and black beans with rice and fried plantains and yucca swimming in garlic and ham *croquetas* and *café con leche*. The Cubans could give my people a close race in making sinful food.

It was in Miami that I finally found pause at the sinfulness of food. It was the first time I ever had a dessert called *tres leches*, a sheet cake of yellow color, topped with icing and drenched in, among other things, sweet condensed milk. Who thought this up? I heard it was a Nicaraguan, but I could be wrong. Whoever he was, I bet he also munched on some pork cracklin's.

Then I went to Cambridge, Massachusetts, and like to starved to death. I lost thirty pounds. I got healthy.

I hated every minute of it—the healthy part, I mean.

I ate sandwiches made on brown bread and—because there was no biscuit for 600 miles—bagels. There were a few barbecue joints, but the Yankees, not being fools, had discovered them, and you needed a hammer and chisel to get inside the door. I would eat dinner at 4 p.m. just to get a little corn pudding.

If it had not been for clam chowder, I would have jumped from a bridge into the frozen River Charles.

Then I went to New York, to the land of the $15 tuna sandwich. I ate at Sylvia's in Harlem three nights a week, ate macaroni and cheese and green beans and chicken and cornbread that had a little too much sugar in it to suit me, but who am I to argue with a legend? I haunted the rib joints. I stalked a place in the Village that had a watery biscuit and gravy.

Then I left for Atlanta.

It would all be OK now.

At Harold's Barbecue, out near the federal pen, I ordered a barbecue plate, sliced, with a mix of tender inside meat and crunchy outside skin, and Brunswick stew, coleslaw, potato chips (they come with the meal, lest you think I am a glutton) and hot cornbread with cracklin's.

Within six months, I had gained back every pound I had lost and the doctor was looking at me with something very close to alarm. He told me to lose some weight, and I said yes sir and meant to get started on it right away, but I had been invited to Thelma Grundy's place near downtown and that day she had sweet potato soufflé and, well, you know how it is.

I was there a few years, within two hours' drive of my home in Alabama and my mama's beef short ribs and spoon burgers and barbecued pork chops, and it is a wonder I did not die on Interstate 20, from joy.

After a while, I left for Miami again, but I was in my late thirties and had not slung a hay bale for a long time. I got most of my exercise running through airports and worrying about the future, and the latest in a long line of doctors kindly told me what all the others had. Exercise, she said.

Fine, I said.

Diet, she said.

I hung my head.

I cut down from six *croquetas* to three. I ordered a *tres leches* for the table, took two bites, which gave me a reason to live, and pushed it away. I ate the same damn roast-chicken *panini*—I think that's a word—sandwich every damn day for a damn year. I drove past the Kentucky Fried Chicken like it was a mirage.

I slimmed down to a lean, mean 245, and my butt was about as fetching as it had ever been.

Then I moved to New Orleans.

Help me, somebody.

I live around the corner from Franky & Johnny's joint on Arabella Street. They make pies out of shrimp.

There ain't much more that needs to be said about that.

I live a few blocks from Domilise's po'boy joint. They make sandwiches out of fried shrimp and oysters and French bread. I eat them with Zapp's Crawtators and a root beer. I guess there's not much more to say about that, either.

About ten minutes away is Dunbar's, a fried-chicken-and-red-bean emporium that offers potato salad on Fridays. I actually believe they make the potato salad on other days, too, but are hoarding it from me.

And get this. When you eat all your chicken, a woman who sometimes calls you "Pookie, my baby" will walk up and ask you if you would like another leg and you always say, "No thank you, ma'am," because, of course, you are on a diet.

So I wander this land, trying to diet with a Southern belly. I want to do right. I really do. But, Lord, it is just so hard.

It would be easier to ask me to go ice fishing. It would be easier to ask me to join the ballet. It would be easier to be an astronaut. I think they still squeeze all their food out of tubes.

I wonder if you could put some cream gravy in there.

# BACK TO THE BAYOU

*Bon Appetit,* November 2004

———

I loved a Cajun woman once. It was her eyes, I believe.
When I was a little boy, just because it is the kind of things
boys do, I would look at the hot sun through a green, sweating
bottle of 7UP. The sunlight seemed to freeze in the middle of the
bottle, and glow.

She had eyes like that.

I was afraid that coming back here, to her Louisiana, would
make me think of Her. And sure enough, every mile, every road
sign, tapped me deeper into that green bottle.

The Bayou Teche, seeming more mud than water, did not flow
or even crawl, but just lay.

Morgan City still existed on a bubble of oil. Its conjugal beds left
half empty by men who worked rigs out in the deep blue. Along
the Atchafalaya River, blue herons, their beaks like stilettos,
stabbed into the dark water and came back out with wriggling
silver victims. Alligators and rumors of alligators haunted Lake
Henderson, where gray trees raised stumps of arms into the haze.

All of it gritty, lovely, like Her.

My heart hurt, a little.

And my stomach growled.

The air on the side streets and outside the wood-framed
restaurants smelled of crab boil and crawfish and hot lemons.

In the roadside stores, big countertop Crock-Pots simmered with boudin, the sausage made from pork, liver, onions, rice, and spices. Iron pots in open-air cookshacks rendered tiny cubes of fatback into golden cracklin's, and old men and little children stood in gravel parking lots and ate them like M&Ms. In the evenings, in dives and fine-dining establishments, chefs took the ingredients of their liquid country—the rice, crawfish, shrimp, oysters, okra, duck, trout, crab, catfish, turtle, and drum—and turned them into dishes that tasted better than the mere ingredients should have allowed.

With every bite I felt a little better, as if there were a tonic in the turtle soup—as if, since I had been hexed in the swamp, it was the swamp itself and its people that had to heal me.

They did their best. Descendants of French Canadian exile who drifted south to these swamps and prairies in southern Louisiana more than two centuries ago, they have long been accused of fusing magic with their food. I ate it in oil towns and shrimp shacks and interstate gas stations, in themed restaurants with stuffed alligators swinging from the ceilings, and in late-night bars where there was more swinging than I care to remember.

I ate to forget.

## LE TRAITEUR

The smell swirled from underneath the roof of the cooking shed and permeated the air over the parking lot, the smell of a million skillets of bacon all sizzling at once.

But it was a witch's cauldron of fatback, roiling, the cracklin's bopping up, the size of postage stamps, all crunchy skin on one side and thin layers of crisp-fried fat on the other.

Some people argue that Eddie Goulas makes the best cracklin's in Acadiana in his cook shed in Ruth, not far from Breaux Bridge. "I never did like cracklin's," Goulas said, as he and a few helpers trimmed the lean from big slabs of fatback, diced it, and fed it into the pots.

"I guess I thought if I can make them where I would eat them, they must be pretty good," he said. His face intent, he watched the trimming process, kept an eye on the heat. "It's not hard to do something," he said, "when you ain't guessing."

In the parking lot, I ate cracklin's from a paper sack. I listened to people speak to each other in French and smiled like an imbecile.

"The food, the music, it's the joy of life," explained 68-year-old

Claude Simon Jr., as he handed me his business card—"Custom Woodwork, Antique Repair, Cowhide Furniture." At the bottom of the card, he has written in a single word: *Traiteur.*

Like his papa before him, he is a treater, a healer, someone the Cajuns—the ones who still believe—would ask to heal bellyaches, arthritis, or general malaise with herbs, roots, and prayers. His papa was a grand *traiteur.* Even when he was very old and in a nursing home, people came to be treated.

Sometimes evil spirits invade us, Simon explained, and make us forget to enjoy life. I nodded, my mouth full of cracklin's.

Before he left, Simon mentioned that he also does exorcisms.

"I don't charge. It's the Lord's work," he said. "I do accept donations."

## LENA AND PAUL

I was healed a good bit more in Carencro, about a block from City Hall. Here, in a place called Paul's Pirogue, a spirit helped stir the pot.

It was a poor man's dish called catfish court bouillon, just a few catfish pieces smothered in stewed tomatoes, onions, and other good things. Paul's served it with some of the best potato salad, with Cajun spices in the mayonnaise.

I asked the man at the cash register: "Who cooked the catfish?" He told me he had, mostly, but his grandma, who has gone on, might as well have.

"It comes from her—I learned from her," said 43-year-old Terry Soignier, who manages Paul's Pirogue. "She lost her first husband in the yellow fever, I believe, of '46. Her name was Lena. My oldest brother had epilepsy, and she would sing to him in French. When she cooked, he was always on her hip."

He spoke about them both, the food and his grandmama, with such love that I expected to see her standing there. "A black cast-iron pot," he said, thinking back. "Fresh onions. Catfish, pulled from the bayou."

"Not a bad memory at all," he said.

I ordered a shrimp po'boy because I had seen one go by, and I lusted after it. It was deep-fryer hot, the shrimp spiced and peppery and served on the best French bread that I have ever tasted. It did not crumble into dust, like delicate, airy French bread, but was chewy, buttery, comforting.

I am sure someone's long-dead grandpapa kneaded that bread.

I walked out feeling loved.

## T-SUE'S BREAD

I met the hands that had kneaded that bread, and I was half-right. Phillip "T-Sue" Roberts owns the bakery in Henderson that furnishes Paul's Pirogue—and much of the Atchafalaya Basin—with bread. The recipes go back to his grandparents, Pete and Delia Patin, who ran a family bakery in Cecilia from 1934 until 1975. It is not designed to be French bread at all, but just good bread.

Roberts' grandparents gave him his skill, and even his name.

"What does T-Sue mean, anyway?" I asked.

"Little drunk," he said.

"Oh," I said.

It involved a bottle of Crown Royal. "I was 13," he said, "and it was the first time they let me out of the house. It was an adventure."

I told him I reckoned so.

"I danced all night at the American Legion," he said, "whether the music was playing or not."

Someone told on him. His grandfather started calling him, in French, *tee soux*, or "little drunk."

That became T-Sue, and that is what he named his bakery.

I ate a piece of bread stuffed with boudin from Charlie-T's Specialty Meats in Breaux Bridge. I can't write well enough to tell you how good it was.

## LIKE CHICKEN

The waitress was pushing the alligator at Prejean's, the big Cajun restaurant in Lafayette, but I don't like to eat things that are said to taste like chicken—snake, alligator, iguana—when what they really taste like is snake and lizard. Instead, I ate delicious corn-and-crab bisque, and asked about dessert.

How about the *gateau sirop*, the syrup cake?

"I don't like it," she said.

It was dense and dark and tasted of molasses.

"Did you like it?" the waitress asked.

"Yes," I said.

"A lot of the older people do," she said.

The bakery chef's name is Roe Zenon, a smiling but no-nonsense woman who eyed a single fly in her bakeshop like it was a flying gopher. She told me she learned from her mom, Bulia Zenon, who called it spice cake.

Her mom would call to her from the porch, "and the kids in the neighborhood would smell that cooking and all come with me.

'Your mama cooking?' they'd ask me. She always was. Mama would say, 'We always got something burning.' "

The children ate their spice cake with Kool-Aid.

I ate mine with gratitude.

Before I left, the folks at Prejean's made me try the alligator. "We just use the tail meat, not the lung meat, and never from a gator over 6 feet," said Dean Dugas, the general manager. I didn't know what that meant, but it was good.

## FOOD OF LOVE

Dickie Breaux and Cynthia Breaux, once married but still partners in Café Des Amis, the restaurant they founded more than a decade ago, are still bound. Their love of the Breaux Bridge restaurant, and its food, survived their breakup.

"I believe you and I were brought together to create this thing," Cynthia said to Dickie one night at dinner.

If that is true, then maybe I was left standing in a driveway in Miami, watching taillights fade, just so I could be healed by barbecued shrimp and a slab of white-chocolate bread pudding. All I know is, it is hard to feel heartsick when you are eating crawfish étouffée served on hot cornbread.

"You have to be raised in the atmosphere of the food," said Dickie Breaux. "We just cook better than anybody else. A Cajun knows he's got it right when, after it's done, you can throw away the meat and just eat the gravy."

The gravy, then. The gravy is the antidote.

That night, I ate the best turtle soup I have ever had. I listened to people who love food talk about how it can hold something fine together that might otherwise have come apart. I knew I couldn't face my bed-and-breakfast on the Teche.

I knew I wouldn't sleep.

So I asked the question millions of men like me have asked.

"Know a good beer joint?"

## SQUEEZE BOX

The dance floor at Pat's Atchafalaya Club was packed with a hundred, more. Geno Delafose wore his squeeze box low, like a gunslinger, singing in French and English as white people and black people and old people and young people danced like it was their last night on this earth.

Crawfish corpses littered the tables. The band never took a break. The dancing never stopped. A big woman in a pantsuit looked at me a little too long, and I got scared.

The next morning, a Saturday, Café Des Amis opened for breakfast, but a breakfast like I had never seen. A zydeco band tore up the small stage at the front of the restaurant, and people danced between tables loaded with bacon and eggs.

A lot of the people dancing were the same ones I had seen the night before. One of them, Ted Couvillion, said hello.

"My wife died of cancer two years ago," he said. He vanished into his grief, until his friends dragged him out dancing. Now, every week, he dances and dances his way out of heartache.

I can't dance a lick. But I have two bags of cracklin's in the trunk of my car.

# TRAVELING FOOD

*Southern Living,* Southern Journal: May 2011

———

I t was always dusk and, it seems, always summer. My aunts would steer their Chevelles and Monte Carlos onto the gravel at Pee Wee Johnson's joint. Change purses clutched in their fists, they would step into line with mill workers, pulp-wooders, and downy-faced soldiers destined for Vietnam. That takeout window in Jacksonville, Alabama, united us all with a common desire: the perfect footlong. These came skinny, dressed with yellow mustard, thin, hot chili, and Spanish onions, the whole mess weeping into waxed paper. Their aroma filled the car and the world beyond, and every turn of the tires tortured us until we finally found a picnic table or shade tree somewhere down Alabama 21. But often we just ate on the go, wiping chili off vinyl, listening to the Happy Goodman Family on the radio, and feeling, somehow, a little more free.

It was not fast food but traveling food, a paper-sack delicacy we grabbed before an all-night gospel singing in Sylacauga, or on the way to buy a truck in Cedartown. It can be found on gas station countertops and off forlorn interstate exits, advertised on badly wired marquee lights that blink FRIED CHICK N, or on plywood that screams BOU-DIN!!! It might be pickled eggs at a fish camp on Lake Okeechobee, Saran-wrapped fried pies at a truck stop outside Laurel, Mississippi, or good wings and crisp potato wedges at a Shell Station on Highway 78 near Winfield, Alabama. In a wasteland of tepid tomatoes and mummified chicken fingers, there still exist across the South some fine dishes, served on paper plates, prepared by people who have solved the great mystery of simple food.

Drake's Citgo on Highway 411 in Leesburg, Alabama, served a mouthwatering pork cutlet on hot biscuit, or about any other part of a pig that can be made to lie flat. Drake's is now Coosa Corner, but to my big brother, Sam, it will always be Drake's. "The ol' boy who owned it had a dog that, if you threw a rock in the river, would dive down and get that rock," Sam said. "That *exact* rock."

Stories like that season a place. Most food joints leave you with, at best, a commemorative cup. Louisiana may be the wonderland of traveling food. Years ago, after being dumped by a Cajun, I drove through that wet country to eat my way free of a broken heart. I ate rice dressing on Bayou Teche, and boudin at every other gas station. I ignored signs for alligator, because it tastes like an unholy union between a chicken and a Gila monster, and my heart never has been broke that bad.

Some foods need to travel with you, taste better if they do. At Ted Peter's Famous Smoked Fish in St. Petersburg, you can eat a plate of mullet, potato salad, and coleslaw at the restaurant, or out a few miles away, propped against a hump of sand, looking out at the Gulf. Mullet are like bad whiskey, cheap and strong, but not at sunset, not here.

It is the same with a Hicks' tamale, in Clarksdale, Mississippi. It tastes fine indoors. But when you peel it at the edge of an endless field, on the hood of your car, there is just the pudding-like texture and smooth, hot, garlicky taste, because there is nothing else out here, as far as you can see, but lonesome.

There used to be so many more such places, before the chains. But there are still good fries at T-Ray's in Fernandina Beach (they must fry them twice to get them that crisp and greasy) and drive-by barbecue at 1,001 places in North Carolina. In my hometown, there are still perfect, dripping hamburgers, at the Rocket and Cecil's, and at Tweeners, owned by Pee Wee Johnson's girls.

I guess that is why I don't like to fly. There is no good food, only the rush and wait, the airplane seats fit for gymnasts. But in the Memphis airport, I found an antidote: Interstate Barbecue's thick-cut, smoked bologna sandwich, topped with coleslaw. I ate it at 30,000 feet. I expected to see Pee Wee's angel, flying alongside.

# FULLY DRESSED

*Southern Living*, Southern Journal: November 2013

———

T he word "stuffing" had a lot of connotations when I was a boy. None of them had anything to do with food.

Sofas had stuffing. But then again, I rarely heard the word "sofa." We sat on "couches." The first time I heard the word "sofa" I thought it was "Sofia," and I never did figure out why anyone had to sit on the poor woman. Once, I heard someone say they had to restuff their Sofia. This haunts me still.

I digress. Teddy bears had stuffing for insides. Baseballs had it. We were urged to "knock the stuffing out of it." If you caught a big fish, or shot a deer, or even a big gobbler, you could have them "stuffed and mounted." I was mightily confused.

Thanksgiving turkeys, however, did not have stuffing, though sometimes my Aunt Jo did shove a whole stick of margarine in there. Stuffing, I would be educated, was another word for dressing. And our dressing, as God intended, was cooked separately, in a shallow baking dish or pan.

It was not something the great cooks in my family were willing to debate.

"Stick your hand up the back end of a raw turkey?" said my Aunt Gracie Juanita, shaking her head violently from side to side. "That is not natural."

"Ain't even human," my mother said.

But the word stuffing was everywhere, come November. I heard it on the television, usually accompanied by images of a massive turkey with a golden cascade of breadcrumbs tumbling from its insides. Was I missing out? Why didn't we have stuffing if they had stuffing on *Father Knows Best?*

"You ain't missing nothin'," my mother told me.

I would learn that, like so many things I struggled to understand, it was a Southern thing, like why a faucet inside the house was a faucet but outside the house it became a hydrant. And Southerners, especially mine, did not tolerate in-the-bird dressing.

I would learn it stemmed from a generational fear of under-cooked poultry. How could the turkey cook all the way through, my people reasoned, if the heat could not swirl around inside the bird? Onions, lemons, butter, and other seasoning were allowed, but a thick gob of breadcrumbs was salmonella waiting to happen. But even if bacteria were not an issue, the cooks in my family would have shunned stuffing for one simple reason: taste.

Our dressing started with an iron skillet of cornbread, mixed with onion, sage, and the fatty, golden nectar from boiled turkey or chicken, usually the pieces that would otherwise be thrown away. It was baked until a golden crust formed on the top, leaving the inside firm but creamy. Too dry and it set up like cake. Too wet and it was a watery mess. It had to be perfect, and usually was.

Years ago, I stood in a supermarket, staring at a "stuffing mix" of spices and prepackaged breadcrumbs—tiny, hard little cubes. Mama, I thought, was right again. But when I mentioned that we were having turkey and dressing at my house, my Yankee friends looked confused. You mean, they asked, the stuff you put on salads?

It is a miracle we fought only one war.

# YOUR FIRST OYSTER

*Garden & Gun*,  February/March 2010

————

The first one I ate tasted like river mud.

It was not that earthy, pungent, essence *du monde* that well-traveled people like to go on about over their *quenelles aux huîtres*. It tasted like wet dirt, only slicker, fishier, like what a tadpole would taste like if you sucked it right out of the ditch, or a wet hoofprint.

Of course, I was not a gourmand then. I was a sun-scorched boy in a dockside restaurant in Panama City, intoxicated by the aroma of coconut butter suntan lotion and piña colada lip balm, and flabbergasted by ten thousand teenage Baptists in tiny two-piece bathing suits. I wanted to eat oysters because it seemed like a thing a man of the world would do in 1971, like being a spy against the Communists, or owning an MGB. But that taste, and that horrible consistency—somewhere among raw chicken liver, Jell-O, beef tripe, and Dippity-do—haunted me for years.

"What does one look like?" one of my brothers asked me at the time.

"Well," I said, "it's gray-lookin'."

"What does it taste like?" he asked.

"Well," I said, "it's...it's..." but it was just beyond me then.

How could people eat something I could not even say?

Maybe, I remember thinking, they might not be so damn awful

if they were cooked. I mean, I suspect that a pork chop would be pretty grim if you had to eat it while the hog was still kicking. But later, in high school, one of my mean girl cousins gave me a fried one from her seafood platter, and even though it was entombed in batter and well and truly dead, it still tasted like tadpole, but crunchier this time.

I spit that one out. At least, back then, I did not have to pretend to like them, to fit in. That came later, when I became a writer.

There are just some things that male writers, of a certain ilk, feel they have to do. I call it the Curse of Hemingway. We have to like to fish. We have to be proficient in blowing birds from the sky with shotguns. And we have to love oysters. We have to sit around a table in some sun-blasted shack on some desolate, mosquito-infested cay and slurp 'em right out of the shell. Or they take our vowels away.

I love to fish. I am not good at it, but I love it. In my youth, I slaughtered some birds, though it seemed like a lot of firepower to get a few mouthfuls of meat—and I still think quail hunting is just an excuse for biscuits and gravy. Then my wife put a dozen bird feeders in our backyard, cooed over finches, hummingbirds, and cardinals, and made me deeply ashamed.

But, even as I got a more sophisticated palate, I could only tolerate oysters. Oh, I put up a good front. Any real man can eat one oyster, two, even three. He just bellies up to it, chews, and gulps. There were worse things. Snails, I guess. Sushi. Turkey bacon.

But I could not make myself like them in my first forty years. I thought moving to Florida, twice, would change that, would at least break down my resistance. But that, too, had no real impact on my revulsion, and the young, oyster-hating man I was vanished into old age.

The change, when it did come, almost makes me believe in magic. And like most magic, here in my South, it happened in New Orleans.

I remember the moment. I believe I was sitting in a cool, dark place in the French Quarter, one of those places that Katrina would drown and remove, forever, from all but fond memory. It was fall, which means it was only eighty-nine in the shade, and as I recall I was mildly drunk on brown whiskey, though it could have been some sickly sweet rum drink and I am just embarrassed to say.

I went in for some crawfish bisque, not the creamy kind but a gumbo-like concoction that was redolent with onions, peppers, and little bitty crawfish heads stuffed with, well, stuffing. It was a reason to live.

I do not know why I ordered the oysters—maybe because I saw the words *half dozen* and thought this might be my chance to try them again and not be so wasteful. I did not try to slurp them from the shell, but carefully prepared them in the fashion I was told my grandfather ate them, when he drifted down to the Florida Gulf coast in the 1950s, to roof houses, fish, sleep on the sand, and eat things he could not find in the foothills of the Appalachians.

I took a saltine, plopped down an oyster, forked on some cocktail sauce, daubed on a fingernail-size spot of horseradish, squeezed a lemon over the whole mess, and popped it in my mouth.

Like I said, it had to be magic. One minute you hate, the next you love. But it was *good*.

I know that oyster purists will say I did not truly taste the oyster, that I am a commoner, but they can kiss my #*!.

The cocktail sauce and horseradish did not mask the oyster, only provided a little misdirection, a little sleight of hand, and I chewed and liked it. They say you can taste the sea in it, and I think that is true. I even ate the last one naked, with just a little lemon, and it was pretty fine. It had to be New Orleans, I believed. In New Orleans, you walk on roads flecked with crushed oyster shell, and there is a whole culture of oysters, a mystique. Oyster recipes and oyster lore naturally pooled there, some of them indigenous, some trickling down from other places.

"One time my mother bit down on one and there was a pearl in it," says Jim Davis, director of the Center for the Book at the State Library of Louisiana. "My daddy took it and made her a ring out of it. We don't know if the fact that it was cooked made it any less valuable."

In New Orleans, oysters are almost an art form. You eat them covered in spinach and garlic and bacon and cheese, eat them roasted, baked, even grilled over an open flame in their shells.

And I came to like them all. At Upperline, one of the great restaurants of this world, I ate them in oyster stew, in heavy cream, but you could have dropped a coaster or a matchbox in there instead and it probably still would have tasted pretty good.

In a half-dozen kitchens around town, I had them in oyster dressing, which I consumed in such quantities I wanted to die, and in gumbo so good you would pray, quietly, that the cook would say, "Babe, you want me to put this in some Tupperware, so you can take some home?"

And of course, all over town, I ate them in po'boys and oyster loaves, dripping with hot sauce and tartar sauce, with cold root beer on the side. I was not just eating food, I was consuming culture, and as I came to love the city, I came to love its oysters.

But it was not just the place, as it turned out. Once my resistance was broken, I ate them in Florida, ate them on the Alabama coast, and loved them, too. Maybe there is no magic to it at all. Maybe—as my mama always told me—as I get older I come to appreciate more of the world around me. Someday, she told me, I will even like butter beans.

Recently, I got to eat dinner with one of the great writers of our time at one of the great restaurants of our time, Highlands Bar and Grill in Birmingham. Pat Conroy ate about 10 oysters, with nothing but a smile.

I ate four, four of the best oysters I've ever had, and prepared one more—in the way my grandfather ate them—for my 15-year-old stepson, Jake.

He gasped and choked only slightly, and fought it down.

"I know, son," I said, and gave him a pat.

"It will," I said, "get better."

# BAD SLAW

I almost lost my mind once, over coleslaw.

I don't mean I got miffed, or a little bit upset, or even perturbed.

I mean, I got spitting, deranged, hollering-at-the-furniture, kicking-a-fencepost mad. The kind of mad that makes people reach for their children, and go, "Shhhhhhhhhhhh, Betty Lou. Just keep walkin' and don't make eye contact with the big crazy man."

Coleslaw is one of the easiest foods to prepare, at least in regard to steps in the preparation. It is slightly labor intensive, as in the cutting of it, but there is really only one hard and fast rule.

Don't let it go bad.

When it does, do not put it under the noses of good people.

They might, in good faith, take a bite.

And this, I feel, should be a crime.

What if I really had gone crazy, from wilted cabbage and tainted mayonnaise?

I don't think we, as a Southern society, should have to live with this abomination.

Somebody should have to pay.

It was a year or so back, when I had enough. I had a fried chicken craving going pretty strong. I had not had any good chicken in a while; I hadn't even had any bad chicken.

I am not a chicken snob. I believe Gus's fried chicken, from the one on Front Street in Memphis, is the best chicken in the known world. Snobs, the ones who think fried chicken should be honey-drizzled or beheaded when it's not looking, will tell you about this great little place in Soho... We will ignore them because they are ... well, we will ignore them because I say so.

Anyway, I needed some chicken, and Gus's was nowhere close, and no one—at least no one who was speaking to me in my rough zip code—was going to fry me any, so that meant fast food or supermarket delis. I am enough of a snob to say this is not often a good idea, but I was hungry.

I do not usually do deli-fried chicken because of the fatal flaw in the supermarket fried chicken apparatus. The chicken is often fine, though I am still fairly certain that several hours under a heat lamp has never done fried chicken any good.

But that's not the big flaw with supermarket chicken. The flaw is that, while the chicken (though perhaps old as Abraham) might taste fine, the condiments will not. Specifically, the coleslaw will not taste like anything approximating food.

The coleslaw in the deli counter even looks like something that does not approximate food. The slaw, even in your high-end supermarkets, appears to have suffered greatly from time. I don't know what happens to slaw in a deli case but it ain't nothin' good. It ranges from mightily shriveled to Spanish moss to, "Oh, Sweet Lord." People there try to fool us by making slaw out of broccoli, or apples, or other unnatural things, but there is just something in the chemical properties of cabbage that does not respond to being encased in a counter next to some dessicated teriyaki chicken wings. But I digress.

Some do not even have slaw prepared in-house. The option is the mass-produced, trucked-in slaw that you can buy in a vacuum-sealed plastic tub. This is not food, in any culture. Cabbage, unless pickled, does not respond to the passing of weeks. Neither, ugh, does mayonnaise. The rule—if I was king I would make it an edict—for coleslaw should be that it should never be anywhere near a truck. I will not eat Gulf shrimp in St. Paul. Coleslaw should not take to the highway.

But, they sell it. They sell it because people eat it.

God help us, they do.

So, I go see the Colonel, or drive through at Popeye's, or another fast-food option.

The Colonel is not with us anymore, and it's probably a good thing he left this world before he even suspected that, someday, his beloved chicken restaurants—I mean, the man used to drive around to his restaurants to taste-test the *gravy*—would someday share a building with fast-food burritos.

I simply cannot abide this. I do not brag about awards that much, not now that I am old and no one who knows me even cares, but I am the winner of the coveted James Beard Award, which makes me a blue ribbon-wearing, bona fide expert on the preparation of food.

That is, of course, a big, fat, hairy lie. But let's at least assume that, as the son of one of the finest cooks who has ever lived, and a man who has dined all over the world, I know the difference between a rice cake and a plate of sausage gravy. And this son of the true South cannot get his mind around the fact that the teenagers behind the glass of the drive-through are forming tacos in the same assembly line that should be devoted, heart, mind, and soul, to my three-piece dinner.

But it's still pretty good chicken, as is the chicken offered by most of the others. (Though, Popeye's kind of bothers me, too. I mean, it's called Popeye's. Why is there no Popeye? I loved Popeye. But there is not one cardboard cutout or action figure or ... not even a Wimpy. I do not miss Olive Oyl. She always kind of bothered me.)

Anyway, these chains, along with a handful of others, are the logical alternative to the troubling slaw that accompanies the otherwise fine deli chicken. And so I am a fairly regular customer of their drive-through windows.

As I was that day I had that awful fried chicken jones. I went through a drive-through, got me a whole bucket and the appropriate condiments, including slaw. Slaw is perfect with chicken. It cools and balances the meal. It is said to be healthy, before you whip in a quart of mayonnaise.

I went home, turned on the Atlanta Braves to see if they have, in the past five years or so, found a way to manufacture a run, and sat down for the perfect evening, just me, my chicken, and four hours of stranded runners. I mean, my grandma could lay down a bunt.

The first bite of chicken was heavenly.

The coleslaw never made it to my lips. It had gone bad. It had probably gone bad two days before. I slam-dunked it in the garbage.

It did not matter that everything else was fine. I had counted on that coleslaw. I needed that coleslaw.

I balled up my fists. I might have cursed. Yes, I did. I did curse.

I am not one of those people who will return to the drive-through and rant. I don't call. What good does it do?

So, I just slumped on the couch, morose.

The Braves, their slump broken, were gleefully circling the bases.

———

Does it have to be this way?

It would be one thing if it were just fast food, where quality control often consists of, well, nothing. But I have stared suspiciously at coleslaw in even high-end places.

One of my favorite restaurants, in Baton Rouge, gave me coleslaw that, I believe, was held over from ... well, dinners past. And I had just written about how good it was.

I think, among the myriad signs of the decline of life as we know it, this is, sorta, one.

It's as if chefs and cooks and drive-through mavens have decided it is not real food, that it is not perishable at all, like a packet of ketchup or a shaker of salt.

We must stop this. We must rise up, as a people, and say no to rancid coleslaw, must stand strong in the rushing tide of apathy that threatens not just our quality of life, but life itself.

For I fear that bad coleslaw can actually kill you.

The next time you are served a half-pint of tainted slaw, do not just pick at it, regretfully and in silence. You know you have done this. You *know*.

No, you must raise the offensive article high above your head and shout, "Nay!"

Or go ask for a fresh one.

———

I make it myself now. I coarse-cut red cabbage—we call it purple cabbage—and fresh carrots.

They need to really snap when you break them. Mix in mayonnaise to taste. I use my hands.

Some people like seasonings, but it is the taste of the cabbage and carrots that I like, so I just sprinkle on a little black pepper.

I will eat it the second day, but never, ever the third, and certainly not if it has anything resembling a whang. We all know the whang. More than half the time, when we eat slaw, there is the whang.

Life is too short for the whang.

Rise up.

Make T-shirts.

A whang, with a slash through it.

The Colonel would wear one, if he was still alive.

You know Popeye would, too.

# NEVER-ENDING GRACE

*Southern Living,* Southern Journal: November 2012

W hen I was a little boy, the words seemed to last forever. It seemed like we were walking the Exodus ourselves, one paragraph at a time. Surely, I figured, thousands of little boys had starved to death between the words "Let us pray..." and "Amen."

The bad thing was, from where I sat, hands clasped but one eye open, I could see it all, and more than that I could smell it all, this wonderful feast laid out hot and steaming: Thanksgiving, my favorite day on the calendar, better than the Fourth of July, Halloween, and Presidents' Day all lumped into one. The pinto beans bubbled in the battered pot, molten with the fat from big chunks of ham. Hot biscuits rested under a warm towel. Mashed potatoes, creamed onions, cornbread dressing, sweet potatoes, macaroni and cheese—all waited, each one sending its own perfume wafting through the house. And in the middle of it all sat the big turkey, its sides trickling with melted butter, specked with black pepper, so close—why, a drumstick was just a side step and quick grab away—and yet so far.

But it would all be cold as a Confederate statue on Christmas morning by the time we got any of it. Between me and all this bounty stretched what we have called and will always call "The Blessing." It consisted, as near as I could tell, of reading the King

James Bible front to back, then holding a discussion on its finer points. While I now see the beauty in those words and in this tradition, I was an ungrateful heathen back then, thinking only of my belly and my own little self.

Before anyone fires off an angry letter pointing out the heathenness I have already confessed—I have learned that admitting to such things in some preemptive hope just makes people mad at you for robbing them of the opportunity to flog you unencumbered—let me say that I know how selfish and ignorant I was to wish for a shorter blessing, a more truncated thanks. I know. I get it. I was a bad child. But I was suffering.

I grew up with Pentecostals, and they do not have a short blessing in their lexicon. They are not like some denominations that see prayer as a fixed ritual; the Congregational Holiness go to town with a prayer, and they do not turn loose of one till they have wrung it dry. So I suffered.

Sometimes, they would have a child do a blessing, and I would grow hopeful, because surely they would not have so many words at their disposal, and older ladies would pat the good child when he was done and say "How precious." But I came to know that this was only a warm-up to the main event, and that a grown-up, a deacon even, would take over, to close the show.

What would happen, I once wondered, if I just broke down in the middle of the litany of things we were thankful for, and snatched a wing? I could be halfway across the pasture and into the deep woods before they ran me down. But it was too awful, the eventual consequences, to even talk about with nice people.

So I suffered.

Now, it is one of those things I wait for all year. My uncle John does the blessing now, and he is a man of honor and brings to us a gentle message of great warmth and dignity. It is a simple prayer of thanks for this one day, for the grace that has allowed us to gather here for one more year. I think anyone, of any faith, or of no faith at all, would see great value in it. It is never too long, this message, though the older and older I get, it is sometimes over much too soon.

# THE PLANE TRUTH

*Southern Living*, Southern Journal: March 2015

———

I f you fly in from Birmingham you'll get the last gate,
    *If you blew in from Boston, no, you sure won't have to wait,*
    *And I'm learning...*
—Hank Williams, Jr.

All I wanted was a peanut.

"We have no food on this flight," the flight attendant said.

A sip of water, then? Or, though I knew it was an impossible dream, a drop or two of ginger ale?

The duration of the flight did not permit it, I was told ... in coach.

Time, like all things, is just bigger in first class.

It is hard these days, to be a Southerner in the wild blue yonder, to be a boy from Alabama who tries to slip the surly bonds of earth. The grand days of Southern flight might not be over, but it is sure different, if you need to go from Memphis to Mobile or Baton Rouge to anywhere.

You can get a peanut up North, on a long flight, but you will play heck getting one as you fly over Georgia and Alabama, which is where they come from. But I can do without a salty snack. I do not need ginger ale. It's everything else that makes me want to Go Greyhound.

The conversations have a sameness to them these days, up high.

I noticed it when I was halfway through a long book tour, doing the same crossword for the third time. People around me thought I was real smart. Night was falling, and the young traveler next to me was trying to get home to Tampa after working in Louisiana. The young traveler showed me a picture of a bulldog puppy and said they would see each other again, someday, after connections in Miami and I think Saskatchewan. I did not tell the young traveler that, by the time he finally got home, the dog might not love him anymore.

It did not used to be this way for the ragged, hypertensive Southern flier. I remember a gilded age, when carriers here flew to actual places we wanted to go—in the region and beyond—on real planes with seats designed for adult humans, an age when every single flight from every decent-size city did not have to connect in Atlanta or Charlotte or Nepal. I remember flying nonstop from Birmingham to Tampa, New Orleans, Fort Lauderdale, Nashville. I remember when planes were not pitiful; now, some are so skinny I feel like I am being shot out of a cannon. Disembarking, now, reminds me of those tiny cars in the circus, the ones that emit an endless stream of clowns. Some days, I think I shall not fly at all. I will just burn $500 on the sidewalk, line up 50 strangers, and see how many of us we can stuff in a phone booth. With a one-bag minimum.

You can say times are tough all over, but down here the airlines have canceled so many flights that the only way to get around is to hop a freight. It would not be so bad if they did not rub it in. Many nights I sit in front of my television as sparkling, majestic planes glide through the clouds, the reclining passengers sipping Champagne on the way to Paris. The next day I board a Sopwith Camel and stumble off wild-eyed, smelling like jet fuel and something called Bloody Mary Mix.

And you can keep your dadgum pretzels.

# MAGIC ON THE PLATE

*Louisiana Kitchen*: June 2012

———

I t may be the magic is real. Here amid marked-down voodoo and dime store gris-gris, between piney-woods preachers and deep-swamp fortunetellers, may swirl real spirits that enrich this place, or at least permeate the food that delights us and drinks that lubricate us. Here, where something as humble as a wooden spoon can seem like a magic wand, where ghosts of ancestors stir a little something extra into recipes passed down 150 years, things routinely taste better than the chemistry of ingredients or the alchemy of preparation should allow. I tasted it for the first time more than a quarter-century ago, swirling up and into and through me, from the bottom of a glass.

———

It was on the balcony of the Columns Hotel on St. Charles Avenue. I was sitting in a wicker chair, just decrepit enough to be comfortable, drinking a glass of Jim Beam on the rocks. I am not a big drinker, but there has always been something comforting about brown liquor. After one, I always felt like I was covered in a warm quilt. The secret, across my life and my ancestors' lives, was not to drink seven more, turn the quilt into a cape or a parachute, and jump off something tall.

This time I only had the one. I was down to ice and watered-down whiskey—wasn't it Sinatra who said you had to let it lay in the ice a little while?—when that special peace slipped over and around me, but in a way I had never felt before. The old streetcar, the color of a WWII surplus jeep, clanked and rattled on the neutral ground below with a rhythm I had never heard. From the bar below, a scent of candied cherries and orange slices and spiced rum and good perfume seemed to reach up and out into the dusk around me. The live oaks creaked. The night flowed through the ancient trees like a river. And I could have slept, if that glass had held just one half-inch more. I sipped the last of the liquor—the same liquor you can buy in almost any bar in this world—and my mind emptied for just a few precious minutes of contention and ambition, and filled with the essence of this place, this street, this city, this state. And all the conjurer behind the bar had to do was unscrew a bottle, and pour.

———————

Think of the magic that Celestine Dunbar and her family created in their place on Freret Street, before the waters took it—fried seafood platters that came so fast from the fryer that you could scorch your hands and fried chicken that made grown men damn near cry, served with stewed okra, and sweet potato pies, and good cornbread. You could eat all the barbecued chicken and stewed cabbage you could stand on a weekday, give the nice lady at the cash register ten dollars and have enough left to tip like a sultan, ride the streetcar, and buy a grape snowball. The allure of that fried chicken held me so tightly that after the city drowned I traced it to Loyola, where Mrs. Dunbar would make young people the best lunch in the whole academic world—many of whom had no idea from whence the source of that magic came. I have forgotten most of the food I have eaten in this life. I have never forgotten one crumb of hers.

I know cynics will say it is just cooking. Maybe. I mean, how complicated is this food, really?

You simmer some beans, roast some fat hog, boil some shrimp or some blue crabs, concoct some gumbo. You have been taught, over generations, not to fear the saltshaker, or the butter, or the garlic, and you do not sprinkle cayenne so much as you ladle it. You give onions, green pepper, and celery a celestial name—trinity— to raise them above the mundane of simple ingredients, but it is still just a seasoning.

But how do you explain the difference in grabbing lunch elsewhere in this poor ol' sorry world to sitting down to a plate of creamy red beans and braised ham shank at Betsy's Pancake House on Canal Street, where the fat from the meat slowly, slowly drips down to season the already perfectly seasoned beans, as much like other beans as a Tiffany necklace is like a string of old beads left in a tree. How do you explain how anything—anything—served on a melamine plate with a side of potato salad can rival meals you have paid $200 to enjoy, and, if you were true to yourself, you would actually rather have the plate of beans? For the rest of my life, I will remember watching my teenage stepson devour a plate of Betsy's beans and smoked sausage without taking time to talk or apparently even breathe, then announce that he really, really wanted to go to school in New Orleans. He lived the first 16 years of his life on chicken fingers and cheese pizza. But he knew magic when he tasted it.

It is the same outside the city, from corner to corner, pocket to pocket in this state. You can even be hexed in a Holiday Inn.

In Gonzales, just off the interstate and affixed to a chain hotel is a Mike Anderson's restaurant that prepared a crawfish bisque that is nothing like the chalky, fake mess most places prepare. It is a rich, brown stew, redolent—I have always liked to say redolent—with onions, bell pepper, crawfish tails that do not taste like they came from a hold of an oceangoing freighter, and crawfish heads stuffed with a dressing that is best devoured by fishing it out with a crooked finger. Local people—not just tourists and weary travelers—piled in by the carload on weekend nights, proof that it is not just the visual or sensual appeal of this state that fools us into thinking things taste better here. I mean, it's in a damn Holiday Inn...

Sometimes, though, the spell this place casts settles around me so completely that I wonder if I can ever leave it and eat the way regular people eat. It happened in the warmth of a corner table at the Upperline in New Orleans, on something as humble as cornbread. But here the sweet cornbread came topped with grilled, spiced shrimp, and shaved purple onions, and something that looked like rich folks' mayonnaise but I now think might have been some kind of potion. They only gave me two little squares, about six bites in all. I looked at the empty plate with such awful regret, thinking, "If I had just taken smaller bites..."

It happened again at Commander's Palace, white lights glinting in the trees on the other side of the glass. A waiter brought out a dish called bread pudding soufflé and poked a hole in the top of it with a spoon so he could ladle a rich, sugary sauce deep into the thing. I forgot, after a spoonful or two, that I was bound up like an asylum inmate in my too-tight sport coat, forgot every warning my doctor ever gave, forgot that when you leave this place there are potholes of doom ready to swallow you whole and daiquiri-dazed drivers waiting to run you down.

You forget everything here, in this Louisiana, for a spoonful of time. If that is not magic, I by God don't know what magic is.

# SEASONED IN THE SOUTH

*Southern Living,* Southern Journal: November 2014

———

T he first time I noticed them, Thanksgiving was coming. The knives in my mother's kitchen were black with age, the blades paper thin, wickedly sharp. They made better steel when steel was dear, in a time before world wars, maybe long before.

But most of the points were broken; the wooden handles—only a Philistine would use a plastic-handled knife—were also worn thin, slick and smooth. When I was a boy, I saw hoe handles that looked like that. You don't give up on a good hoe handle, not for a generation or so. You drive a nail through the split, twist some electrical tape around it. And one day, when you are gone from this earth, your grandson will finally break it in two and prop the handle, just the handle, in the corner of the shed, like some old man who has finally retired and does not know what else to do but lean.

But I wanted my mother, the best cook in the entire universe, to have new, proper tools for her most important job of the year: fixing Thanksgiving dinner. I gave her some fancy kitchen knives—it must have been almost a decade ago now.

"Go to town with 'em, Ma," I told her.

I never saw them again. I think maybe she buried them in the backyard, or furtively disposed of them at a yard sale.

There is no good food, she finally explained to me, "cooked on new stuff." It is like there is a memory in it, in the iron and the old wood, maybe some magic. You cannot see it or feel it, only taste it.

"I have biscuit pans older than me," she said.

She will cook Thanksgiving dinner with tools passed down to her from the great cooks of antiquity, not only in pots and pans given to her by my grandmothers, Ava and Velma, but passed along from their mothers, and even deeper back in time. "My cornbread skillet—you know you can't have good dressing without good cornbread—come from your Granny Bragg, and I know she got it from somebody, probably her mama, who got it..."

My mother's little house burned down some 20 years ago, around that skillet. She went and got it from the ashes. How do you hurt a skillet, in a fire?

My Aunt Jo won her turkey pan in a raffle at Coleman's Service Station in Jacksonville, Alabama, about, she believes, 1961. My Uncle John wrote his name on his gas ticket, and the owner of the station, Mr. Coleman, drew it from a jar. It cooked an average of four turkeys a year for about 50 years. It cooks pretty good, my mother allows, for new stuff.

They do not look, these tools, like anything on the food channels. They do not have gleaming copper anywhere on them, except in the rivets on the old knives. They are battered and dented but not rusted. Rust waits on idle metal. These pans, these skillets, are never idle.

"People may not believe it, but you can get iron—that good iron for your body and your blood—from an iron skillet," my mother said.

If that is not true, it ought to be.

# SUMMER SNOW

*Southern Living,* Southern Journal: August 2014

———

I t was long before Katrina, in those hot, sticky, normal years when people complained how dry things had been. The drought made the already insubstantial dirt weak and powdery, and the piers of the shotgun houses sank into the earth. It is not unusual in New Orleans for an old house to lean, drunkenly. My favorite story was about a house that leaned so much it fell on a bar—just collapsed. Top that.

But it is not what you want to hear when you are looking for a home. You want your house to appear, well, sober. The sweet real estate lady gently reminded me that New Orleans was just special like that. The potholes were eternal. The termites were, too. It was all part of the charm.

Then, perhaps afraid I was wavering, she bought me a snow cone. Some few days later, I bought a house.

Since then, I have come to believe that the only real antidote to the mean or troubling things of late summer is a paper cone of shaved ice and a squirt of Day-Glo yellow pineapple syrup.

I am not silly enough to believe any crisis can be cooled this way. If you get a tax lien from the State of Georgia or get pulled over for speeding in a school zone in McIntosh, Alabama, a snow cone may not suffice. But if a red wasp nails you on your eyebrow, or you bounce across a New Orleans pothole and your manifold falls off into the abyss to hit a poor man in China upside the head, then a cherry shaved ice might do it. Or a grape one—you pick. Either way, your mouth turns red or purple and you look like you are 5 years old, and even that makes you happy somehow, so it's all okay.

I like pineapple because, at worst, you look a little jaundiced.

Most cities have snow cones, or snowballs, or snoballs; for some reason shaved ice and poor spelling and grammar seem entwined. I do not write much about grammar here because one reader actually told me that, since I was now writing for educated, middle-class people, I should try not to sound like I fell off a hay wagon. But that is another story.

In New Orleans, a city I lived in for just a few years but will never exorcise from my soul, there seems to be a steady supply: There is a fine snowball stand on Plum Street, not far from Loyola and Tulane. But the proverbial granddaddy of them all, Hansen's Sno-Bliz, still leans on Tchoupitoulas Street.

Hansen's, at the corner of Bordeaux Street, is thought to be the oldest in the country. The story goes that, in 1939, Ernest Hansen saw a man shaving ice from a cart and thought he could do it cleaner and better. He invented a machine that shaved fluffy ice, his wife devised the sweet syrups, and they sold snowballs under a chinaberry tree.

Katrina closed the long-standing location on Tchoupitoulas Street, and the Hansens (both in their nineties at the time) died soon after. But as New Orleans emerged, their granddaughter reopened it with the same methods, the same recipes. People who say change is good are ignorant of a great root beer snow cone.

I am glad such places survive, for I doubt seriously if I will get through this life without a few more bad days. I can't even get through McIntosh.

# THE IMPOSSIBLE TURKEY

*Southern Living*, Southern Journal: November 2011

I am going to write a letter to the editor of this magazine. I am going to type with ill intent, use all the wicked prepositions and strident punctuation I know, and give these people a piece of my mind. If gas were not $19 a gallon, I'd drive to corporate headquarters and get ugly. I mean it—somebody hold me back.

I would not be this upset on my own behalf. But these people have hurt my mama's feelings. And not just this year. This has been going on for decades, right about this time every holiday season.

It has to do with turkeys. My people cook the best turkey in the whole turkey-eating world. "It's tender, and it tastes good," said my mama, who, with my Aunt Jo and Uncle John, have cooked 99% of the turkeys I have consumed. That should be enough. It is enough.

I start to think about it around this time of year, every year. I start to visualize it. For about four decades, they used the same pan, the one Aunt Jo won in a raffle at Coleman's Service Station in Jacksonville, Alabama. The bird, usually furnished by someone's employer in lieu of an actual cash bonus during the holidays, came from the oven half submerged in butter and juices, and cooked—because we country people are terrified of half-done poultry—through and through. And then cooked maybe a few minutes longer, just to be sure. That bird naturally tended to fall apart, but since it fell into butter, no one really cared.

I never even thought about what they looked like. To me, to us, they were beautiful. Then, it happened. Two years ago, Mama stood looking at another thoroughly cooked, wonderfully seasoned, heavenly aromatic bird, and sighed. "Well," she said, "it don't look like the ones on the magazine." She meant the almost annual spread of an immaculate turkey in *Southern Living*.

Those turkeys were, to be honest, things of beauty. They were luscious, plump, and cosmetically perfect. They were not just browned, they were golden brown. The skin was unbroken, wing to wing, leg to leg, gizzard to...well, where they hide the giblets. Sometimes, they even wore little white turkey booties on the end of drumsticks. (I am sure those things have a name, but danged if I know what it is, and I wouldn't admit it if I did.)

It was as if the turkey was actually posing, posing on an impeccable tabletop, with real cranberries sprinkled around. I told my mama her turkey was beautiful, because it was, and always will be. I told her not to give those tarted-up show turkeys another thought.

Then, we feasted. There was cornbread dressing, the best I have ever had—my Aunt Jo always says she ruined it with this mistake or that mistake, but it is always perfect, dense, the kind of thing you can cut a slice from at one o'clock in the morning two days later and eat cold, all by itself. There were the best mashed potatoes in the universe, and pinto beans, seasoned with big chunks of ham. There were hot biscuits and cabbage and carrot slaw—because country people do not celebrate anything worth celebrating without slaw—and cranberry sauce, the kind that makes a sucking sound as it slides out of the can. (We do not abide any cranberry sauce that does not make a noise.) There were green beans, pulled from the garden and canned by my mama months before, and my favorite thing of all, a kind of creamed onion, cooked slowly in an iron skillet in bacon grease, softened by adding water. And, in case we were a tad short of carbohydrates, there was a big pot of macaroni and cheese.

My Uncle John said grace, with the dignity of ages. My mother's beautiful turkey always falls off the bone. I eat a leg, and then a wing, unless my shirt buttons start to pop off. It will be that way this year. It will be that way forever, because it has to be.

Now forgive me. I have a letter to write.

# HONOR THY MATRIARCH

*Southern Living*, Southern Journal: June 2015

———

D eviled eggs always make me want to cry.

It happened again the other day, when my mother told me, "Look in the 'frigerator, hon, and see what we got," and inside was a platter with about a hundred deviled eggs. I ate two standing up in the yellow glow of the open door, and then went where no one could see me, in case I made a fool of myself.

It's not that I cry over deviled eggs, themselves. They trigger a memory hard to live with, even after all this time. As my people would say, "some things just stand for things."

You will see when I am done.

My grandmother, Ava, was our matriarch, but not in that solid, steel magnolia way you think about with Southern women. She suffered from mild dementia early, and in her old age suffered more. She required someone to watch over her.

Yet every June, on her birthday, the whole clan gathered in her backyard to celebrate a life, to pay respect as she sat in her lawn chair in the shade of the hardwood trees. I can still see her, hair bound in a turban of some kind of manmade silk, pale blue eyes seeing nothing, everything, behind thick, yellowed glasses that had not been adjusted since Pearl Harbor. There was always a child on her knee. She could not, as she failed, be trusted to be by herself, but she could be trusted with a child.

They honored her for what she had been, for the fact she lost a baby in the Great Depression from simple dehydration, in a time when poor people died from such things, but she saved seven others, saved them by doing without, herself. They honored her because she stuck by a husband who was a good man in almost every way, but drank, and the bottle took him down. And when he died she lost a little bit of her mind.

They honored her for living through. They came in Vietnam-era Chevrolets and work trucks that rattled with logging chains and, in a few, rusted beer cans that had drowned sorrows they could no longer recall. This was a celebration, so grown-ups came in church clothes, though it was Alabama in summer so the men did leave their shirttails out. They came bearing fried chicken cooked in iron skillets and potato salad that did not come from a plastic tub. The Georgia people, as our kin across the state line were called, brought cases of Double Cola, which we considered exotic since you could not get them west of Carrollton. And three or four of the best cooks on this earth brought deviled eggs, speckled with black pepper or cayenne. It was the only time we had them, and so they always make me, as foolish as it is, and as I am, a little sad.

It is not just that I miss her. She has been gone for decades now. It is the fact that, as she failed, I rarely went to see her. I lived from a duffel bag, always moving. I chased selfish things, chased prizes that, now, shine no more than the folded-up pieces of Juicy Fruit wrapper that the old woman used to hide, like jewels, in her room.

Things stand for things.

# REQUIEM FOR
# A FISH SANDWICH

*Garden & Gun*, August/September 2014

———

I love fishing stories, which some people equate with lies. I do not believe this is always true. I think weird things happen when you step boldly off firmer earth, and commence to float. This is my new favorite.

Jimbo Meador, outdoorsman, writer, and other things, was fishing the Yucatán about forty years ago. Not far away, a tiny man, a Mayan he believes, was fishing with a hand line from a tiny boat. Suddenly, the tiny man and his tiny boat went shooting across the water. The tiny boat did not have a motor.

He had hooked a Goliath grouper, and it was taking him for a ride.

"Like *The Old Man and the Sea*," said Meador's friend Skip Jones, who grew up, like Meador, not far from Mobile Bay.

The tiny man hung on, and on, and on.

Finally, he had his prize, and got the weary fish, hundreds of pounds of it, back to the dock.

The tiny man ran a rope through the grouper's massive maw and gills. "Tied it to a post," Meador said, like a horse.

There was no electricity there, no ice. So they tied the live fish to the dock to swim, to keep, till they decided it was time to eat.

Meador told it at lunchtime over fried chicken, since there was no grouper to be had. As the story hung in the air, as all good stories will, I was not thinking of hot weather in exotic places, or fish fights, or Hemingway.

I pictured a five-gallon bucket of tartar sauce, and a hundred hamburger buns.

Just how many sandwiches, I wondered, would that big ol' boy have made?

But it seems all the great grouper stories are old stories, now. The Goliath grouper, fished relentlessly, is a protected species, other types of big grouper have been sorely depleted, and the grouper sandwich seems, sometimes, more like a dream.

I remember a recent birthday when all I wanted was a grouper sandwich. It was late summer, ninety-five degrees in the descending dusk. I had been waiting for two hours; you should not wait two hours for anything in this life except surgery, and at least then they have the decency to knock you out. As I waited, I sat on a hard bench in the humidity and watched children play in dingy sand and scream, which is to say they mostly just screamed. One little boy was flinging sand—I think it was mostly dirt—high in the air.

Children are not wise enough not to look up, or close their mouths, when a dirt cloud falls.

The restaurant had about the same seating capacity as Legion Field, one of those places on the Redneck Riviera where we, as a Southern people, have been conditioned across our lifetimes to sit and sweat into our aloe-vera-anointed sunburn for many, many hours for some fried and blackened seafood, all the while clutching one of those flasher-buzzy things in our slick palms, or anxiously waiting for our names to drift from a loudspeaker like Saint Peter calling us home. A restaurant in Destin, Florida, asks to keep your car keys, lest you run off with its priceless buzzer-flashy. I am not making this up.

I recall that, down the bench, a young man with numerous eyebrow piercings and more tattoos than a harpooner from *Moby-Dick* was enthusiastically trying to suck the lips off a young woman with blue hair. I am pretty sure I sighed. I do not know why we submit to all this for a sandwich, even a grouper sand-wich; I guess because we think that, when it comes, it will be hand delivered by a backstroking Weeki Wachee mermaid. But it never is.

In such times, I often slink back into the past, into nostalgia, where the passing years have rubbed and buffed all the rough edges from things. I closed my eyes and thought of grouper sandwiches long ago, as the lovers slurped, and the children screamed.

————

I will never forget my first. It was more than twenty years ago. I arrived in Clearwater, Florida, dead broke, except for rent money and some change in a pickle jar. I came to write for the Clearwater bureau of what was then the *St. Petersburg Times,* one of the great newspapers. I have always had a fascination with palm trees. The Gulf Coast seemed exotic, and still does; I don't care how many snowbirds cross my path in black socks and Bermuda shorts. But by the time I paid for a concrete-block, one-bedroom apartment, I did not have money for furniture, or food. I lived three weeks on banana sandwiches, washing them down with cold water from plastic jugs my mother filled before I left home. Florida water, she knew, was not fit for drinking or even putting out a brush fire. I read a paperback copy of *Lonesome Dove,* twice, on a bare terrazzo floor, and listened to my stomach gurgle. After my first paycheck, reporters invited me to lunch for a grouper sandwich. The only fish sandwich I had ever had came in a sack with an action figure called a Hamburglar.

My expectations were not high, but I was *hungry.*

To this day, I do not know if it was the sandwich or the scenery. The sand of Clearwater Beach stretched wide and white to water the color of emeralds. Mermaids were everywhere. The place was called, I believe, Julie's, one of many there known for their fish sandwiches, for grouper, and mahi. The grouper was grilled, dripping with cool, lemony tartar sauce and dressed with a thick slice of genuine, ripe, non-gassed tomato, an antidote for every pink, bad tomato I ever had. God ripened that tomato, just for me.

The first bite was clean and not fishy, but the thing I remember most is the consistency, the flesh firm, thick, and meaty, with none of those gray streaks of nastiness that taste like fish gone bad. I would have them, over time, grilled, fried, and blackened, from almost every kind of grouper in the Gulf, Atlantic, and Caribbean. I remember whole days of my life better because of them. I loved them, me and everyone else, and I guess we loved them about to *death.*

Most people, younger, have never had them the way they used to be. It was not, in fact, a fillet at all. It was a slab. *"Three inches thick,"* recalls Pete Blohme, a chef, owner of the landmark Panini

Pete's restaurant in Fairhope, Alabama. "I sure do miss 'em. Brings tears to my eyes, just thinking about 'em."

It did not look like fish, really, those sandwich fillets. There was no taper to the fillet, just an irregular, fat, square chunk, one of many fat, square chunks carved from something massive.

"I was eight years old, the first time I saw one, and we had just moved to South Florida...Fort Lauderdale," says Blohme, whose café au lait and beignets are a Saturday morning tradition in Baldwin County. His father had taken him to a seafood warehouse, a place where massive fish lay or hung, waiting to be cleaned and processed. Stone crab claws were piled on ice. But it was the grouper that fascinated him.

"I saw grouper bigger than me... a hundred pounds, more. "They were huge."

"Beautiful," he says.

Then, he had his first taste.

"It tasted like the ocean. A little salt, a little brine. It was like that smell," that smell when you stand by the open water. "You take a bite, and go, 'Aaahhhh...' You knew where it came from."

Like the redfish, which became so symbolic in Louisiana cooking it was almost eaten into extinction, the grouper became shorthand for the beach, a vacation delicacy.

"It was common," Blohme says. "By the late 1970s, grouper was king."

They hung like great cows in the murky water, and would bite almost any bait, live or dead. In the 1980s, deep-sea fishing boats, on the Gulf and Atlantic sides, unloaded them like slabs of beef. By the late 1980s and into the 1990s, marine biologists warned that without careful management many kinds of grouper would virtually disappear. I know it makes me a hypocrite, since I did my part to eat them into oblivion.

"I guess they fished all them big ol' fat fish out," Blohme says.

Sometimes, I suspect the grouper inside the bun may be fooling me.

The fillets are scrawny, and look like, well, catfish.

"Sometimes, it's that counterfeit grouper," Blohme says.

---

I was still a young man when I arrived in Miami the first time, almost a quarter century ago, to write about one of the most compelling places on earth. I have never liked mornings, but there was something about the morning light in Miami, something golden. I would get in my '69 Firebird convertible and rumble out to Key Biscayne, to a cool, dark bar at the Silver Sands motel. I would order a grouper sandwich for my 11:30 breakfast, and watch the European mermaids play in the calm, flat water. I remember the grouper inside the bun was good, fresh, real, and delicious, every time. It was Florida. I thought, in that cool dark, I had the best life a man could live, right then, right there. I know, I have buffed this memory. I know, nostalgia is a veil, a piece of colored glass. I know. But I had a fried grouper sandwich and onion rings for breakfast.

Other people were staring at shredded wheat, and hoping to live forever. But I bet forever is a long time with shredded wheat.

There are many kinds of grouper, most at one time either threatened or protected, in varying degrees of commercial appeal and distress. There are black, gag, red, yellowfin, yellow edge, red hind, rock hind, or speckled hind, and, of course, Goliath, easy to identify because they have been described as being the size of a Mini Cooper, and are prone to lurk under fish boats and eat hooked fish like Tic-Tacs. One tried to eat Cameron Diaz once, but that is another story.

State and federal protections ebb and flow, ease and tighten, but people who grew up by the water say the grand days of grouper are over. Competing restaurants squabble—some even use DNA testing as proof—over who is serving real grouper. On the Alabama coast, it can be hard to find a grouper sandwich like the slabs of old, or one of any kind, though I did find one a few miles inland that tasted of cat food. Gulf Coast restaurants largely feature mahi, or use sutchi, triggerfish, or other fish as an alternative to grouper. In the Gulf, overfishing is not the grouper's sole peril, since the Deepwater Horizon spill.

Marine biologists have warned it may be years before the lingering impact of the disaster comes to light. For now, people here continue to celebrate the recovery, a return to normalcy. Sometimes, the past is not better. This part of our past may haunt us for a long, long time.

One of the last holdouts from the old plenty of the grouper seems to be the Tampa Bay area, where the grouper sandwich is said to have been invented, where places like Frenchy's Rockaway Grill, in Clearwater, and Dockside Dave's, in Madeira Beach, and the Sandbar, in Anna Maria, still consider the sandwich a signature dish. Down in Miami, the grouper sandwich at Garcia's is frozen only in time, a fresh slab of the way things used to be. Such places are often the first stop I make, to taste the past.

———————

I almost drowned once swimming off Bean Point on Anna Maria Island, within sight of the Sandbar. There was a hurricane in the Gulf and the waves were massive. I had always liked that phrase "storm-tossed," and I felt big and brave, thrown into the air, till the undertow got me. I staggered into knee-deep water, finally, exhausted. That afternoon I had a fine grouper sandwich, to celebrate being alive, and at dusk joined a group of elderly ladies doing water aerobics in the shallow surf, which I often did then as protection from sharks.

This was as much of a man of the sea, I decided, as I needed to be.

———————

I was in my final hour of hell at the big seafood restaurant, my final hour of toddlers apparently raised by wolves. My number was up and I shuffled like a man on a chain gang to a table made to look like one at a tiki bar. The sandwich, when it came, was not grouper, but then the menu had not claimed it was. I had not known, as I languished, that there was no grouper sandwich here, but it was too late. I do not know its origin, that fish, though it was fine enough. But I decided, then, to travel across the Gulf to Anna Maria someday soon, to see if they still make as good a sandwich there as they used to, there at the Sandbar or places near, and maybe see if any of the old mermaids from that water aerobics class still know my name.

# PART 3
# PLACE

# SOUTH TOWARD HOME

I t suits me, here.

My people tell their stories of vast red fields and bitter turnip greens and harsh white whiskey like they are rocking in some invisible chair, smooth and easy even in the terrible parts, because the past has already done its worst. The joys of this Southern life, we polish like old silver. We are good at stories. We hoard them, like an old woman in a room full of boxes, but now and then we pull out our best, and spread them out like dinner on the ground. We talk of the bad year the cotton didn't open, and the day my cousin Wanda was Washed in the Blood. We cherish the past. We buff our beloved ancestors till they are smooth of sin, and give our scoundrels a hard shake, though sometimes we cannot remember exactly which is who.

I wonder if, north of here, they might even run out of stories someday. It may seem silly, but it is cold up there, too cold to mosey, to piddle, to loafer, and summer only lasts a week and a half. The people spit the words out so fast when they talk, like they are trying to discard them somehow, banish them, rather than relish the sound and the story. We will not run out of them here. We talk like we are tasting something.

I do it for a living, which is stealing, really. Li'l Abner, another not-too-bright Southern boy, had a job once, testing mattresses.

People ask me, often, why I love a place so imperfect, where the mosquitoes dance between the lukewarm rain and the summer heat turns every stretch of blacktop into a shimmering river of hot tar, where the football-mad fling curses and sometimes punches and forget their raising on call-in radio, and the politicians seem intent on a return to 1954. I merely answer: How do you not love a place where the faded beads from a parade six years before still hang in the branches of the live oak trees.

I love the big carnival floats that lumber through the streets of New Orleans and Mobile to rain treasure on the streets below, causing the people there to leap and snatch at the air as if it was real swag instead of aluminum money and Moon Pies. I love the mountain churches along the Georgia-Alabama line, love the hard-rock preachers in their Conway Twitty sideburns who fling scripture with the force of a flying horseshoe at congregations who all but levitate in the grasp of the Holy Ghost, and every old woman's purse in every pew smells like a fresh stick of Juicy Fruit. I love the cry of a steel guitar on a makeshift stage in the Appalachian foothills, where a fierce old man who looks like he just walked out of a fire reaches for a shorted-out microphone to holler "Rollin' in My Sweet Baby's Arms." His grown son does a buck dance on a concrete slab. How do you not love such as that?

I love tomato sandwiches and fried oyster po' boys and pineapple upside-down cake and biscuits and sausage gravy, and love the Southern doctor who offers me antidotes, and prayer. I love roiling caldrons of pork cracklin's on the first frost, and great pits lined with smoking, fat-dripping pigs, and jars of crabapple jelly that gleam like rose gold in my mother's windowsill. I love old men who talk tools and transmissions over black coffee in the Huddle House and pass around heirloom pocketknives with more pride than they do pictures of their grandchildren. I love big-haired waitresses who call me baby, and fat Shriners who ride little-bitty cars in the Christmas parade, and stained and faded recipes for tea cakes passed down from the Yankee war. I love lightning bugs. I love winter without snowdrifts, grief, and pain.

I love the Delta and its empty, uncluttered land, love a recidivist guitar man named T-Model Ford, who, when asked how many men he'd killed, asked if it counted if he "done it with a Pontiac." I love the music of Hank Williams, and the mockingbird of Harper Lee, and a Louisiana accordion player named Rosie Ledet. I love to see a speckled trout fight the line through the flats of Tampa Bay, love the black dirt of the lower South and blood-red clay of the highlands and the glittering white sand of the Gulf, love the smell of sawmills, and the ever-fading, irreplaceable shake and stamp of the cotton mills and what is left of the broad-shouldered South of my boyhood. I love all-night gospel singings and flea markets four miles wide, and hounds that wail on the mountainside while the raccoons they chase double back on the trail and steal the cat food off the front porch. I love café au lait, and clanking, squealing streetcars, and boiled blue crabs too hot to touch, love the summertimes that smell of bourbon and orange slices and crushed cherries and that old, clinging waft of decay. I love the scent of a million flowers, a riot of flowers whose names I have never taken time to truly know.

I love, I guess more than anything, the ghosts of my people, spirits who are always close, always riding in my memory like a good luck charm in my pocket, like the late aunt who will forever walk between rows of red and yellow roses on the Alabama coast, whispering to her elderly sisters, who hold tightly to both her hands, that they are the most beautiful roses she has ever seen.

It is the South, and so spirits are welcome here.

You have to love that, too.

Because, despite what they believe in Savannah, the party does sometimes end, no matter how deep your to-go cup might be as you warble down the street. There are times when I cannot escape the melancholia of this place, like when I drive the seemingly endless blacktop between walls of dark, between the curtains of the pine barrens and silver-white glow of the vast cotton fields and other lonely stretches where even the glares of Atlanta, Raleigh, and New Orleans are snuffed out by the sheer breadth of the empty miles. To be a Southerner, or to live Southern, is to feel, well, *something* special even in the quiet, something fine in itself after all those rebel yells and fight songs have finally faded into silence. The great Texas writer Larry McMurtry once wrote of a man born beside a river of melancholy, and I have always loved that line. To be a Southerner, born or replanted here by fate, is to drive through that stillness of landscape and spirit and feel it, and we mumble a few lines of a song from childhood, to gather the ghosts of our tribe around us.

*When I was a little bitty baby*
*My mama would rock me in my cradle*
*In them old cotton fields back home*

One recent fall, on the last night of a book tour that had taken me from New York to Miami and much of the in-between, I rolled through the Tennessee Valley, across a bleak landscape of fallow fields and black trees already stripped by the winds and rain of the season. It is not real work, writing books, not like roofing, or carrying concrete blocks, or swinging a hammer, but I was tired and a little gloomy and, in this rare time, saw little beauty in this region that had nurtured my life and my livelihood. Then, just before the thinnest sliver of red sun sank below the flat horizon, the gloom around the speeding car erupted, exploded, with a million blackbirds, whirling first left and then right in a great column of black wings before vanishing into the dark that fell, right then, like a heavy curtain. It was like they just winked out, just, in a blink, claimed the air around me, and then ceased to exist. Maybe I am easy to impress, but it was one of the most beautiful things I have ever seen. I grinned, and laughed out loud. I guess they have blackbirds everywhere, but I will stash that memory away with all those things about this South I love, there in that imaginary box with all the rest of it, next to my grandfather's fedora, and the little scraps of silvery chewing gum wrapper that my grandmother saved, for some unfathomable reason, between the pages of Deuteronomy, the *Farmers' Almanac*, and a decades-old edition of *Life* magazine.

I have always tried to write of this South in a way beyond clichés, and that is why, most often, I have pulled my writings from the memories and stories of my own blood. The most interesting thing about my South is not juleps on the veranda and sweet tea in a Mason jar (though I have enjoyed both). There is more to us than deer hunting, or NASCAR; the Yankees have all but wrested that from us, anyway. There is more to us, even, than football, and no matter how many sportscasters might say it, it is not *truly* our religion; it engenders far too much cursing for that, though we have prayed to our Lord and Savior on third down and three, and like to tell that joke about St. Peter walking on water in Bear Bryant's hat. I have never seen a Confederate saber over a mantel, though that may just be because I'm not invited to the good parties. But to me, the actual South, the actual adventure, is so much better than clichés. My Uncle Jimbo never challenged a man to a duel to defend his honor, but he did win a $20 bet by eating a bologna sandwich while sitting on a dead mule. My grandmother prayed a tornado away, and punched a city woman in the eye.

I've lived other places, colder places, where the first snow does not send the population screaming out the door to empty all the bread aisles. I waded knee-deep in running slush in Boston, cursing, and saw whole cars vanish under walls of hard-packed snow. But even in the thaw I never felt at home anywhere but here. I got a $400 parking ticket in Los Angeles my first ten minutes in town, and tried to learn to surf, which was really just buying a really small boat and practicing to drown. I ate a $35 chicken salad sandwich in New York City, with a $4 pickle, and while it was a fine pickle it still left me feeling like I had been thoroughly had. I have, along the way, seen some lovely things. I got to see the elephants before they are all in fences, and a Cape buffalo under a lightning-blasted tree. I have seen vast deserts and deep chasms and rolling seas and camel trains on a horizon a world away, and sometimes I told stories about those places and sometimes I even made a little sense. But I think sometimes I told them the way a tourist would, because I knew, as I left, I might never see those places again.

I am home now. If it snows, more than an inch, I will scrape it from the windshield into a mixing bowl, stir in some sugar and Pet milk, and make ice cream, not because it tastes all that good but because my grandmother did it that way. If I get a parking ticket, I will still have to pay it but pay it by mail, because I am always unsure about the statute of limitations on things I did in 1973, and people know me at the courthouse. It won't be more than $20 anyway. If I want a $35 chicken salad sandwich, I can get one in the Atlanta airport.

I am home.

I am an imperfect citizen of an imperfect, odd, beautiful, dysfunctional, delicious place.

But at least we ain't dull.

I have been told, a thousand times or more by kind people, that it can be like looking in a mirror, looking at people, places, and things that are more than familiar, and at feelings that seem lifted from their own hope chests, sock drawers, recipe books, and family secrets. Maybe that is what writers mean, when they talk about a sense of place.

# WHAT STANDS IN A STORM

*Southern Living,* Southern Journal: May 2011

———

Almost nothing stood.
　　Where the awful winds bore down, massive oaks, 100 years old, were shoved over like stems of grass, and great pines, as big around as 55-gallon drums, snapped like sticks. Church sanctuaries, built on the Rock of Ages, tumbled into random piles of brick. Houses, echoing with the footfalls of generations, came apart, and blew away like paper. Whole communities, carefully planned, splintered into chaos. Restaurants and supermarkets, gas stations and corner stores, all disintegrated, glass storefronts scattered like diamonds on black asphalt. It was as if the very curve of the Earth was altered, horizons erased altogether, the landscape so ruined and unfamiliar that those who ran from this thing, some of them, could not find their way home.

We are accustomed to storms, here where the cool air drifts south to collide with the warm, rising damp from the Gulf, where black clouds roil and spin and unleash hell on Earth. But this was different, a gothic monster off the scale of our experience and even our imagination, a thing of freakish size and power that tore through state after state and heart after Southern heart, killing hundreds, hurting thousands, even affecting, perhaps forever, how we look at the sky.

But the same geography that left us in the path of this destruction also created, across generations, a way of life that would not come to pieces inside that storm, nailed together from old-fashioned things like human kindness, courage, utter selflessness, and, yes, defiance, even standing inside a roofless house.

As Southerners, we know that a man with a chain saw is worth 10 with a clipboard, that there is no hurt in this world, even in the storm of the century, that cannot be comforted with a casserole, and that faith, in the hereafter or in neighbors who help you through the here and now, cannot be knocked down.

I know this to be true because I came home to it the day after the storm. My street, a quarter mile of small, historic homes and lovely trees, had looked as though it were painted on canvas and hung on the air. It was ruined April 27, and also spared. No one died in Glendale Gardens, while, yards away in Rosedale, rescue workers pulled the dead from houses blasted as if in war. It is why, even as they piled their neighborhood into trash heaps two stories tall, my neighbors said, over and over, how fortunate they were.

Our little white house, on the edge of a mile-wide tornado, was hammered by flying 2 by 4s, stripped of its shingles but, somehow, still standing when we returned from New Orleans. My wife, Dianne, cried when she saw it, and cried more as she looked down our street. A third of the houses were destroyed. Others will be torn down. The trees that gave this place its name were gone or splintered. In our yard, a single, ancient dogwood survived, my wife's pride, a reminder of what this used to be.

People say it will never be the same. I don't know about that.

———————

It had been a bad spring. The sirens screamed every few days, in Mississippi, Alabama, and beyond. In Tuscaloosa, just days before the big storm, Mary Kate Jemison Cochrane and her daughter, Emily, walked through the family house in Glendale, looking for a place the 91-year-old Mrs. Cochrane could shelter when the weather turned. They settled on a hall closet, removed two Electrolux vacuum cleaners, silent since antiquity, and put in a chair. When sirens did sound on April 27, Mrs. Cochrane stepped inside and shut the door.

She passed the time by looking through things, forgotten and dusty. She picked up a cookie tin, and pried off the lid. Neatly rolled inside was her christening gown, the one she wore as a baby, almost 92 years ago. She had been looking for that.

She is hard of hearing. Inside, with her memories, she did not hear the destruction. She felt the house shake, but it had shaken before. Then she heard someone calling her name.

A neighbor, Michael Carr, had huddled as the storm tore at his walls. The first thing he did, when it passed, was break into her house, damaged but intact, and shout for her. It was the same all along the street, as people ran from house to house, shouting, hoping.

Carr called for her again. The closet door swung open.

"Well I am fine, Michael," she said graciously, "and you are just so kind, to come check on me."

She stayed here because it was where she raised her children, where she once found a live horse in a bedroom, where every cardboard box bulged with history. It took the storm of a lifetime to move her. She walked through the ruin, and rode away. But she sent Emily back for the gown.

There will be great-grandchildren to baptize. They must be properly dressed.

Outside, minutes after the winds died down, people gathered in the street. Tammy Elebash—our boy took her daughter to prom— held a phone. "I see the Pittses...I see the Petrovics...yes, Mrs. Brannon is fine. She's on my arm...." Inez Rovegno and John Dolly had grabbed their wedding album and crawled into the tub. Mary Pitts had hidden with her triplets in a hallway as flying glass stabbed the walls. Beverly Banks had held to her big, white dog as her house disintegrated around her.

Then, one by one, people noticed the change. The once verdant place was laid open, stripped, flattened. You could see things you had never seen, like a water tower that used to be invisible behind the curtains of green. It was like the storm had picked these people up and set them down someplace ugly, broken, new. How awful it would have been, to have landed there alone.

---

I have seldom felt helpless in my life. I hold to the hillbilly standard that there is no situation so hopeless that, through perseverance, I cannot make worse. It is why my wife will not let me have a chain saw—"You will cut off your own head"—and will not allow me on the roof. So there I stood, giant trees across my driveway, my roof naked, helpless. What happened next still seems like magic.

Within a minute of stepping into my yard, I was met by a never-ending stream of neighbors, some I only slightly knew, who left their own crises to help me clean up mine. There are too many to list here—I would leave someone out—but they came, capable men who knew how to run a saw, or twist a wrench. Some came, worked like a dog, and vanished before I could thank them. I hope they are reading this, men and women who lifted and dragged tons of trees, and almost killed me and my stepson Jake, trying to keep up. Every church group in Tuscaloosa, it seemed, clawed rubble out of my yard, or out of the playground across the street, meaning I can never again say anything mean about the Episcopalians. I came to enjoy the company. That first afternoon, I straightened up from tugging on an unmoving limb to see Allen McClendon, the husband of my son's music teacher, saw through a tree that blocked my drive. He brought his father, Rick, and an old, brown dog named B.J., and we told duck hunting stories and I don't think any lies, but it was hard to tell over the roar of the saws. And then they, too, were gone, to help someone else, somewhere down the road.

There was no end to this generosity. Food just appeared. No one would take a dime. The college students on our street, the ones I had yelled at for driving too fast, cooked all the meat from our melting freezers, and let me pet their puppy. Mrs. Cochrane's Emily asked if we needed a generator. Our boy's friends brought gasoline. Folks with gas water heaters offered hot showers. That night, I went to sleep under the luxury of an electric fan. The next morning, my neighbors were in my yard before I was.

So I wonder. If a street is made of people, not oaks and tulip trees, how can this place not be as fine as it ever was? I think the best I heard it put was by Mary Pitts.

"I always thought we lived on a good street," she said. "Now I know."

---

A few days after the storm, on a Sunday morning, I awoke to a tap-tap-tap on my roof. I should have gone to see what it was about, but after a while the rhythmic tapping got to be almost soothing, and I ducked inside a dream. Later, I learned that my neighbor James Mize had scaled the roof and tacked down some covering that had blown loose.

He did not ask me where I went to church, or how I voted, or who my family was. He did not climb that ladder for money, or attention, or even thanks.

He did it, he said, because it looked like rain.

# NO PLACE LIKE HOME

*Southern Living*, Southern Journal: August 2011

---

Sometimes, to break a spell of death and destruction, you just have to drop a house on a witch.

Our boy moped into the den last spring to announce, after much sighing, that his teachers had settled on *The Wizard of Oz* as the final production of his junior year. Over the years, Jake had swaggered across the stage as a tortured drifter in *Picnic* and mugged as the mad dentist in *Little Shop of Horrors.* He had hoped for serious theater, Tennessee Williams maybe, but instead got a "little kid's play."

"I think I'll try out for Scarecrow," he said.

"That's the one looking for a brain?" I said.

Holy Spirit is a small school. The stage is a plywood platform in the gym. There is no curtain, but that does not mean there are no curtain calls. For three years I perched like an elephant on a beach ball in those tiny plastic chairs, watching teenagers sing, dance, and emote their hearts out. I gave standing ovations, in part because it allowed blood to flow again in my legs.

But this Oz, despite my boy's grumpiness, promised to be a grand production. It would be a schoolwide showpiece, gathering older students into starring roles while providing unlimited bit parts for little children. You can have an Oz without flying monkeys—they give me the creeps—but how do you pull it off without Munchkins?

They were churning through rehearsals in April when, on the 27th, tornadoes tore through the South and gouged into Tuscaloosa. Fifteen of the cast's 65 students were touched directly by the storm, their homes damaged and destroyed.

Annie McClendon, the music director, thought the play was finished. In a city so wounded, how do you put on a play about the house plucked from the earth that lands on someone, even a witch? It would seem insensitive. But Kelly Taylor, the drama director, convinced her that, if canceled, the play would be only one more normal thing the storm took away from these children.

You could see a change in the actors when they returned, some arriving from borrowed houses in cars patched with duct tape. The Wicked Witch was sad. The Munchkins had learned that not even the walls of their houses could keep out bad things.

"My kids saw trees knocked down they used to climb and saw the street where they used to ride their tricycles destroyed," said Philip Pitts, whose triplets, Henry, Kate, and Anna, played Munchkins. "And they learned that their daddy can't protect them from everything."

But to abandon the play would have been admitting things might never be the same, said Maxwell Elebash, whose daughter, Augusta, played the bad witch. If not now, with this, then when? With what?

They set up chairs for 150 on opening night, but the people kept coming, 200, 300, more. The gym filled. People came who had nothing to do with Holy Spirit, to be part of something normal, too, and hear a 3-foot-high thespian squeak: "You've killed her so completely that we thank you very sweetly." People said it was one of the best performances of *The Wizard of Oz* they had ever seen. Even the part where the Wicked Witch—circling the gym floor on her bicycle, shrieking—accidentally crashed into a baby carriage.

It will not fix everything. It will not raise walls. But Jake had worked like a man, digging stumps, hauling limbs, never complaining that his new car was now filled with broken glass. That night he danced across the stage with a girl in ruby slippers in his arms.

Sophie Petrovic, whose house just down the street from mine was ruined, cavorted in a blur of Munchkins, as if all evil winds were just props on stage.

The show does go on. Ding-dong. The witch is dead.

# TRADE DAY

*Southern Living,* Southern Journal: June 2011

F ive years ago, my brothers and I drove to a vast flea market in Collinsville, Alabama, to buy a bantam rooster for our mother. We left with two ducks, two chickens, a Hamilton watch, two fig trees, a sack of green onions, a bone-handled pocketknife, a bushel of sweet potatoes, a four-way lug wrench, a goat named Ramrod, and a ball-peen hammer.

The goat, the size of a Shetland pony, butted my Ford Bronco so hard it rocked on its springs. That was why I bought the hammer. I was not riding back with that thing unarmed.

"Couldn't find a pistol?" I asked my brother Sam. Sam, who has always been serious, said he could have found one, easy, in the endless stalls and milling throngs of people, if he had known I needed one—that, or a banjo, a croquet mallet, or a rhesus monkey. The goat just glared at me, kind of walleyed. "Ain't he a dandy?" said my little brother, Mark.

It may have other names, this place. But for generations, my people have referred to it as Trade Day. Every Saturday, an eroded hillside explodes with color and sound, covering acres of gravel, rock, and mud with junk and treasure. If you want it, ever wanted it, or think you might want it someday, you can find it here. Quilt scraps and new and used clothes blow like banners, and ladder-back chairs and mule shoes sell next to Bear Bryant clocks, velvet matadors, mood rings, top-water lures, Dale Earnhardt action figures, and Burt Reynolds commemorative plates. I could not conjure such a place even in a fevered dream.

There are others around the South, but this is ours, a kind of clearinghouse for the vanishing skills of my people. Old men in overalls stroll with bundles of carved ax handles sanded so smooth they would not snag a silk stocking. Old women unfold patterns first traced on flour sack dresses in the time of the WPA, or Reconstruction, or The War. Crab apple jelly shines in the sunlight next to jars of honey, the comb glistening inside. There is macramé so intricate it would make a spider quit his web, just steps from bins of rusted drill bits, crosscut saws, ancient cutting boards, sunflowers the size of truck tires, hammer dulcimers, hickory nuts, and gingham bonnets, just like my grandmother Ava wore every hot day of her life.

I can mark most years of my life with purchases here. A baby duck, when I was 6. I carried it home inside my shirt to keep it warm. At 10, a harmonica I would never play, except for one long, asthmatic moan. A ukulele, at 12. I never learned to play that either. At 17, it was a Creedence Clearwater eight-track tape (it stuck on "Run Through the Jungle") and racing mirrors from a '69 Camaro.

My cousin negotiated a pistol. "Does it shoot?"

"Oh, yeah."

I have never seen a monkey for sale, but that doesn't mean they never had one. High on the hill—upwind, inevitably—are fightin' roosters and guinea hens (said to eat snakes), Poland China piglets, rabbits, and some of the finest dogs I have ever seen. I love to linger near the coon hunters with their redbone, bluetick, and black-and-tan hounds with bloodlines that reach back to the Bible, and listen to the lies...I mean testimonials. "Does he hunt?"

"Oh, yeah."

I guess there is some junk here, but I never took any of it home. Only treasure. We secured the goat with logging chain. "If he gets loose," I said as I turned the key, "I'm bailing out, and leaving him with y'all."

# LOST IN THE DARK

*Southern Living*, Southern Journal: October 2014

———

I have always been haunted by wrong turns, by high beams on asphalt I have never seen before, in the Halloween landscape of the Appalachian foothills. Everybody is afraid of something, and this is the time of year that you can admit it and smile at your foolishness—then eat that half-pound bag of baby Butterfingers you hid in the shaving kit next to your blood sugar medicine.

I grew up in the country, where rows of brittle cotton stalks rustle in the black of the evening and the wind hisses through the thick pines. They do whisper, as the old songs said. I have seldom been afraid of the dark; there is peace in it, when the cool evenings chase the snakes into their holes and send the spiders scurrying to wherever spiders go. In the evening you can hear coon dogs crooning on the mountainsides, and the far-off singing of a chain saw, and rusted-out mufflers of distant pulpwood trucks.

But here, there is no stripe down the side of the asphalt, just the wall of black trees, and the voice of the GPS is just one more Yankee lost in the woods. You are fine as long as you stick to the roads you know, past the fields and rolling pastures. Even at night there is enough moonlight to hold your imagination in check.

But now and then you tell yourself you will try a new way to get over the mountain, and make that turn that changes everything. It is worse this time of year, when the weather does not know whether to be hot or cold and storms transform the trees from sunbursts of orange and gold into naked, jagged spikes.

I blame my people, who will not use main roads. They insist on the shortcut, as if anybody has ever really been late to the dollar store. Are they going to run out of onion dip, or Roll Tide-themed polyester shorts? They say it is because they are saving time, but it is really because our ancestors could not drive through town or down a main highway because they did not have a driver's license, or a tag, or more than one headlight, or sufficient sobriety to do anything except creep along a forlorn road, drifting till they hear the whippings of Johnsongrass against the bottom of the Rambler.

I have my people's proclivities, but no sense of direction. Plus, I have been gone from here a long time. So I drive, forever, headlights on high beam, so I can see the ghosts peeking from the ditches, and though I have lived in these hills all my life, I do not recognize a thing, just trees and black and an occasional sign that seems to read "Dead Lake," or worse.

But I do not panic, because I know my part of the scary world is only so big, and I know that at least some of the spirits swirling around me have my last name, because where else would they wander but on some road to nowhere, and they would not let anything happen to me.

It is foolishness, but sometimes I even smile when I see a car with a missing taillight far ahead, or a one-eyed truck rattling toward me. And I always find my way home.

# THE ETERNAL GULF

*Southern Living,* Southern Journal: July 2012

———

To pick one day on this water, one above all the rest, is like trying to hold on to the white sand with your scrunched-up toes as the receding waves pull it from beneath your feet. The Gulf occupies a shining place in our memories, of rushing, crashing blues and greens against a shore so white it hurts our eyes, of flashes of silver through shallows clear as branch water, of pink babies screaming with laughter as they outrun an inch-deep wave onto safe, dry sand, as if winning that race was the most important thing in their lives, till the next one. And when they are old it will still be that way, because waves are always waiting, one more summer, to race again.

I wondered if we would lose it all that spring and summer of 2010. Some old men, who know things like tides and the habits of fish, told me not to fret, that there was too much water out there to be killed by even such a gout of oil. Other old men, tears in their eyes, told me the Gulf only seemed eternal, that mankind could kill it like any other living thing. Now, two summers after, the crisis fades in our memories: The highways south are busier, the waits for a shrimp platter drag on a little more. And it is easy to believe again that it will always be there, a cradle for the fish, or just a place to ease our souls.

I will never forget the hopelessness of 2010, because little has been done to ensure it will not happen again. But it is not what I choose to remember.

I will remember a day when I was a young man in a small boat, drifting on the currents where the flats of Tampa Bay flow into the Gulf, water changing to a deeper blue, shadows of sharks in the shallows, me cursing at cormorants who snatch my bait as it hits the water. The Captain, Joe Romeo, told me fish stories as rays glided like flying saucers across the bottom, till it was time to unwrap a Cuban sandwich and open a freezing can of Coke. I could stay, I remember thinking, stay and fish and tell stories and live on speckled trout and grits. But I would not. I would give in to ambition, and give this up. But before we quit that good day, I hooked something different, a glittering silver torpedo that, even now, remains one of the most beautiful things I have ever seen. "Lady Fish," Joe Romeo said matter-of-factly, as if some other fool had caught a fish this pretty and it had not made the newspaper. We let it go, but I never let go of it. I catch it, in my memory, over and over again.

Or maybe I will remember the day my mother, aunts, and little brother came to see me in Clearwater, bringing fried chicken cooked in an iron skillet and homegrown tomatoes and five plastic Purex jugs of water from Germania Springs, because everyone knows Florida water is not fit to drink. They got up the next day before dawn because they just do things like that, and we drove to a deserted beach. A pod of dolphins arced through the calm, flat water, and my mother hollered for me to get back because she believed them to be sharks and believes that to this day. When I told her they would not stroll ashore and get me even if they were sharks, she told me I might not ought to be so full of my little self. I watched my family drive away, waving from a butternut-colored Chevelle.

Or maybe I will not remember a day at all, but a night in Pensacola. After hours wide awake in a hotel bed, I dragged the bedclothes out on the balcony where the Gulf wind rattled the palm fronds and shifted the patio chairs. I made a bed from a comforter and a 99-cent air mattress, wrapped up in a giant beach towel, and let the rhythm and rush of that water, invisible in the dark, sing me to sleep.

# DONKEY BUSINESS

*Southern Living*, Southern Journal: May 2015

————

I am a miniature donkey rancher. Wait, let's begin again.
That makes me sound like a tiny man, with tiny donkeys.
I am a rancher of miniature donkeys. No sense in making
it sound worse than it is.

It all started with cows, with a whole pasture full of noble cows.
Purebred, white-faced, rust-red Herefords, including a bull or two,
fed in the mountain pasture below my mother's house. A man
with cows on his property is a serious man. A man who has bulls
on his range is even more serious. No whistle-britches will even
climb in a fence with a bull.

They were already on the land when we bought it, but I loved
having them there. You see, I have always been just a little
ashamed of being a writer. To my people, it is not serious work, not
something a real man would do. On airplanes, it seemed I always
sat next to an oil driller, or a welder on the pipeline. When I told
them I was a writer, they looked at me like I cut out paper dolls for
a living.

But when we inherited those cows, I would merely squint at
these rough men, and mumble:

"I raise bulls."

Eyebrows lifted.

Respect did, too.

Then my mama made me get rid of them.

She called me and told me a bull had chased her when she went down to the stock pond to feed her fish. I had told her she did not have to feed the bass and bream there. She ignored me and, every day, took them a loaf of white bread, leaving us with the only fish in the state of Alabama with diabetes. But that is another story.

According to her, one of the bulls chased her out of the pasture, so of course we had to get rid of my cows. Not long after that, she told me the pasture looked lonesome.

"I sure would like to have two of them miniature donkeys," she said, and because she dragged me on a cotton sack when I was a baby, I got them for her.

Bucky and Mimi.

The day they arrived, from a miniature donkey conglomerate in Baldwin County, Mimi snuck up behind me while I was scratching Bucky's nose and bit me on the tendon behind my knee. Bucky kicked me so hard I staggered. Things have pretty much spiraled downward from there.

But my mother loves them, calls them her little "dah-lings" and talks to them like they are people.

"They love me," she said.

"They love you more with a feed bucket in your hand," I said.

But there is a kind of magic in them. It is impossible to look at them, with their potbellies and big heads and tiny legs, and not smile, not feel better.

So, I am in the donkey business. That mostly means I buy feed. A lot of feed. And call the vet. And, when no one is watching, rub them on the nose.

I am a jackass man. I am a muleteer.

And on the plane, when one of those rough ol' boys asks me what I do for a living, I look them in the eye and hiss:

"I'm a writer."

# ARMADILLO

———

**I** am 55 years old.

I have seen, roughly, one million dead armadillos in my life.

I have seen, at most, three live ones.

I think maybe it's time someone started pulling for the armadillo.

This is a kind of love story, I suppose, for an unlovely thing.

I am not a fan of invasive species, on the whole. The South, in its wildest places, belongs to the bass and bream, and perch and catfish, and, yes, even the vile water moccasin. It belongs to the yearling deer, and the rabbit, and squirrel, and black crows as big as fighting roosters. It belongs to the fierce red-tailed hawk, and mosquitoes the size of a paper airplane, and fat groundhogs, and mockingbirds. It belongs to the bull alligator, with its eyeballs glinting red and orange just above the dark water, and the blue heron, the brown pelican, and snapping turtles that bite down like a bear trap. It belongs to the gopher, and the possum, and the raccoons that are at least as smart as we are.

But, just in my lifetime, invasive species have made this their paradise, and I am not just talking kudzu. Killer bees hum in the trees. Fire ants have conquered this region from the rocky tops to the red clay to the Gulf sand. Our waterways, some of them, are clogged with carp. The fanged snakehead fish, the most repulsive of all, can walk on dry land; not even a Southern drought can kill a snakehead.

Python, if you believe the nature channels, are eating the American alligator down to its teeth and claws, and moving on Miami itself, slithering up the canals. Monitor lizards, like something from a Roger Corman film, devour the native species of the Keys, and silence the birds.

The South is their buffet. They have, mostly, no natural predators, so they flourish here, kind of like that Yankee third cousin from Michigan who takes up residence in a motor home in the side yard, wears out your washing machine and eats all your Popsicles. Some people, Yankees, mostly, say the solution is to eat the carp and snakehead and the rest out of existence, a kind of farm-to-table solution. That will never happen until the South runs out of sausage biscuits. You can make jelly out of kudzu; it hasn't made a dent.

But the armadillo does not seem to do much harm to anyone. Its main talent seems to be for getting run over.

It is, I believe, the most singular creature I have ever seen at the side of the road. Their name means "the armored one" in Spanish, and across the ages their carapace of horn-covered bone protected them from wildcats, wolves, and bears. But the Creator must not have counted on a speeding Chevy Tahoe loaded down with lawyers on their way to catch red snapper in Panama City.

The Aztecs called them "turtle rabbits," which seems to fit their modern-day fate a little bit better.

Hating them would be like hating a speed bump.

You see them, it seems, every few miles, usually toes to the sky. Armadillos die ugly, and often. But there has to be more to them than this.

I realize the armadillo is hardly exotic to, say, Texas. I know y'all of the big hat and beef barbecue South have lived amongst the humble armadillo forever, so long that it is a native species. But my childhood would have passed in ignorance of them, if not for the writer of the great children's books *Old Yeller* and *Savage Sam*, Fred Gipson. In his writings, set in the Texas hills of the 19th century, he paints a picture of how the young scamp, Arliss, tries to drag a determined armadillo by its tail out of a hollow log, but the armadillo puffs itself up and plants its feet and plugs that log like a cork in a whiskey bottle.

That story was the beginning of a lifelong fascination with armadillos, if a lifelong fascination meant I went to the library at Roy Webb Elementary and looked them up in the *World Book*.

I learned that they came from South America, and had migrated northward, into Central America and then Mexico and finally the roadside ditches of the United States, as far north as Nebraska but at home in the South, particularly. I would learn that the armadillo came in several exotic sub-species, including the tiny pink fairy armadillo, which is less than 6 inches long, and the giant armadillo, which can grow to almost 120 pounds. If I saw a 120-pound armadillo, I would ask my physician to adjust my blood pressure medicine.

But here, we have only the pedestrian nine-banded armadillo, about the size of an obese house cat. It is armored with solid plate across its shoulders and hips. Its back and sides are protected with hard bands connected with leathery skin, which to me makes them look a little like a Slinky.

Their belly, oddly enough, is not armored, but since most of the Deep South is fresh out of bears, wolves, and cougars, I reckon they don't really need it. If it wasn't for highways, we'd have more armadillos than Carter's got pills.

The armor would seemingly be inconvenient, as to swimming. Like a conquistador who falls off his horse in the middle of a river-crossing, the heavy plates make conventional swimming hard for the armadillo. But even in this, it is remarkable. The armadillo can, before entering the water, fill its stomach with air, blowing itself up like a beach ball, to compensate for the weight, and float across to dry land. Or, because it can hold its breath for several long minutes, it sometimes just walks the bottom like a kind of submarine.

They are timid, harmless. You never hear someone say, "Yeah, little Tater Bug was out in the yard playing with her Taylor Swift action figure and she got attack-ded by that vicious possum on the half-shell."

They do have teeth, and sharp claws, which they used for digging up grubs. There used to be a 500-pound armadillo here, a rhino-like creature that roamed the coastal South some 10,000 years ago, but its modern-day descendant is more likely to run or curl up in a ball and play dead if threatened. But who would want to abuse an armadillo?

You can eat them, I guess. But who would want to? Though I guess they do come in their own pot.

Their sole purpose on this earth seems to be to perish on the blacktop. But that is not true, either. The armadillo has long been used in the medical research of leprosy. The microbe that causes the disease is difficult to grow in a laboratory culture, but the armadillo is oddly susceptible, a kind of walking petri dish. Research involving the armadillo at the Hansen's Disease hospital in Carville, Louisiana, helped in the science of leprosy, and helped improve life for the people who were once shunned in their own communities and closeted on the hospital grounds. If that is not a noble creature, I don't know what one is.

I have never struck an armadillo, and I hope I never do. I have never placed a bumper sticker on my car, though I think if an "I BRAKE FOR ARMADILLOS" one is out there, somewhere, I would consider it. It seems to me, with all the good the armadillo has done mankind, right here in the South, it should not be considered an invasive species at all. Maybe we could bump off one of our indigenous species, to make room for it. I would be willing to give up the chigger.

# DIXIE SNOW

*Southern Living,* Southern Journal: January 2014

———

T he yellowed photograph, the size of a playing card, is tacked to the wall in my mother's house, right above my desk. It shows a tiny frame house blanketed in white. An old woman, my grandmother, stands in the open door. You need a magnifying glass to read Ava Bundrum's expression, but on her face appears to be a look that is part fascination, part suspicion, as if she is trying to decide whether to step off into this alien stuff or duck back inside and wait it out till the thaw.

No one here seems to remember how that picture came to be, but I fixed it to the wall because I like looking at it, because it makes me smile. It is proof of the Southerner's never-ending wonderment with snow.

Ava never went north of Lookout Mountain. She lived her life in the low hills along the Alabama-Georgia line, and seldom saw deep snow. Though, one year, a late snowfall did all but cover the buttercups she had planted inside an old tire at the edge of the driveway. And because it was so rare, it was always wonderful and, in a way, maybe even a little frightening.

She had sayings for the weather. If thunder shook the house and a big rain turned the air around her to gray, she would mumble: "Ole devil's beatin' his wife." But she had nothing for snow. It was too infrequent. She would merely stand and look at it, through the thick glass of her spectacles.

When enough of it had fallen onto the cars and trucks in the yard, she would wrap a shawl around her head and slog through it, a dishpan in one hand and a spatula in the other. She would scoop a gallon or so of the snow into the pan, then hurry inside. Working fast, she would mix in sweetened condensed milk and a little sugar, and maybe some vanilla flavoring. Then she would portion it out to us boys, her grandsons, and announce to us: "Snow cream." And it was good.

The Yankees say we don't know how to drive in it, how to walk on it, or even stand. They may be right. But if they had not come down here to live among us, abandoning the tundra of home, they would not be here to know.

I like that people here are not used to it. I have walked hip-deep through the dirty gray snow of New York and Boston, and have seen whole cars disappear under grimy snowplowed ice, along with my fascination.

I still feel it, some, when I see children rush into a snowfall that could not cover pea gravel. I see them using spatulas and spoons to scrape up enough snow to make the saddest snowmen you have ever seen, more red mud that anything else. They last a day, or a morning, and then become forlorn lumps. I have seen children make snow angels in what, mostly, seemed to be slick gravel. But I love to see them try.

Ava never went to a place where such things were mundane. The snow was always exotic, and if the Yankees had any sense they would recognize that she was exotic, too, a kind of hothouse flower, surviving in this one special, humid place. I miss her all the time, but more when the ground turns white.

# MERRY AND BRIGHT

*Southern Living*, Southern Journal; December 2014

———

Some things we cannot duplicate here; we will never celebrate Christmas inside a picture postcard. We have no winter wonderland, though once, inspired by a snowfall seen on the black-and-white television, I did scrape a handful of ice from the inside of the freezer to throw at my brother. By the time I got to him, all I had to fling was a handful of rain.

What we do have is electricity. As long as the Tennessee Valley Authority can light up the Southern night with strands of color, shining from every mansion and mobile home, twinkling 'round the baby Jesus, they can have their white Christmas. I have seen lights encircling hay bales, hung on rusty tractors, and wrapped around mailbox posts. In the country, you need a whole lot of drop cord to electrify a mailbox.

I have seen them strung across the grilles of Peterbilts. My mother never takes down her lights, strung on a cedar beam in the living room, though she does unplug them eventually. The rich folks have switched to white lights, a lot of them, to be elegant, I suppose. But it will always be lights of color, shining through a night that smells of cut pine and woodsmoke, that mean Christmas to me.

I have written that I find it hard, as the years tumble by, not to live in the past, especially in a time of year when I would do anything to see the world again like a child. It is why I fill the refrigerator every December with chocolate-covered cherries and buy my brother fruitcakes at the day-old bakery outlet—fruitcake is impervious to time—and watch, for the hundredth time, those oddly animated, 50-year-old Christmas specials about Kris Kringle and the evil Burgermeister and the elf who wanted to be a dentist and the Island of Misfit Toys.

It is important that some things stay the same, that, at some point this season, someone will say, "We're goin' to look at Christmas lights. Wanna come?"

I go sometimes and sometimes just say no; it is enough to know someone is going. I have a fine memory stashed away of the lights; I do not want it to grow less than it was by heaping a Walmart's worth of new lights on it.

I remember it was first grade, and the big, ramshackle house we lived in, just for that winter, was haunted; but it's really the people who are, I suppose. I was afraid of that house at night. It creaked, and the wind hissed around the eaves. One cold evening, my aunts came by to take us for a ride in an old Chevrolet, rescuing us.

As we drove through the foothills, my face pressed against the window, I saw that the very dark had been conquered, chased away by miles of light, tracing the outlines of ragged trailers and leaning frame houses. Now and then, one of my aunts would mutter, "Their light bill's gonna be high," over the Christmas songs on the radio, and I went to sleep that way. Later, someone carried me inside. I remember I was embarrassed by that; I was a big boy. But the women in my family are strong.

I wish you a merry Christmas, and a very hefty light bill.

# SHOPPING

---

I knew, the day I saw my first pair of skinny jeans *on a man,* that I no longer have any place in this world, and should probably just go live by myself in a hole in the ground.

I am immune to fashion.

I am loathe to shop.

If I cannot find a hole to crawl in, give me a shovel and I will create one. Just, please, Oh, Lord, do not make me wander one more day in the wilderness of the Belks or the Dillards or the Abercrombie and whatever the heck it is, there amid the endless racks of shirts sized for jockeys and gymnasts and the chicken-chested who actually like their shirts to fit *tight.* Do not abandon me to tunnel through mountains of pants designed for short, fat men and 7-foot-tall anorexic ones, only to find that the one normal-size pair, the single, lonely pair that will fit me, comes only in Kelly green.

I do not love clothes, and you cannot make me. I do not believe, as a Southern man, that I am supposed to like them. The pictures of my ancestors all show men in worn-through overalls and battered fedoras and work khakis, in threadbare jeans and canvas shirts that look like they have been mutilated a million times in a Sears & Roebuck wringer washing machine, or beaten on a rock. But they by God look comfortable, like something a man could live in.

New clothes are not comfortable.

New clothes make me uneasy, the same way that snooty cocktail parties do. You know what I mean. Oh, the people there may look fine across the room, but when they get right up on you they make you itch.

New shoes feel like you are shuffling around in a box of saltine crackers. They even sound wrong. They squeak, and squeal. Shoes should not be heard. You should be able to sneak out of a cocktail party unheard, in the right kind of shoes. New shirts feel like somebody left the hanger and cardboard in them, and have too many sharp edges. Cloth, by its very nature, should not have too many straight lines. You can hear a new shirt, too. Think about it.

New pants? I do not really know you well enough to explain why I am terrified of new pants. Let us just say that, on some of my pants purchases, the best thing I can say is there was no lasting injury.

So, I have decided not to shop for clothes again, ever. I have examined the number of clothes in my closet and tried to calculate the amount of wear and tear they can absorb over the next decade or so, and have come to the mathematical conclusion that I can be dead and naked at about the same time.

It is not just that I detest new clothes, but I detest going to get them. I do not love to shop, the way some men do, and no matter how many flyers you stuff in my mailbox or how many e-mails you fling at me or how much societal pressure you bring to bear through your endless loop of television ads, you cannot make me go to your store unless I *have* to go. I will go when I stare into my sock drawer and see only one lonely tube sock looking back at me, or when the posterior of my favorite jeans gets worn so thin that an elderly woman behind me sucks in her breath and shudders an "Oh, my!"

I know what you are thinking. Few men do love shopping for clothes. I hear women say that all the time. "Scooter would just go naked if he had to buy his clothes." I think that might have been true, back when all men could change their own tires and did not think an adventure was cheating on their golf score. Sneak a peek in their closet and tell me what man needs 47 pastel Polo shirts? What man needs 132 pairs of khaki pants ... Dockers. With something called a forgiving waistband. You see men wandering the outlet malls of the Deep South loaded down with shopping bags from Eddie Bauer, arms straining under loads of Old Navy, and you know they ain't never been nowhere near a battleship.

I do not have such largesse. Well, there is plenty of largesse in my waistband, and I guess a little elastic never hurt anybody. But my point is that in the Southern man's closet, there should not be pleated, unpleated, cuffed, non-cuffed, etcetera. Pick a damn style and ride it into the grave.

Part of it, I admit, is the bleak truth told in the mirror. If I had the dimensions of a department store mannequin, and roughly the same intelligence, I might be more shopping-inclined. But there is no designer on this planet who has ever fashioned a garment with me in mind ... and the camo rack at the Walmart does not count.

My clothes are not selected with most of your finer aesthetics in mind, not your higher fashion. I follow a few simple rules:

First, does it actually itch? That immediately excludes most wool and all polyester, and especially this frightening man-made thing called rayon. I will not wear anything that sounds like it was named for a death beam from a B-movie from 1952.

Does it bind? Does it make me wish, after about two or three hours, that I was dead?

Does it make me look like a doofus? Or, to be accurate, more of a doofus. This includes all relaxed jeans, golf shirts since the advent of time, fanny packs, sweaters from the fjords, and T-shirts without sleeves or T-shirts that advertise those bearded guys from Louisiana, the ones that remind you of a bunch of unshorn Kardashians.

But I digress.

I wake up in the morning and assess my wardrobe, and often spend long seconds deciding what to wear ... actually, it only takes that long because sometimes I have to look under the bed to locate the other shoe.

I look in the drawer and assess the sock situation. Socks come in two varieties: white and black.

The white socks are divided into two sub-groups: the comfortable ones, and the soon-to-be-left-behind at the first Hampton Inn I come across. It does not matter if the black socks are all that comfortable because I only wear black socks with suits, and I do not actually own a suit, so that solves that problem.

I have two black jackets, one heavy and one light, and a khaki-colored one made out of something called "firehose canvas." I think perhaps it would stop a bullet. I have two pairs of black dress pants, in cotton, to give me what seems to be a suit if you do not look too close. I only wear this somber black ensemble if I do a talk in front of rich folks or go to a funeral, because even in Florida they will not truly let you go to a funeral in a pair of flip-flops and a roomy pair of swim trunks and a faded blue cotton T-shirt from Panama City 1974.

Shirts are as close as I come to being particular. I have five white-cotton button-downs, soft and worn. I am ashamed to admit that some of them have that little horse and that stupid polo player embroidered on them, ashamed because, when the company made the uniforms for our Olympians a while back, the company saw nothing wrong in the fact the uniforms had been manufactured in China. Plus, I just feel stupid with a polo player stitched on my chest; I think if my grandfather knew I wore a polo player on my shirt he would claw himself from the grave and slap my jaws. But they are fine shirts, and I will choke down my shame so as not to itch.

In fact, I plan to have a tailor either sew me a pocket over the polo player, to hide it, or just stitch a black line through it, in protest. The horse is fine. Horses, even ones subjected to the indignity of polo, look good on anything.

That brings us to pants, and frustration.

I have four good pairs of jeans, not skinny, not relaxed, just human-sized. Jeans should look like, well, jeans. It has taken me 11 years to find that many pair that fit.

I sometimes take my brother Sam with me when I go to the store not to buy pants.

I cuss, and I rave.

I walk out muttering.

But if I do not have him there with me, I fear that—seeing a man my size cursing into the surrounding air—the people at the Burke's outlet store would call the law. I admit I may not shop at the finer establishments. Most of our mothers shopped the bargain stores, and so we do, now. As a friend told me once, he was almost grown before he knew his pants size was not IRREGULAR.

Still, why is it that the manufacturers of pants think that all men are either 28-34, or 46-30. Are all men egrets, or beach balls? Is it too much to comprehend, to fathom, that some men are big men but not unusually wide, not thin, yet still tall. Is it too much to ask, for a 38-34? Apparently, it is.

"You need to get you some of that anger management," my

brother Sam will say, as I grind my teeth.

Do not tell me to go to Big & Tall. I am too small, for the Big & Tall.

My brother Sam never gets mad in the store. The fact is he seldom gets mad at anyone, at anything. He has the same dilemma I do, but just rolls with it.

Once, as he finished working his way methodically through a mile-long rack of jeans, I asked if he had any luck.

"Naw," he said. "They didn't have nothin."

He held up a pair of pants that would have cut high water on the Keebler elf. Then he went to try on hats.

But what really kills me, what really makes me go crazy mad, is the fact that the sizes on the clothes DON'T MEAN ANYTHING. A 38 in the waist can fit me like a pair of maternity pants; a 44 can be so tight it looks like I am auditioning for the Bolshoi.

Do not tell me to try them on. My people were and still are Congregational Holiness.

We do not undress in public behind a swinging door that looks less substantial than the one Miss Kitty hung on the front of the Long Branch. You can *see people* as you take your pants off.

To make it worse, I am told by some rocket scientists at the men's department that I have "a long torso," which means I need to always buy tall clothes, tall shirts and jackets, even though my arms are regular length. This means that the sleeves hang 6 inches below the tips of my fingers, making me look like a 4-year-old boy playing dress-up in his daddy's clothes.

No, I will just wear what I have, for as long as it lasts. I will patch, and mend ... or find someone who can patch and mend. My Aunt Gracie Juanita once re-covered the seats on my Uncle Ed's 1967 Chevrolet dump truck; I bet she could easily re-cover the seat of a pair of Levis.

I don't mean to sound like a Luddite. But there are just indignities in this world I am no longer willing to endure. Do not ask me if I want a Nautica charge card, as I wander the mall, eyes watering from the cloud of toxins sprayed into the air in the beauty aisle.

Just let me go smooth and ragged down through the years, my feet in soft leather, my soul at rest.

Let me fray, and unravel.

And use what is left of me for soft rags, to shine the bumper of an old, comfortable car.

# MY KIND OF TOWN

*Smithsonian*, June 2009

———

I grew up in the Alabama foothills, landlocked by red dirt. My ancestors cussed their lives away in that soil, following a one-crop mule. My mother dragged a cotton sack across it, and my kin slaved in mills made of bricks dug and fired from the same clay. My people fought across it with roofing knives and tire irons, and cut roads through it, chain gang shackles rattling around their feet. My grandfather made liquor 30 years in its caves and hollows to feed his babies, and lawmen swore he could fly, since he never left a clear trail in that dirt. It has always reminded me of struggle, somehow, and I will sleep in it, with the rest of my kin. But between now and then, I would like to walk in some sand.

———

I went to the Alabama coast, to the eastern shore of Mobile Bay, to find a more forgiving soil, a shiftless kind that tides and waves just push around.

I found it in a town called Fairhope.

I never thought much about it, the name, till I saw the brown sand swirling around my feet under the amber-colored water ten years ago. A swarm of black minnows raced away, and when I was younger I might have scooped one up. This is an easy place, I remember thinking, a place where you can rearrange the earth with a single toe and the water will make it smooth again.

I did not want sugar-white sand, because the developers and
tourists have covered up a good part of the Alabama coast, pounded
the dunes flat and blocked out the Gulf of Mexico and a large
number of stars with high-rise condominiums. You see them all
along the coast, jammed into once perfect sand, a thumb in the
eye of God. What I wanted was bay sand, river sand, colored by
meandering miles of dark water, a place tourists are leery to wade.
I wanted a place I could rent, steal or stow away on a boat.

A town of about 17,000, Fairhope sits on bluffs that overlook the
bay. It's not some pounded-out tortilla of a coastal town—all tacky
T-Shirt shops, spring break nitwits, and $25 fried seafood platters—
but a town with buildings that do not need a red light to warn
low-flying aircraft and where a nice woman sells ripe cantaloupe
from the tailgate of a pickup. This is a place where you can turn
left without three light changes, prayer, or smoking tires, where
pelicans are as plentiful as pigeons and where you can buy, in one
square mile, a gravy and biscuit, a barbecue sandwich, fresh-
picked crabmeat, melt-in-your-mouth beignets, a Zebco fishing
reel, a sheet of hurricane-proof plywood, and a good shower head.

"Now, you have to look pretty carefully for a place on the coast
to get the sand under your toes without somebody running over
you with a Range Rover," said Skip Jones, who lives on the same
bayfront lot, just south of Fairhope, his grandparents built on in
1939. "We may be gettin' to that point here, but not yet."

It would be a lie to say I feel at home here. It is too quaint, too
precious for that, but it is a place to breathe. I have a rambling
cypress house five minutes from the bay and a half-hour from the
blue-green Gulf—even a big cow pasture near my house is closer to
the waterfront than I am—but every day I walk by the water, and
breathe.

It is, as most towns are, a little full of itself. Some people call it
an artist's colony, and that is true, since you cannot swing a dead
cat without hitting a serious-faced novelist. And there is money
here, dusty money and Gucci money. There are shops where ladies
in stiletto heels pay Bal Harbour prices for outfits that will be out
of style before low tide, but these establishments can be fun, too.
I like to stand outside the windows with paint on my sweat pants,
tartar sauce on my T-shirt, and see the shopgirls fret.

It had to change, of course, from the sleepy town it used to be,
where every man, it seemed, knew the tides, when the air smelled

from big, wet burlap bags of oysters and the only rich folks were those who came over on a ferry from Mobile to watch the sun set. But everybody is an interloper here, in a way. Sonny Brewer, a writer, came here in 1979 from Lamar County, in west central Alabama, and never really left. It was the late-afternoon sunlight, setting fire to the bay. "I was 30 years old," said Brewer. "I remember thinking, 'God, this is beautiful. How did I not know this was here?' And here I stay."

It is the water, too. The sand is just a path to it.

Here are the black currents of Fish River, highways of fresh and salt water, big bass gliding above in the fresher water, long trout lurking below in the heavier, saltier depths. The Fish River empties into Weeks Bay, which, through a cut called Big Mouth, empties into Mobile Bay. Here, I caught a trout as long as my arm, and we cooked it in a skillet smoking with black pepper and ate it with roasted potatoes and coleslaw made with purple cabbage, carrots, and a heaping double tablespoon of mayonnaise.

Here is the Magnolia River, one of the last places in America where the mail is delivered by a man in a boat, where in one bend in the river there is a deep, cold place once believed to have no bottom at all. You can see blue crabs the size of salad plates when the tides are right, and shrimp as big as a harmonica. Along the banks are houses on stilts or set far back, because the rivers flood higher than a man is tall, but the trees still crowd the banks, and it looks like something from *The African Queen*—or the Amazon.

Then, of course, there is the bay. You can see the skyscrapers of Mobile on a clear day, and at night you see a glow. I pointed to a yellow luminescence one night and proclaimed it to be Mobile, but a friend told me it was just the glow of a chemical plant. So now I tell people Mobile is "over yonder" somewhere.

You can see it best from the city pier, a quarter-mile long, its rails scarred from bait-cutting knives and stained with fish blood, its concrete floor speckled with scales. This is where Fairhope comes together, to walk, hold hands. It is here I realized I could never be a real man of the sea, as I watched a fat man expertly throw a cast net off the pier, at bait fish. The net fanned out in a perfect oval, carried by lead weights around its mouth, and when he pulled it in it was shining silver with minnows. I tried it once and it was like throwing a wadded-up hamburger sack at the sea.

So I buy my bait and feel fine. But mostly what I do here is look. I kick off my flip-flops and feel the sand, or just watch the sun sink like a ball of fire into the bay itself. I root for the pelicans, marvel at how they locate a fish on a low pass, make an easy half-circle climb into the air, then plummet into the bay.

I wonder sometimes if I love this so because I was born so far from the sea, in that red dirt, but people who have been here a lifetime say no, it is not something you get tired of. They tell you why, in stories that always seem to begin with, "I remember..."

"I remember when I was about 10 years old, maybe 8, my mother and sisters and I went through Bon Secour and some guy in a little boat had caught a sawfish," said Skip Jones. "And I thought this thing can't be real—like I felt when they walked on the moon."

A lifetime later he is still looking in the water. "Last year I went out on the walk one morning at about 6 o'clock, and I looked down and there were a dozen rays, and I looked harder and they were all over the place, hundreds of them. Well, we have a lot of small rays, but these had a different, broader head. And I went inside and looked 'em up and saw that they were cownose rays that congregate around estuaries. I called my friend Jimbo Meador and told him what I saw, and he said, 'Yeah, I saw them this morning.' They came in a cloud and then they were just gone. I don't know where. I guess to Jimbo's house."

I would like to tell people stories of the bay, the rivers, the sea, tell them what I remember. But the best I can do is a story about cows. I was driving with my family to the bay, where a bookseller and friend named Martin Lanaux had invited us to watch the Fourth of July fireworks from his neighborhood pier. As we passed the cow pasture, the dark sky exploded with color, and every cow, every one, it seemed, stood looking up at it. It was one of the nicer moments in my life, and I didn't even get my feet wet.

# THE LOST GULF

*Garden & Gun*, August/September 2010

———

E verybody feels something when they look at it, unless they are hollow. Standing in that sand, looking into that blue-green, liquid forever, I felt relieved. It was forty years ago this summer. I was going on 12, a boy from the red dirt, what people call the Alabama highlands. My leather work boots, my future, lay under my bed in Calhoun County, three hundred miles away. I didn't need shoes here. I felt the sand pulled from beneath my toes, felt clean water rush around legs as pale as bone, because a serious man, a working man, did not strut around in short pants. My bathing suit was a pair of cutoff jeans, and when I turned the pockets out I found a handful of sand, white as a wedding dress, pure as salt. For some reason, a reason my grown-up mind cannot see, I laughed out loud.

What I do recall, more than the lovely dunes and raucous seabirds and tiny fish that rode the waves straight into my cupped hands, was a feeling that I stood at the edge of something, not a place to fall off but to float away. The Gulf of Mexico, so vast, was just the beginning of a big world that did not end at the terminus of a dirt road, or a mill gate, or a bald hill stripped clean of pulpwood. From here, why, a fellow could go almost anywhere.

And my mama thought she was just taking me to Pensacola.

People seemed happy here—sun blasted and smelling of squid

bait and fried fish and maybe a little drunk, but happy—or at least that was how it appeared in the summer of 1971. Their pockets were picked clean by overpriced seafood joints and souvenir shops, but they would wear that T-shirt into rags when they got home, to brag that they had been to Panama City, or Gulf Shores. For generations of Southerners, this was the most escape they ever got, as if a five-night stay in the Castaway Cottages was a hole cut in a fence. It broke a lot of hearts, of course, because it was just a feeling, and a feeling can't save you, really. It can only give you, as it gave a 12-year-old boy, a cool taste of hope.

I have felt it all my life, though now walking in the shifting sand hurts my hips, and the sunlight bouncing off the water hurts my eyes. I did see the world, as it turned out, or at least the dark side of it, but looking at this water always made me feel better, somehow, like a laying on of hands.

And now they have fouled it. The oil giant BP and its contractors built a rig in water too deep for common sense, too deep to repair if it all went bad. With some Americans slobbering "Drill, baby, drill," the worst happened. Eleven people died on the rig Deepwater Horizon as a fireball climbed into the sky, the rig sank beneath the waves, and oil jetted into the Gulf and the life within. The oil company, it would turn out, had no workable plan to plug a leak five thousand feet down, at least none that did not take months to accomplish. The failures mounted and the oil billowed from the sand as April faded into May and May into June.

They have left us haunted, and guessing.

How bad?

How long?

My whole life has been bathed in these waters. I lived through a thousand undertows, ten thousand hush puppies, two honeymoons, five hurricanes, a never-ending sunburn, untold jellyfish stings, a dozen excellent drunks, two Coast Guard interventions, a hammerhead as long as a Boston Whaler, and one unfortunate misunderstanding in the Breaker's Lounge. Here I saw the most beautiful mermaids God ever constructed, the ugliest oyster I ever ate, and a hermit crab with a Rebel flag painted on its back. As a child I moved ten tons of sand, one plastic bucket at a time, and as a grown man I waited two hours outside Captain Anderson's in Panama City for a piece of grouper and some French fried potatoes.

Now I wonder. I wonder if the only way I will see my Gulf in the future is through the open window of a dented Chevrolet Biscayne,

Porter Wagoner on the radio, vinyl seats crammed with cousins, beach balls, fried chicken, cold biscuits, and a Coleman thermos full of sweet iced tea. We rush to it, slipping through speed traps, watching for the shrouds of Spanish moss, the first long bridge. And then there it is, the sand white, the water clean. I can keep it that way. I have the power, as long as memory holds.

The first time I saw it was 1965. My mother was convinced the sharks could crawl on shore and snatch us, so we darted in and out of the water like magpies, my brothers, my cousins, and me. My grandmother wandered the shoreline, talking to herself and her dead husband under the brim of her bonnet, filling an apron pocket with shells. They found, him and her, some pretty ones. My mother and Aunt Juanita rolled up their blue jeans as if they might wade in, but just stood on the sand, looking. They rode a full day, changed a fan belt and a radiator hose, just to come down here and look. My big brother, Sam, unafraid of bull sharks, or sea monsters, waded in chest deep and did not cry when he stuck his hand in a jellyfish, a creature not of this world. We saw the remnants of sand castles, eroded ruins, but the bedtime stories our mother told did not involve keeps or castles, so we did not know for sure what they were. But we understood moving earth. The descendants of well diggers, we dug a hole almost 5 feet deep, buried Sam up to his neck, and caused my mother a small heart seizure, because she was convinced every trickling wave was the incoming tide. At dusk we sent cannonballs pounding into a swimming pool the size of a stock trough, the water spiked with so much chlorine it turned our hair green and our eyes the color of cherry cough drops. That night we wandered aisles of coconut monkey heads, embalmed baby sharks, and plastic grapefruit spoons, putted golf balls through the legs of a cement dinosaur, and begged to stay just one more day. Later, our sunburn slathered in Avon lotion, we ate tomato sandwiches and barbecued potato chips by a rolling television screen. Matt Dillon had yet to make an honest woman of Miss Kitty, and paradise cost fourteen dollars a night, if you remembered to drop off your key.

In one awful moment, an oil company accomplished what a drumbeat of hurricanes, pollution, and insane overdevelopment had been unable to do. It threatened the sanctity of the Gulf in a way most of us could not even imagine, sending a stain from horizon to horizon across the surface, and giant plumes of oil, miles long and miles deep, drifting through its depths.

The oil came first to Louisiana, to the marshes, bays, and delicate ecosystems that are the Gulf's cradle of life, as people elsewhere on the coast just waited, waited, for their bad dreams to drift ashore. In Mobile, across the bay from my home, it first slid into Mobile Bay on the oil-slimed hull of a giant freighter, peeling away at the impossible dream that, somehow, all this might pass us by.

In the fifth week, Spencer Johnson sat behind the counter of his Fairhope Fly Shop, looking at a chart of the tides, talking about how a man could catch all the speckled trout he could stand if he cast not from the Fairhope pier but at it, at just the right time in the evening, with just the right fly or bait, and only if the pier lights were shining, and…and then he began to think of the oil. The lovely way he talked of fishing seemed to grow dull, as if the colors had been bleached away, and he began to wonder if he would recognize his Gulf and its sisters, the bays, as the oil drifted closer and closer.

"I'm 67," he said. "I won't enjoy the bay again in my lifetime."

Now, suddenly, every big one that got away is suddenly bigger, more important.

"It was three years ago this June, in the Gulf on the *Lady Ann*, four miles southwest of an oil rig called the Beer Can," he said, thinking back. It was deep water, and something—he thinks probably a wahoo but maybe a shark—took off with his fly, fought, ran, then took it down to coral, "and cut me off." Now he wonders if there will be another fight, another chance.

The island was called Anna Maria, on the west coast of Florida where the Gulf swirls into Tampa Bay. The captain's name was Joe Romeo and I was his third mate, behind a grandson who was in grammar school and whoever else was in the boat. The truth was I was such a poor seaman that I would have been third mate to a tackling dummy or a mannequin at JCPenney. But Lord I did love to go fish with that man. He knew where the specks lived on the flats, and if we caught enough—and we always did—his wife fried 'em up and we had fresh trout and grits and it was a reason to live. In the early evening, a bad time to swim, I would choke down my fear of sharks and wade out to my neck, hugging close to a circle of old ladies who waded out there every evening to do exercises. I learned a good bit about burial plans and assisted living, bobbing in their orbit. They say Ponce de León believed the fountain of youth was here somewhere, but I don't know about that. But I can tell you where to find a good early bird special, or a comfortable shoe.

It may be it will not be as bad as we fear. Some places will be poisoned, some begrimed, some spared. But by summer, even as the bulk of the oil still rolled offshore, people along the Gulf began to speak of their way of life here as something lost, something ripped from them. They began a massive cleanup and animal rescue in Louisiana in what would be called the greatest ecological catastrophe of its kind in U.S. history, and the hateful thing was the oil still poured.

All this misery, because our government believed an oil company—an oil company—when it said trust us, we got this, it'll all be fine. Republicans called it Obama's Katrina, and Democrats blamed a culture of greed and collusion in the past administration that set the stage for a disaster. Meanwhile, BP gouged at the leak with robots, tried to cap it with a big mixing bowl, shot trash and golf balls and mud into the breach, and generally flopped and floundered until it became clear to the people of the Gulf Coast that the oil company did not have the smarts or skill to repair such a snafu, and no solution—no timely one—had ever really existed. They made jokes about it on *Saturday Night Live,* about the hapless oil company, as the stain spread, but it wasn't all that funny.

Smart people, people with doctorates and others with decades of experience in the oil fields, worked for a solution, thought hard, thought long, but eventually, every time people onshore heard the term *brain trust* at a press conference, their hopes sank a little lower, and they ground their teeth.

My daddy loved to drink and he loved to fish, and though he took me with him drinking a dozen times, he never took me fishing. I never had a boy of my own. But when I married Dianne in 2005, I inherited a 10-year-old boy, Jake. He can whup a guitar like it's going out of style, and sing like a fallen angel, and I am glad that he is mine, at least part of the time. I took him fishing in the Gulf because that is what a good man does, or at least a man trying to be. We left from Orange Beach and went out in the blue with a friend of his we called Taco, because he likes tacos, and we caught fish after fish, red snapper and mackerel and fish I had never seen, and I would have liked it if the boy and I could have talked about life a little bit, or adventures, or maybe even dreams. But instead he and his buddy just hooted and giggled and acted like the dumbasses little boys are as the spray from the speeding boat drenched them on every bounce, and they laughed out loud.

At first, people just wanted the comfort of numbers, how long their Gulf would be fouled, how many fish or birds or turtles would die, how many shrimpers, oystermen, fishermen, hotel maids, short-order cooks, and all the rest would be wiped out, run off, how many families who made their living here for generations would be ruined, or just leave. Then, as attempt after attempt failed, they began to imagine the unimaginable, that the whole damn thing would become a dead zone, a kind of poisoned lake, leaching into the Atlantic and beyond.

The skeptics and the old salts said such people were just a bunch of Chicken Littles, said there was just too much water out there to worry about doomsday, that the Gulf would cleanse itself, even as the oil rolled into balls of tar in the waves. It was just thin oil, they said, not thick crude, and chemical dispersants would break it up so that the microorganisms in the Gulf could just gobble it up. When it did not immediately foul all the beaches, bays, and estuaries of states east of Louisiana, indignant, desperate sea captains and chamber of commerce officials said it was just a scare, that it was environmental types who were really putting them out of business, with rumors and lies.

And then came the pitiful proof. Oil-slimed pelicans struggled to lift off the glistening water and just hung there in the mess, confused, beaten. Tar balls rolled in the dingy surf, gummed up the beaches. The fish and the shrimp and the turtles and the crabs ingested the toxins, and began to die.

People strung booms, built berms, prayed.

In June, the oil rolled just offshore in Baldwin County. We went, my family and I, to wade, and bob in the water, and just look at it, before the oil crept in. But it was no good. Every cool wave just reminded me of what would be lost. I thought of that line from Tennyson, about casting a shade, a shadow, on such a delightful thing as this, and I wanted to beat the water with my fists.

# THE YANKEE MYSTIQUE

T he cold had teeth in it, in '93. I walked from the old house in
Cambridge, Massachusetts, and I felt it bite me through my
clothes, before I had taken a second step. There was snow on
the ground but it was old snow, weeks old, glittering, frozen hard
as marble. By my third step my legs were already going numb. It
was dark, just a few steps from Harvard Yard, from those great
halls of enlightenment, but the Southern gothic in me could not
help but wonder if I might just freeze stuck to the ground in this
foreign place, freeze into a statue that the students would gaze
upon with great curiosity in the morning light. I turned around
and almost leapt back onto the porch, snatching at the door,
almost clawing for the warmth inside. Say what you want about
these Northerners, but don't call them weak-willed, don't call
them soft. A creature that can live in this, live like this, deserves
our respect, even our admiration. But I could not help but wonder
if maybe my kinfolks had been right, when I was a child. Maybe
the Northerners are an altogether different people, maybe even a
different species. "They ain't like us," my kin used to say. Well at
least, I thought as the door closed behind me and the feeling came
back in my legs, they have much finer long underwear.

The next winter, a record one for nasty cold on the island of
Manhattan, I stood at the doors to my apartment building in

Midtown as the doorman looked at me with something close to pity. He was a nice man, a New Yorker to his bones, and was especially kind to me after he heard my hillbilly accent. He told me everything twice, to make sure I understood. I steeled myself for the bite, that cold, cold bite, and stepped boldly onto a sidewalk crowded with Northerners who thought this was just brisk. I hit a patch of hard snow before I made it a block and a half, to slide and stumble spectacularly onto iconic Broadway itself, where a sea of dirty yellow taxis flowed around me as if I was Moses. No one even blew a horn. And again, I had to give them respect. Say what you want to about these Northerners, I thought, but these people do know how to drive in the snow.

I lived two winters up there, among them. I learned a lot.

I learned that, if you are a Southern boy, keep your behind at home.

---

I think I was 7 years old before I knew it was not a bad word.

I grew up just 20 miles or so from a big Army base, in the era of Vietnam, so the Northerners, though a distinct minority, were always among us. I would hear these accents I could barely understand, accents that sounded like the speaker was chewing on something that tasted unpleasant. I would look to the grown-ups for some kind of explanation.

"Well, son," my uncles would say, "they're Yankees."

"Oh," I would say.

"They can't talk no other way," my aunts would say.

"Oh," I said.

"Bless their heart," my aunts said.

In time, I came to understand that the mysterious Yankees, bless their heart, were from a place far, far away, a frozen land where people cut holes in the ice to fish.

But that part sounded made up to me.

I was told by the grown-ups that the Yankees sometimes had to wait till spring to bury their dead, and were sewn up in their long underwear in September because it wasn't coming off till July. I was told they did not sell grits in their stores and did not even know what the word meant, did not like cornbread of any kind, and looked down on *us* because of the way *we* talked, or at least some of them did.

I was told they ate sardine-and-onion sandwiches and something called scrapple that was rumored to be even nastier than chitlin's, and they drank heavily from a clear spirit called vodka, which was manufactured from the heathen potato and not the sacred corn, as God and my whiskey-making ancestors intended. I was told they wrapped their tires with chains to traverse the frozen earth, that the never-ending snows piled so high and heavy on their houses it crushed them to sticks, and they had to shovel it out twice a day just to back out of the driveway to get a loaf of white bread, which they ate three meals a day. I was told their cars disintegrated into piles of rolling rust, from all the salt they spread on the iced-over roads, and only a fool bought a Yankee car. I was told they sometimes got hung up inside their own heads when they tried to pronounce the names of their *own* places, like *Baaaaa-ston*, and *Mine-soooooo-tah*.

I was told we fought a great and bloody war with them a long, long time ago, and lost because they had all the cannon, and that the rich folks down here never really got over that ... though the rest of us had more pressing concerns, like college football bowl games, where teams from the tundra sometimes beat even the vaunted Crimson Tide, and the Devil quite possibly hailed from a froze-hard place called Notre Dame.

I would learn it was a whole lot more complicated than that, this wonderment and animosity that swirled around the Yankee. But as a child of Alabama, in the insulated foothills of the Appalachians, it maybe took longer than it should have to figure it all out. In time I would discover that the Northerner was profoundly different yet still roughly the same species as me, even if they did sometimes wear cheese on their head.

I blame my slow development on the first Yankee I ever met, who was, oddly enough, my distant kin.

I might not have even met a Yankee, at least not until high school, had it not been for the great northern migration of working-class Southerners to Detroit, a migration that began even before I was born. By the time I was old enough to walk, in the early 1960s, it seemed every other family down here had a second cousin up in Michigan, living on white bread, searching hopelessly for grits and hanging bumpers on Cadillacs. They married up there, to women who had never even seen an iron skillet, and brought their funny-talking progeny home to mystify us at family reunions and sometimes Christmas.

One of them, a cousin, came down to live among us.

I was maybe 5 or 6, but intelligent for my age. You might not understand everything that is said, when you are so small, but you can feel unease, tension, the same way a dog can. I like to think I was at least as observant of the human condition as your average Golden Retriever.

This young man, in his late teens, acted like he had fallen from the moon. He looked around this corner of the South, at us, at our small wood-frame houses and our food and the way we lived, and spent every moment after, it seemed, gazing longingly back at the moon.

One day, after doing some work with other young men in the family for a farmer who lived close to us, the farmer paid them and told them, if they wanted, they could go into the garden and pick a mess of turnip greens to take home to their mamas.

"I ain't gonna eat them weeds," the Yankee boy said.

The old farmer nodded.

"I'd rather eat manure," the boy said.

The old farmer nodded again.

"Well, son," he said after a while, "I guess it all depends on what you're used to."

It was about then that my extended family gathered for a barbecue, and I remember it as one of the most elaborate I had ever seen. It had been a good year for hogs, and I can still see the clean, white butcher paper that was wrapped around what must have been fifty pounds or more of pork. The men of the family had built a pit out of concrete blocks and wire grate that seemed about as long as a Studebaker. On it, after the coals were cooked down, they laid on fresh ham and pork chops and about 1,000 weenies, basting the cooking meat now and then with homemade barbecue sauce they had mixed in half-gallon jars.

I think I ate six pork chops and two hot dogs and would have had more but my mother was afraid I had injured myself; that, and the fact someone had prepared a banana pudding in an honest-to-God washtub, and it was calling my name. When I was done with my chops, my mother carefully raked them off into the trash, to the great distress of the hounds and beagles milling around, begging.

You have to be careful with pork chop bones, which can be jagged, and brittle. Like chicken bones, they can splinter in a dog's mouth, and choke them to death. My mother and aunts policed the bone disposal, since none of the men could be trusted with anything that required that much forethought and common sense.

The Yankee cousin had eaten the pork chops like they were

going out of style, like there would never be another pork chop on this earth. He was a big boy to begin with, in a white tank top that might have covered his belly five pork chops ago, and what little had missed his mouth, he was wearing on his shirt. I say this not as indictment, since I was wearing barbecue sauce in my eyebrows. Bless my heart.

"What did you do with your bones, son," he was asked, as he presented a paper plate all but licked clean.

"I eat 'em," he said.

Then, to demonstrate, he sucked all the meat off a good-size pork chop, and then went to work on the bone with a sound like breaking sticks.

The story is legend. It was told year after year, as testimony to the strangeness of Yankees.

But now that I have had a lifetime to think about it, now that I have lived among them, I now feel a little sorry for that boy. Was he not as displaced as I had been, my years in the tundra? How he must have felt, being dropped into this caldron, this swamp? I wonder if he ever looked into a Southern sky, a sky so hot, so thick with haze, that it was more white than blue, and felt a long way from home?

Instead of sliding out into traffic on the hard ice, did he walk out into the air as thick as cotton and feel as if he could barely breathe, feel as if he could barely lift his arms? Did he stare out across fields of empty? Did he stare up into mountains of silence? Did he dream of the crash and bang of assembly lines?

Did he stand in the middle of a crowd of Southerners and wonder why some of us talked as if we had a mouthful of seedless grapes, others grunted their words and still others were so in love with the language that they told stories without end ... and sometimes without purpose, just to talk, just to tell?

Did he wonder why every old man had a jaw full of Brown Mule?

Did he recoil at the stifling clouds of snuff?

Did he almost hurt himself the first time he heard a rebel yell? Did he even know it was a human sound?

Did he wonder if his head would explode, in conversation with a Southern belle?

People are strange, when you're a stranger. I think that's a song. Still...

I guess it just depends on what you're used to.

# COTTON

W e go looking for the young woman, from time to time. We know where she lives, but she only appears in September, around picking time.

We know where the old woman lives. The old woman lives in the mirror, although my mother remains unconvinced, even after all this time, of her true identity. "Where did that old woman come from?" she says, and though it is something she says all the time we still smile, because it is so odd to hear this woman talk about vanity. She is beyond it, I believed. I guess I believed she was above it, too. She had first heard about the old woman who lives in the mirror in a poem, or a story, but it is an old joke now and she cannot remember how it started, and like a good hat she appropriated on a stormy day and forgot who she borrowed it from, she wears it comfortably, often, and without regret.

"I don't know how that old woman got in my house."

But the young woman, now ...

We know where we left her.

We find her, year after year, in the cotton.

It is a myth that you pick cotton in the broiling heat of summer. You pick it in the early fall, usually after the first frost. The great machines pick it now. They tear through the fields and devour the bolls atop the dry, brittle stalks, stripping a field in a day. The men and women of the fields, the ones who worked hunched over in the rows, are a thing of antiquity.

But my mother can still see a solitary figure there. We seek her out every season, riding past field after field here in the small, pocket crops that still survive in the foothills of the Appalachians along the Alabama-Georgia line. There are fewer and fewer of them, it seems, every year, but as long as there is even one left, the young woman will be there. It doesn't matter that no one else can see her in those fields; my mother can, and over time, so can I.

I guess we all see something different when we look across it, across this most Southern of things. I know there is little romantic about it for some Southerners. Some look out across that sea of white and bitter green and see a history of human bondage; others see great wealth, see the bedrock of a failed society, as if they were looking at the foundation of a house that no longer exists.

My mother looks down the rows and sees youth, sees a serene and beautiful woman that time had not yet torn down, that hard work and sorry men and needy, grasping children had not seemed to mark at all. When I was a baby, she dragged me up and down those rows season after season, and I even slept there on that canvas sack as she pulled, and picked, trading the extra pain, the weight, to have her baby close to her, to sing to, to talk to. When my baby brother took my place there on the sack, I played in the cotton wagon and listened to old women, black and white, sing about streets of gold. At quitting time I would stand at the edge of the field and wait for her blonde head to reappear over the rise in that field.

That is who she sees now, as we roll past, sees that young woman there under the sweat, inside the whorls of wind-whipped dust, and she says the same thing, a hundred times or more.

"Ain't it beautiful."

People who do not know any better would think she was just talking about a cotton field.

For my people, the working-class whites of the highland South who picked it across the generations for a handful of dollar bills, it has always been complicated, this crop.

My big brother, Sam, sees the industry in it, sees the science, sees the history in this plant that made fortunes for the big people and broke the little people's hearts.

"You don't remember the year the cotton didn't open?" he asks me, like asking if I remember the plague years.

He cannot recall the year, but in his childhood, when drought and other factors caused a perversion in the bolls. Instead of bursting open after the first frost, the boll, hard and thick and guarded on the end with needle-like spikes, remained sealed, and the cotton began to rot in the fields. People took big sacks home with them, built fires in the hearth, and pried them open by hand, burning the bolls in the flames. The stunted cotton came out in tightly pressed wedges, like orange slices. People who pick cotton make their money by the pound. This was a bad year.

He was the last in my family to pull a sack. There was no romance in it, just great uncertainty. He went to work in the cotton mill in my hometown when he was older, in the nerve-stripping crash and clatter of the machines that filled the workers' lungs with dust and bacteria that cut short their lives. "Made more money than I'd ever made," he said, and the day it shut was the first and only time in his life that I think he almost, almost cried.

Me, I looked across those fields as a little boy and saw *everything*.

I had never seen what was on the other side of that field, not when I was so small. Back then, when I was still playing in the dirt with a borrowed spoon, I believed it was all there was. The cotton field, just steps from my bedroom window, was the first thing I saw when I woke up in the morning, and the last thing I saw at night. I have never slept all that much, not even as a boy, and from my tiny bedroom at the back of the quiet, sleeping house I would stare across a field that seemed to have no end, that rose from the edge of the backyard in a gentle slope that blocked out everything beyond. In the daylight we played hide-and-seek in the stalks and beat each other bloody with the red-dirt clods that had baked hard as stone in the Alabama heat, but in the dark I sent my imagination out into that field to play. Between those rows lived all the ogres and elves and howling beasties that I could conjure, all the tigers and bears and biting things my imagination could invent. Here, Indians in lurid war paint crept through the green-black, chest-high plants, and whole battalions of goose-stepping Germans stomped through the moonlight and the rising dust. I could hold them off till morning with my lever-action Daisy BB gun, as long as my ammunition held out, and I had a three-year supply of that; you could buy a million BBs at the Western Auto and still have enough change left over from your dollar to buy a lead sinker, a Sugar Daddy, and a week-old edition of *The Jacksonville News*.

Sometimes, looking out across those rows under a full moon, I barely had to squint at all to see what I wanted to see. I cannot reach that far back anymore, to most things in my childhood, but I can still see how the moonlight washed across the rows and turned the whole field a shining, ghostly silver-white, more like something from another world, from the black-and-white B movies on the television screen. You expected a flying saucer to wobble from the stalks, expected little green men with helmets like goldfish bowls to glide across the tops of the cotton bolls to stare bug-eyed through the still blades of your shorted-out electric fan. I could not tie my shoes properly yet, every time, but there was nothing wrong with my five-year-old imagination in 1964.

Once, twice a season, the crop dusters came to spray the fields—and us, I guess—with cotton poison, what I now know was DDT. The planes looked like something from forgotten wars, and probably that was true. They swooped in ridiculously low, almost to the height of the stalks themselves, it seemed to me, before pulling back and climbing, climbing, only to plummet again and again. It was death-defying work, I was told. But in my imagination it was even more dangerous up there in those clouds of cotton poison. In my imagination there was not one plane, but two, and the endless cotton fields became a bombed out row of hedges, in war-torn France. The clouds of DDT were gunsmoke from the chattering machine guns of the Red Baron as he chased the other pilots from the sky. The dogfight, somewhere over Walter Rollins' chicken house, seemed to last all day. I remember that the crop dusters always waggled their wings at me there on the earth, jumping up and down, as they flew away, and I took that to mean that only them and me knew what really happened up there in the sky.

I will always remember the day I snuck away from my mama and walked a single row, determined, till I reached the other side, remember how I pushed through the ragweed at the edge of it all and found not one dragon. Here was not the drop-off into nothingness you would expect at the end of the world. It was just more dirt, and more Johnson grass, and a fat snapping turtle the circumference of a hatbox, which was impressive enough but not much to look at if you were expecting crocodiles. I could even hear my mama calling to me, faintly, from the other side. "Well," I remember thinking, "this is disappointing." But it wasn't, really.

It was exactly what I needed it to be, that field, when I needed it to be that way. My imagination, my dreams and daydreams, grew in that rust-colored ground, crop after crop.

I look for those things now, those ridiculous things, and I cannot find them. I see just the white, the lovely white.

But the young woman, now...

We know she is real.

# STILLNESS

*Southern Living,* Southern Journal: May 2013

---

I remember a quiet so complete a lone cricket was a cacophony, a single drop of water boomed like a stick hammering a bass drum. I remember space, vast and long, remember cotton that stretched to the end of everything, interrupted only by ribbons of blacktop that led to exotic places like Leesburg, Piedmont, and Rome. I remember a darkness complete, not only the absence of light but a thing that could swallow light altogether, the way a mud puddle does a match tossed from a passing car.

It was the early 1960s, in a place called Spring Garden, Alabama, where I would lie in my bed in a big, ragged house and wonder if the whole world had stopped spinning outside my window. I would have asked my big brother, Sam, about it, but he would have just told me I was a chucklehead, and gone back to sleep. I have never slept much; I think I was afraid I would miss something passing in all that quiet dark.

Then, sometime around midnight, I would hear it. The whistle came first, a warning, followed by a distant roar, and then a bump, bump, bumping, as a hundred boxcars lurched past some distant crossing. They were probably just hauling pig iron, but in my mind they were taking people to places I wanted to be. A braver boy would have run it down and flung himself aboard.

And then it was gone, without warning, and I would go to sleep, grudging, and dream about oceans, and elephants, and trains.

I miss the stillness. It is an antique in this shrill, intruding life, an all-but-forgotten thing of no real value, like inkwells. It is as if we have tried to fill up what stillness there is with all the mindless claptrap we can conjure, as if a little quiet or a patch of peaceful dark is a bug that has to be stomped before it gets away.

In restaurants, I am forced to eat my meatloaf with the television tuned to two mental giants ranting about a topic they manufactured that morning, apparently from mud and straw. In a doctor's waiting room, a televangelist told me I was going to hell, then Rachael Ray made me a tuna melt.

At any given moment, on a plane, in a lobby, anywhere, I hear the TV at war with a dozen personal electronic devices. I am certain that, if I were sitting on a rug woven from palm fronds and dead army ants in the middle of the Amazon, I could hear the ubiquitous song of an iPhone.

I miss the wind in the cedars. I miss that sifting sound. Sometimes in summer, we sit on the porch of our old house in Fairhope to watch the dark fall, but sometimes the neighbors get to hollering about, well, living, and how do you go over and say, "Excuse me, but you are messing up my dark"?

It is enough to wish for a lightning storm. There's that moment when the lightning flashes and thunder shakes the house. The power flickers and dies, and a dark stillness falls. And you're swallowed up by a pure, old-fashioned silence, free of the hum of the refrigerator or the air conditioner, free from all the man-made background noise that makes you feel less human.

I do not sleep any better now. I live most of the year with sirens and squealing tires. But someone, somewhere, is looking after me, and sent me another train. I hear it bump through the city of Tuscaloosa in the small hours of the morning, and I dream and wonder, again, though I know exactly where it goes.

# PART 4

# CRAFT

# WHY I WRITE ABOUT HOME

*Long Leaf Style*, Summer 2008

———————

I write about home so I can be certain that someone will. It is not much more complicated than that.

Home for me has always been as much a matter of class as location. My home is not the comfortable South, not the big churches, or the country clubs, or the giant waterfront houses on the lakes or the columned mansions on the main drags.

Home for me is not a skybox at Alabama or Auburn, or good seats at Turner Field in Atlanta. It is not even the Kiwanis Club, or the Rotarians.

Home is not a thing of position, or standing. My home is where the working people are, where you still see a Torino every now and then, and people still use motor oil to kill the mange.

It is where the men live who know how to fix their own damn water pump, where the women watch their soap operas on the VCR because they will be at work at mid-day.

It is where the churches are small, and the houses, too. It is where people cheer for a college they have never seen, where propane tanks shine silver outside mobile homes with redwood decks, where buttercups burst up out of mounds of red mud, encircled by an old tire.

These are not the people of influence who have their names carved into the concrete of banks and schools and Baptist churches, whose faces stare back from the society page. As I've said, maybe too many times, these are the descendants of people who could only get their name in the newspaper or the history books if they knocked some rich guy off his horse.

I do not, greatly, give a damn about writing about people who, by birthright, history will handle with great care anyway.

I will write about a one-armed man who used to sling a sling-blade out by the county jail, and a pulpwood truck driver who could swing a pine pole around like a baseball bat.

I will write about dead police chiefs who treated even the most raggedy old boy with a little respect, and old men who sip beer beside the pool tables in Brother's Bar, and then go take some money off the college boys.

I will write about the wrongdoers, because sometimes doing right is just too damn hard, and the sorry drunks, and the women who love them anyway. I will write about mamas, not somebody's Big Daddy. I will write about snuff, not caviar.

I will write and write as long as somebody, anybody, wants me to, till we remind one more heartbroken ol' boy of his grandfather, or educate one more pampered Yankee on the people of the pines.

I will put on my necktie and do my best to fit in the more comfortable places, and it may be that I have come to like that too much. But it will never last for me, there, and I will always go back to what I understand and admire, and love.

And it may be that there will come a time when no one wants to know, when no amount of skill will make them want to know, or care. And then I will quit, and I will do something else, or just die, because all this jaw jutting will wear out a man.

But the stories will last whether I do or not, count whether I do or not, and the rich folks will just have to get used to the idea that their stories are only part of the story, and not the only part worthy of the clay, and the pines, and the years.

# THE FINE ART OF PIDDLING

*Southern Living,* Southern Journal: February 2012

———

The obituary made me smile. *Ellis Ray of Moundville passed away Saturday...he was a loving husband, father, and grandfather, who loved to fish and piddle. He will be greatly missed.*

I mean no disrespect. Quite the contrary, I smiled because Ellis, whom I never met, is my brother, bound to me not by blood but by a shared habit. We are piddlers.

Or we were. Now I am left here, an earthbound piddler, to piddle alone. What is a piddler? It is hard to explain to begin with, because piddling is neither one thing nor another, but something in between. It is not rest, not something that can be done with your feet on an ottoman or as you recline in a Posturepedic. But then neither is it work, something that one toils at, sweats at, something one needs a break from, for lunch, coffee. It is certainly not something for which one should ever be paid, and absolutely not something that one does while watching a clock.

The whole idea of piddling is to kill time, but without any great effort at all, or even really meaning to. If one piddles correctly, time just goes away, without regret on the part of the piddler, or even any particular notice. One does not march off to piddle. One meanders. And even when one heads off to do it, one may not go to piddling right away, because one might have to loafer a little first. But loafering is another story.

A piddler does not fix a leaky washing machine, or a slipping transmission, or a hole in a roof. Such work is necessary, and the more necessary a labor is, the farther from piddling it becomes. A piddler may use tools, but only small, light ones, and only on things that are not needed right then. Changing out a car battery in the dead of winter is not piddling, because it is a necessity. But tinkering with a lawn mower in the middle of February is, especially if the grass is deader than Great-aunt Minnie's house cat and buried under a foot of snow. Doing a load of laundry is, of course, not piddling. Organizing one's sock drawer by color and fiber is.

Fishing is not piddling. That is why Ellis Ray's survivors made that distinction in his obit. But sharpening hooks and respooling line is, especially if the bass boat is covered in sheet ice. Going to a baseball game is not piddling. Retying the laces on your cleats is, but only if the only way you will ever again go fast down the first-base line is if someone shoots you out of a cannon.

Some people have to retire to piddle. Dr. David Sloan, a venerated college professor who worked across the hall from me, seemed one of the least piddling men I ever knew. But he said he fully intended to spend at least some of his retirement piddling. I am not so disciplined. I rearrange books, sharpen knives—the ones I am certain not to use—and change knobs on dressers and cabinets, but only if the ones I am replacing were perfectly fine. I rearrange pictures on the wall, and re-rearrange them because my wife makes me. I spackle holes left from the first rearranging, but only the holes that are hidden by the paintings and do not really have to be spackled at all. To spackle a hole in plain sight would be necessary and therefore illegal under piddling guidelines.

My wife does not piddle. She reads, gardens (successfully), and uses her time wisely. When I try to interest her in my own piddling she looks at me with disdain and says she does not have time to waste.

Ellis Ray of Moundville was 68 when he died. I bet he never wasted a second.

# THE COLOR OF WORDS

*Southern Living,* Southern Journal: February 2014

———

The winter is bleak and gray down here, or at least it can seem that way. The sky turns the color of dirty cotton and it rains two weeks straight, then sleets. Wet leaves blow like old newspaper and stick to anything that stands still, like windshields and old, slow-moving dogs. The red mud turns slick, then freezes. The ice storms turn out the lights, and people raid the bread aisle as though this were the end of time.

Often, I gaze at the scudding clouds and icy mist and think of fishing.

"The fish won't bite on a bluebird day," my big brother, Sam, told me many years ago, looking up into a bright, blue sky. I hear it in my head every clear, blue day—and when it's cloudy with a chance of fish.

Or, I think about Mrs. Mary Bird, of Waterloo, Alabama, who sees through the gray and cold. "Still enough blue in the sky," she says, "to make a cat a pair of pants." And I know that the real color and warmth in us, as a people, is not in the landscape or the sky but in our language, the way we lean the words against each other. We are the best-spoken people on Earth, not in the realm of grammar, perhaps, but in the pictures we paint and hang on the air.

If you ask my mother if someone told the truth, she will not answer, "Why, yes, they did." She will answer, "Why, hon', she was

tellin' God's sanction." And that is just prettier. She also does not
say people act a fool, which is cruel. "They play folly," she says.
I have been playing folly, she points out, for 54 years.

We have our own phrases for things, like our phrase for a good
person. If a man is capable, sound, he is not just "steady." He is,
as Sam says, "gun-barrel straight." A man who is not gun-barrel
straight is "a chuckle," which I think is short for chucklehead. I just
know that is what he calls me before suggesting that perhaps
I should go get me "some of that anger management," like it was
something they sold with salt licks down at the co-op.

"And if I tell you a rooster dips snuff," he says, "you can look
under his wing for the can."

I think a lot of people think our language is a bunch of clichés,
like "shut my mouth," or "rode hard and put up wet," usually spat
out when we are "drunk as Cooter Brown." This is not what I am
talking about.

I think about my Uncle Ed, leaning on a shovel handle in the
100-degree heat of an Alabama summer, turning up an ice-crusted
RC Cola before mumbling, quietly, "If the good Lord made anything
better than this, He kept it for Hisself."

Some things we say are just mysterious, like a friend's grandmother
who is prone to blurt out, "Well, I'll be Johnny." We do not know
who Johnny is. I am tired of trying to explain us. I once wrote that
a man had enough money to burn a wet dog. I got a call from
animal rights activists who wondered why I advocated such.
I told them it was only something we said, and I loved dogs, and...

I should have just told them to go see Johnny about it.

# THE BLANK NOTEBOOK

*Southern Living,* Southern Journal: September 2013

---

The long hallways—math to this side, science to the other, social studies down the way—were of ancient, gleaming wood, and always smelled of fresh wax and old misery. How many D minuses had fluttered down to those dark boards? How many "trues" that should have been "falses"? How many multiple choices that left no choice at all?

It was around 1966 or 1967, but September for sure, because September meant that summer was well and truly dead. It was still hot as seven hells outside, but with one halting step into the gloom of that hall you entered a whole other realm, where coaches and even math teachers kept order with long wooden paddles, and a second-grade teacher once kicked my cowboy boot clear off my foot, then, with a running second kick, knocked it clear into the hall. All this, because I left one leg sprawled out in the aisle during her elocution. Still, it was a fine kick for an old woman.

I should have hated that school, Roy Webb School, in Calhoun County, Alabama. I would have, maybe, if not for that notebook.

As much as I hated the end of those hot, free days of summer, I loved that notebook, loved the clean, unmarred lines. Every year I got a new one, divided by subject, and it was always somehow just enough to get me through the year, perhaps because math was completely blank. Except for pictures of hot rods. I used a quarter to get the wheels right.

Mostly, I loved the smell of it. It smelled like... well, I couldn't put words to it, then. Now I know it was the smell of a fresh start, the smell of possibility. I could learn something, if at the end of the year the pages were filled with ideas, maybe even answers. I would start writing on the third or fourth page, because surely there was some finer idea that needed to go first.

I wrote Mark Twain's thoughts here. I wrote every line to "Big Rock Candy Mountain," about how the hens laid soft-boiled eggs.

My books were wrapped in brown paper bags from the Piggly Wiggly, and on those rare occasions I got a new one, the spine would make a cracking sound, like snapping an ice-cream stick, when I first opened it. My desk was always carved at least once with the name of a long-lost third grader, always daubed at least five times with a petrified wad of Juicy Fruit. I puzzled at that. How did he expect to get away with defacing school property when he signed his work? And how did a school that had banned the chewing of gum since the first Roosevelt Administration have desks in such a state? Come to think of it, they had banned pocketknives, too.

But this was the key to my castle. I learned here.

I walk through stores and pick up notebooks and smell them, and I am sure more than one person has shaken their head at the odd man trying to snort up a stationery aisle. It does not smell the same. I think it is because my chance is used up, and the great possibility with it. Maybe only the young can sense it, the ones at the beautiful, unmarred beginning of things.

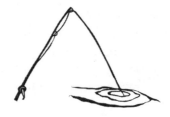

# FISH STORY

*Southern Living,* Southern Journal: July 2013

This is a fish story. That said, it is still mostly true.

"We need to go fishin' out in the Gulf, on my boat," said my friend Randy Jones.

"Not," I said, "if you are driving." I had never heard of any great seafarers from Sand Mountain, Alabama, and had this awful image in my head of him and me playing dominoes in a Cuban prison.

"I'll get somebody good," he said.

There were five of us the day we put out from Orange Beach on Randy's 40-footer, *Earlie Tide.* "Because my daddy's name was Earlie," he told me, and if that is not the perfect reason to name a boat, I don't know what is.

I do not recall the day. "Just say it was the hottest day of the year," Randy said. It was me, him, and my stepson Jake. The skipper was Fred Williams, whom Randy described as "a car salesman and wannabe sea captain." But I looked him in his squinty eyes and knew him to be a capable man. Crewing the boat was Dr. Wayne Hyatt, a pioneering laser surgeon and, Randy said, "the most expensive deckhand in maritime history."

We went 27 miles into the blue, and when we stopped, the sun seemed to be trying to bore a hole through the deck of the *Earlie Tide.* "I got air-conditioning and a big-screen TV in the cabin,"

Randy told me, but I told him, "Naw, I came to fish like a man."
Besides, the TV wasn't hooked up.

Jake was oblivious to the heat, and cranked in fish after fish.
I lasted about two hours and began to perish. My face burned red
and my mouth went white, and I began to see things in the water
that were not there. "We can read your last rites right here," my
good friend told me, " 'cause I ain't givin' you mouth-to-mouth."

But I wobbled around the deck another hour. Hemingway
would have, I told myself, and he would have been knee-walkin'
drunk at the time. Just about then, in my weakened state, I felt that
pull on my line even bad fishermen dream about. I tried to keep
the rod pointed at the sky, but whatever was on the line nearly
pulled me into the water. Do red snapper get this big? Do Spanish
mackerel? I fought and I fought till my stomach began to flop
around inside me, and then with one last pull the hook, bait, and
a portion of, well, something, came flying into the boat.

"It's the jaw of a red snapper," someone said, solemnly.

"Pulled his lips off," I said, tragically.

It takes a man, I told my shipmates, to separate a fish from
his lips.

Yeah, they said, that must be what happened. Then Wayne
posed with it and got his picture made. Most likely, a shark took
the fish as it rose on my line. I choose not to believe that. But it was
a failure, I suppose, another failure for the worst fisherman in my
family line. I asked Randy why we even try. He explained that it
was natural, to try and fail and fail again. We have this man in our
head we want to be, a fisherman.

"So," Randy said, "we go."

# THE QUILL AND THE MULE

*Southern Living,* Southern Journal: April 2011

————

I n one of my most delicious daydreams, I stand at the gates of the Southern Writers' Hereafter, wondering if my name is on the list. Suddenly the gates swing open to reveal a sanctum of velvet drapes, leather chairs, and a bar lined with bottles of brown whiskey. William Faulkner is here, spats propped on his Nobel Prize. Truman Capote drops names at the bar. Flannery O'Connor tells a bawdy joke.

The ghost of Erskine Caldwell takes my arm. "How did you get in?" he asks.

"I rode in," I say, "on a dead mule." We laugh. Zora Neale Hurston slaps my back.

"Son," she says, "didn't we all?"

Scholars have long debated the defining element of great Southern literature. Is it a sense of place? Fealty to lost causes? A struggle to transcend the boundaries of class and race? No. According to the experts, it's all about a mule. And not just any old mule—only the dead ones count. Ask the experts.

"My survey of around 30 prominent 20th-century Southern authors has led me to conclude, without fear of refutation, that there is indeed a single, simple, litmus-like test for the quality of Southernness in literature...whose answer may be taken as definitive, delimiting, and final," wrote professor Jerry Leath

Mills, formerly of The University of North Carolina at Chapel Hill, more than a decade ago. After some four decades of cataloging, he concluded that the true test is: "Is there a dead mule in it?...*Equus caballus x asinus (defunctus)* constitutes the truly catalytic element..."

I have written two dead mules in two books. That's how I know I am bona fide. Southern writers were killing mules even before Faulkner drowned a perfectly good team in the Yoknapatawpha River in *As I Lay Dying* in 1930. The carnage has been written about in *The Southern Literary Journal* and debated at academic conferences. Mules have perished in books, plays, and stories.

"A dead mule was such a big thing my mind couldn't really gather it in," wrote Barry Hannah in *Geronimo Rex*. "I had to think about him in pieces..."

They have been worked to death, bludgeoned, asphyxiated (by accident and on purpose), run over, shot (by accident and on purpose), bitten by rabid dogs, stabbed, starved, frozen, herded into the barren plain to perish of thirst, driven mad by erroneously administered castor oil (the less said about this the better), led out to be murdered on the blind curve of a train track, and, in Capote's *Other Voices, Other Rooms,* hung from a chandelier.

They have been killed by Larry McMurtry, Richard Wright, Reynolds Price, Larry Brown, Robert Morgan, Jack Farris, Kaye Gibbons, Clyde Edgerton...everybody who is anybody. The most inventive is Cormac McCarthy, who had one beheaded by an unbalanced opera singer.

In modern-day literature, whippersnappers who wouldn't know a mule from a hole in the ground are killing mules by the caravan. Faulkner, at least, knew mules. "A mule," he wrote famously, "will labor 10 years willingly and patiently, for the privilege of kicking you once." A painting of one still sits on the mantel of his study at Rowan Oak, overlooking his portable Underwood, like an angel.

I grew up on stories of noble mules. The mule meant survival for my grandparents in the 1930s. I hate to see the hardworking beasts herded off cliffs and broiled in wildfires. Then again, I can cast no stones. In my first mule story, my Uncle Jimbo won a bet by eating a bologna sandwich while sitting on one.

But that mule was dead when we found him.

# WORDS ON PAPER

*Southern Living*, Southern Journal: January 2012

———

H ere, between the shelves, I escape everything worrisome, petty, mundane. In late afternoon, as the weak winter sun begins its slide, pale yellow light washes through the west-side window of my office in Fairhope, Alabama, and something like magic floods the room. I sit in a big, soft chair, and the words that are bound here come loose all around me.

French cavalrymen on white horses charge through shifting shadows on the wall above my desk, as Lord Nelson, Fletcher Christian, and Captain Horatio Hornblower set sail across the floor. In one corner, Bedouins glide on camels across a void of Sheetrock, while, in another, Sherlock Holmes grapples to the death with Professor Moriarty on the lip of a high shelf. Here, Willie Stark sits with Atticus Finch, Ishmael leans against Ignatius Reilly, and the Snopeses rub elbows with Shakespeare. It lasts only a little while, this glow, until the sun descends toward the dark trees somewhere across the Mississippi line, but not before Woodrow Call keeps his promise to Augustus McCrae, George Smiley sends one more spy into the cold, and Elmer Gantry does a hook slide for Jesus in the last, fading light of the day.

I know that the world of reading has forever changed, that, in this cold winter, many people who love a good book will embrace one that runs on batteries. I know that many of you woke up

Christmas morning to find that Santa graced your house with an iPad, or a Kindle, or a Nook, or some other plastic thing that will hold a whole library on a doodad the size of a guitar pick. Some of you may be reading one of my books or stories on one today, which is, of course, perfectly all right, and even a sign of high intelligence. Someday, I may have to read *The Grapes of Wrath* on the side of a toaster myself. I am hopeful when young people say, "I read you on the Kindle," because it means they are at least reading, and reading me, which means my writing life is somehow welcome in whatever frightening future awaits.

But I hope I will never have a life that is not surrounded by books, by books that are bound in paper and cloth and glue, such perishable things for ideas that have lasted thousands of years, or just since the most recent *Harry Potter*. I hope I am always walled in by the very weight and breadth and clumsy, inefficient, antiquated bulk of them, hope that I spend my last days on this Earth arranging and rearranging them on thrones of good, honest pine, oak, and mahogany, because they just feel good in my hands, because I just like to look at their covers, and dream of the promise of the great stories inside.

Here, not far from the shores of Mobile Bay and the white sands of the Gulf, is a limitless world of *Gallipoli, Sanctuary, Tennyson's Poetry, The Comedians, Riders of the Purple Sage, For Whom the Bell Tolls, Of Mice and Men, The Last of the Mohicans, Let Us Now Praise Famous Men, A Christmas Carol, Brave Men, An Outside Chance, Cold Mountain, Adventures of Huckleberry Finn, Blood Meridian, The Prince of Tides, Goodbye, Mr. Chips,* and a slightly molded flea market copy of *Dixie City Jam*.

It is not just the stories, but the physical book, the way I feel when I see the spines, when I read the titles, the very feel of the paper under my fingers as I turn the pages. I see the words *Lonesome Dove* and I see the beauty and great cost of true friendship, played out in a wild, wild West. Every book comes alive in my mind. I like to be in that company.

Cicero said a room without books is like a body without a soul, but I don't know about that. I just know I like to have them close, when the sun goes down.

# WOOD, PAINT,
# NAILS, AND SOUL

*GQ*, June 2002

I t has doves under the eaves of the back porch. I hear them, hear that lonesome, gentle sound, when I wake up in the morning and stagger to the kitchen over the 100-year-old pine planks and nail heads so old they have turned black as pitch.

I stand there and just watch them, sometimes, at the French doors leading out to the plain brick courtyard that is my entire backyard, watch them dance around the barbs of the bougainvillea, the same bush that the winters always kill down to a stob in January but magically swirls out from that dead nub like a purple fountain by mid-May. Winter isn't much in New Orleans, true, but cold is cold and dead is dead, and yet that plant rises like Lazarus without any help from me and does its duty, which is to be as pretty a thing as there is on this earth.

It has ornate, curving spandrels—I call them buttresses but I am ignorant of the finer points of architecture—that support the front porch, and that, along with the wooden, slatted shutters, adds character to this shotgun double that was built for working people 100 years ago. From a distance, and with a bit of imagination, those carvings—what some people call steamboat carvings—make the front of the house look like a ship pushing its way up the black river of Annunciation Street. It is painted yellow, but not a pale, sissy, dollhouse kind of yellow. It is a dark, golden yellow, trimmed in olive and some traces of red, and it looks a little bit Caribbean and a little bit Southern, but mostly it just looks like Uptown, New Orleans.

It has a back porch that runs the length of the whole house, sheltered by a lean-to roof, and I would sit out there a lot more if it wasn't for the mosquitoes that seem to thrive in every season except ice storms, and we haven't had one of them since I've been here. But I ignore them sometimes and sit outside with my friends and tell lies and stories while they sip on Abitas and I nurse a glass of watery iced tea, which has been about the strongest thing I've had to drink in a long time. I don't want to be a drunk writer in New Orleans. I would miss too much. The porch shelters some old, sun-blasted banana leaf chairs that I bought in Miami a long time ago, a cast-iron barbecue grill in the shape of a pig, and a punching bag that I beat the mortal hell out of when I am mad at life and editors and my own damn self. It does not have any wind chimes, hanging plants, garden trolls, welcome mats that say my name (because if anybody ever comes in my house through the back door I had better by God have invited them), ship's bells, cat scratching posts, and hummingbird feeders. I love hummingbirds, but my eyes are getting weak and they are hard to enjoy without squinting. It's like having to bend over to pet a short dog.

It has six fireplaces. It has ceilings so high you have to have a serious ladder to change a lightbulb. It has ceiling fans that spin half-heartedly through the summer heat doing no good at all, and an air-conditioning unit strong enough to chill the world squatting on the roof of the porch like a big Buddha, which does do some good—some heat-spanking good. It would be more picturesque to sweat like a hog in a parking lot, I guess, dripping sweat onto the keys of my Underwood and into the tepid brown lake of my bourbon glass, but as long as I can pay the robber barons at the power company my monthly ransom, I think I'll chill.

It has termites, and though I know it is silly I lie in bed sometimes at night and listen to munching sounds. I only hope that, if they ever do eat the support beams out from under me, I kill a few of them as I fall through the floor. It has, once a month, a palmetto bug the size of a small kitten that darts from under the refrigerator and makes a crazed dash across the kitchen. I chase. I slip. I stub my toe. As far as I know it's the same damn bug making the same damn dash for... for what? All the little @#%!#*% ever does is run out into the middle of the floor until he is certain that I see him, then heads back in the same direction. He may just be messing with me.

It has the pictures of my people, the books I love, the music I hear. I guess it is really just a wooden box to hold a life in, for days or decades, until someone else takes it over. But in my little house at the corner of Joseph and Annunciation Street I have found something good, something solid, even if it does sit 7 feet below sea level in a termite-haunted city that every meteorological expert in America swears is doomed as soon as the next big hurricane comes barreling at us up from the Gulf of Mexico.

It is the same feeling I get when I walk in my mama's kitchen in Alabama, or when I knock on my Aunt Juanita's door and hear her Feist dogs growl, or climb the steps to my Aunt Jo's porch with an armload of Christmas presents on December 24.

I guess it just feels like home.

It is not a rich guy's house. It was built around the turn of the century—that other one—by real craftsmen who did not have nail guns or snarling power saws or prefabricated anything.

Every nail in it was driven with the force of a strong man's hand, and I don't really know why that matters to me but it does. Every piece of wood was handled and measured and cut with that same strength, and that matters, too.

It may be foolish to think it, but I think maybe it is a better house, a tighter house, because of that. I wish I knew who built it. I would like to shake their hand, as if I could divine the artistry there in the calluses and the thick, blackened nails that every good carpenter has.

They built it on the pudding-like ground of the gentle slope of the levee in a time when sweating men still unloaded the massive freighters with pure muscle, built it on piers of red brick sunk deep into the shifting earth that is dry as salt in droughts and gummy, even mushy, when the rain comes down too hard and too much. They did not get fancy, just dropped a frame of good wood on those piers, and over the century the ground shifted under and around it the way the ground does here, but the house stayed mostly level—which makes it a damn good and lucky house.

They hung cypress strips—some people would call them shingles—on the outer walls, and put on a slate roof that someone replaced with Seal-Tab a long, long time ago, and built a gently sloping porch on the front that lets the rain roll off into the bushes. It was a smart man who built it, a man—I'm guessing it was a man—who built it to last in a place where the rain falls down in sheets and the earth crawls.

Now, most likely, he lies under this same shifting earth—the wealthy and middle class lie above ground in crypts here, but a simple workman may have been interred in the soil itself, and I wonder if he, too, is nudged gently back and forth by that movement. This may be the one place on earth in which the dead do not ever really, completely, lie still.

I had another house, once, a Florida bungalow with a tile roof and terrazzo floors and leaky sliding glass door that I used a dump truck full of caulking trying to seal up right. It was my pride and my joy and I bought it with a future in mind, as all people do. It was a lovely white house covered in ivy, a house on a street lined with oaks and flowering shrubs. It was in Coral Gables, a rock's throw from the Miami city limits, and the backyard crawled with lizards and hummed with insects and was home to a mangy black cat that I ultimately named "Come Here You Fuzzy @#%!#*%." I named him other things, but that was the one that stuck. He never let me pet him and I didn't much care. But he lived in my backyard and decimated the lizard population, living on fried chicken and spare ribs and McNuggets—and lizards I suppose. He was fat as a volleyball some days and other days looked half-starved, had a broken tail and chewed-up ears and didn't take stuff from nobody. Sometimes when I sat in the backyard he would come and sit just out of reach and was content to just be there, close, unless I tried to pet him or made any sudden moves. Cats are funny, that way.

It was a mighty fine house, too. But the future I had in mind when I first planned on moving to Miami just didn't ever firm up—one that had once included a beautiful Cajun woman from Morgan City, Louisiana, a woman with eyes like chips of frozen sea, who was the most beautiful woman I have ever seen when she smiled. But that future just wore out over time, from circumstance and neglect and bad damn luck that was every bit my fault, and I sold the house and left there for New Orleans, which is where a lot of people go when they need a new future.

New Orleans is forgiving, and lets a man pick a future—sometimes even a new identity. I hated the day I sold that house in Florida, I guess for all the feelings of loss that it entailed.

I also hated it because, just as I was getting ready to move to New Orleans, the 2000 election somehow failed to elect a President and Florida was the reason, so I lived in hotels for months as the democratic process worked itself out in a dignified and orderly process that involved a whole lot of "spokespeople" and finally it was done and I was free and headed to the Easy and the future and a mustard-colored house on a street just steps from the dock.

It was everything the Florida house wasn't. It was not built of brick and stone and concrete, and was almost flimsy in comparison, and looking at it I wondered if it would hold up through a hurricane or even a good washing.

My real estate agent, Linda Roussel, just nodded sagely and pronounced: "That house has stood the test of time."

I signed the papers and left for a few days and, when I returned, discovered it was also the neighborhood dumping-off place for the buggies from the Winn-Dixie.

Ain't no place perfect.

———

But in the days that followed, I found in this house an antidote for imperfect futures. There was a warmth in it, in the wood, in the high air of those tall ceilings, in the very feel of the floors that glowed yellow when you turned on a lamp.

Of course, that might have been because the air conditioner soon died, but even after $6,000 and change, the air was cooled but the house still had that warmth.

I painted, I sanded, I tacked down floorboards that popped up with a twang when the earth moved, but mostly I lived in it.

I sit on my front porch and watch, over my left shoulder, the endless trains that run between the levee and Tchoupitoulas, watch the conning towers of the massive freighters as they glide by. I watch the cars that slow to a crawl, when the children are too engrossed in their cross-over dribble to hear them coming. Some people pass by and wave and I wave back, which is an Alabama thing to do, really, but it's nice to see, nice to do. Almost nobody gives me the finger, and the garbage men only drag my garbage can a half-block down the street before leaving it there, which is not bad for New Orleans, I am told.

I sit for a long time, sometimes, just living.

———

It leaks a bit. When the winter rains pound for three days at a time, stripping the cypress tree of its dead leaves—more like needles, really—and clogging the gutters, a little water will slip down the wall and drip over my stove or inside my cabinets, and I curse the house and the weather and cypress trees in general, and then feel guilty, as if I had verbally abused some great-aunt or a well-meaning Bible salesman.

That is when I know I love this house. I do not talk to it, yet, but I may, maybe when the first hurricane trembles its foundation, or when I am so damn old that all I have left to talk to is the walls.

# GRANDPA WAS A CARPENTER

———

The place is immaculate, the cleanest building I have ever seen that smells of grease and oil and rust. My brother Sam pretty much lives in his workshop, the place he goes when he gets off work from the job he is paid to do, or, as Mark Twain writes, obliged to do. Here, in his shop, he works to unwind from work, and finds peace in that. Work is the true value of a man, in his mind, and a man cannot work without tools. He is surrounded by them here, floor to ceiling, and I believe their proximity makes him feel the way that stacks of books comfort me. The difference, in his mind, is that it is hard to plane a door with a first edition of *The Great Santini*, or drive a nail with *The Mystery of Edwin Drood*. To him, a man without tools is a pitiful thing. He had to bring me a lug wrench and a jack one time when I had a flat tire on my '69 Mustang on Alabama 204, and he has had little respect for me since. That was 1974.

In his workshop, sheltered by the big pines behind his house, is everything a working man needs or thinks he might someday need; you never know when you will need a horseshoe nail, or a fender clip from a ... well, I don't know what it's from. Here, there are a hundred well-oiled and freshly cleaned power saws, drills, mowers, other machines, and an untold number of carefully cleaned and sorted handtools, not one out of place, not one put away wet, or begrimed. I think if he knew a three-sixteenth socket was left out of its designated slot in his big red toolbox, he would be unable to live with himself.

The most precious tools he has there, the most valuable, are rarely used, though they have hung on one wall of his crowded workshop for as long as I can remember and will hang there long after we are gone. No one with our blood would dare take them down from their altar here. They were already black and pitted with age in '29, when rich men leapt from the windows on Wall Street. I have never understood those men, never understood how a broken dream could send you flying, your necktie and coattails aflutter in the wind. The men who used the tools on my brother's wall were different, and in some ways the tools made them that way. Their lives were hard in the beginning, hard in the Depression and the recessions to come, and hard in the end, but as long as their muscles held out and could power their tools, drive them, then they could beat out a life, a noble life. I get that.

They were poured from hot steel in American mills and stamped out, smoothed and sharpened by men with little white scars on their arms from the whorl of sparks they worked within, a thing I know only because my kin worked in steel mills back when the blast furnace fires still lit up the skylines of Birmingham, Bessemer, Gadsden, other places. My grandfather and men like him rolled steel in the Gadsden plant, and when that work vanished in '29 they picked up their hammers and handsaws and buckets of tar and built many of the houses you see along the thin ribbons of asphalt that run through the hills of my home, here in the highlands of the northern third of the state.

There are wrenches, hammers, saws, roofing hatchets, chisels … all stained with a hundred years of grease and soot and, finally, after a century or more, coated with an unavoidable rust, but still good, still waiting for men—or women—with the muscle and know-how to take up and, by God, make something. They are what is left of my grandfather's tool kit. They might as well be smelted from silver and gold.

I never saw his face, his living face. But Sam did. It is, I believe, why he can make anything, do anything, and I am the worst carpenter, the worst mechanic, in my family line. I am also the worst fisherman, but I can only deal with one great shame at a time.

The story of them, the old man and the baby boy, is one of my favorites, one I know only because I overheard a conversation between my mother and a young woman who was writing a story about her. The young woman, a much better journalist than I will ever be, asked my mother to tell her about the best day of her life. I tried to appear modest as I waited for my mother to tell the young woman of the day I showed her the first copy of a book with her face on the cover, or the day I won some big prize.

"I believe," my mother said, thoughtfully, "it was the birth of my first son."

I slunk away, but not so far I could not hear.

My mother told the story of giving birth to the boy they named David Samuel, and how, since the man who would be my father was nowhere around and almost certainly drunk, my mother had no place to take the baby but home to her mother and father's house, to Ava, and Charlie.

The baby did not cry. I do not believe he ever has cried. He was a man all his life, serious and capable. My little brother, Mark, likes to joke that when Sam was born he "dusted himself off and walked home."

The morning after the boy's birth, my grandfather pretended to chastise my mother, saying that while the baby had slept soundly, she had not, and stayed up all night. "Margaret, you kept us up all night," my grandfather told her, "a'talkin' to that blame boy."

The young reporter asked my mother what she said to the baby, but it took my mother a moment to answer.

"I never had a doll," my mother said, not looking for sympathy, just stating a fact. A child of the Great Depression, she had had almost nothing nice, nothing, in a house crowded with children, to call her own. And now there was this thing, this beautiful child.

"And I just kept telling him, 'You're mine.'

" 'You're mine.' "

My grandfather, the master carpenter, worked every day he was physically able to rise from his bed. Sometimes it was a roofing job, or framing up a house, or digging a foundation, but sometimes, to be honest, he was nowhere near a hammer. He augmented his carpenter's pay by making liquor. When he came home, sometimes smelling like sweat and sawdust, and other times smelling like sour mash and wood smoke, he would reach down with one big hand and snatch up the baby and sit him on his knee. Sometimes he would talk to the boy like he was grown, about floor joists and shingles and such, and sometimes they both went to sleep in the straight-backed chair, the child on his chest. When he was a year old, the baby began to go through the pockets on my grandfather's overalls, curious, searching, always busy, so my grandfather took to hiding a piece of soft candy there, for the boy to find. I like to think something fine passed between them, there in that chair.

And then, when my brother was not yet 3 and I was not yet born, the white whiskey that my grandfather had drunk most of his life took him from this world, and then there was nothing, really, except those tools. A toddler does not remember much, truthfully, although people, being romantic, like to say they can. But I swear, something passed between them, maybe nothing more than plain genetics, like a fine tenor voice, or a strong nose, or big feet. But something broke off the old man and stuck in the mind of the boy.

By the time he was walking, he was working, putting together junk and taking it apart and putting it back together, to make it slightly better junk than it had been before. He made wagons, and rafts, and tree houses, and then bicycles out of abandoned pieces. I called them Frankenstein bicycles, some of them so ugly you would leap off the thing when you saw a girl coming and hope it'd get swallowed up by the weeds. But they rolled, man. They took us down the road.

He could build anything, and I was his unskilled labor. We built dams, and stopped rivers ... well, creeks, but when you are 3 feet tall anything bigger than a roadside ditch is a raging torrent. We built boats ... well, plywood rafts, and sailed them around the world or at least as far as the depth of Mr. Paul Williams' cow pasture creek would allow us to go. We built treehouses that reached into the clouds ... or at least eyebrow high on a tall man. We built clubhouses where we threw lavish parties ... really just a shed, but it was straight, plumb, and watertight. We sat there with our cousin and listened to Creedence Clearwater Revival, and sharpened our pocketknives. I guess if I am being truthful I let him sharpen mine. "A dull knife ain't no 'count," he told me. He sharpens mine still, because I did not draw from that blood the skills a man needs.

In construction projects, I toted wood.

I sawed crooked, at a slant, ruining the precious lumber we scrounged.

I bent nails, on, it seemed, every swing. I hit my own fingers every fourth or fifth lick, and once, with my big brother looking, not only missed the nail but missed the *board.*

And in time, in all construction or mechanic jobs, I became the boy who held the light, when the sun sank in the middle of a project and we were intent on finishing before our mother chased us into the house. A chucklehead could hold the light. But even in that, I was inept. I got bored, and shone the beam on every other place except the board Sam was cutting, or the head of the screw he was feeling for in the dark. Come to think of it, he never hollered at me, much.

In time, in junior high school, I fell in love with books, and I abandoned my family's legacy almost completely. I tried, now and again. As a young man, I came into possession of a great Saint Bernard dog named King, big as a Shetland pony. I had to build a fence but wire was expensive, so I borrowed some one-by-eights from behind my Uncle Ed's house and commenced construction. I sank some creosote posts, nailed on some two-by-fours, and then tacked the one-by-eights onto them, to make a respectable 6-foot-tall fence ... respectable until the first windstorm, when the whole thing began to lean drunkenly toward the house in some sections, and away from the house in others. I rode by there not long ago to see if it had survived, but I guess the new owners of the house were ashamed of it.

In New Orleans, I tried to build a shelf in my office and gouged out holes in the wall so big you would have thought someone was looking for a time capsule.

In Tuscaloosa, I destroyed whole walls just trying to hang a picture. The contractor said if I would promise not to try to put any more nails in the wall, he would promise not to write a book.

In Miami, I built bookshelves too big to get through the door when I moved. I fled in the night.

In Fairhope, after a thousand-year flood sent water into a basement that had been bone-dry since the Johnson Administration, I went into something very much like a rage and took a shovel to some wet drywall. It cost $5,000 to fix what I did. It might have been too much tool for the job.

"A shovel?" the contractor said.

"Yep," I said, and did not try to explain. I am not sure I could.

My brother looks at my projects with an undeniable pity, but he has tried not to be unkind. He listens to my ideas for home improvement, and offers sensible suggestions, like, "Don't."

Still, I like looking at those old tools. They are our history, my brothers and mine, our legacy. The rich folks have their Confederate sabers over the mantel. These tools, that rusted roofing hatchet, that old box-end wrench, is our crest, our insignia. My brother Sam hits the nail head every time, dead and true. Even my little brother, Mark, born years after my grandfather's death, has the ghost of my grandfather in him, can sight down a board and tell you, to a fraction, how much it is warped, how far it is off true.

Me. Well, surely I inherited something.

I am told, now and then, the old man was a good storyteller.

# STUCK FOR GOOD

I guess the best way to tell the story of how I glued myself
to the wall of my house, how such a thing could even happen,
is to tell it chronologically. Otherwise, I might appear stupid.
But if I walk you through it, tiny misstep by tiny misstep,
you will come to see that such a thing could happen to almost
anybody, even a smart person.

It began, as all great disasters do, with a plausible theory.

It began with the simple thought, *I can fix that.*

I have a rambling old house in Fairhope, Alabama, made of
50-year-old cypress that has turned hard as iron. It all sits on
ancient bricks shaped by men who are only ghosts now, and is
shaded by long porches on the front and back. It's not a fancy
house but one with sheltering trees and rocking chairs and
screens to keep the stinging, buzzing things at bay. The bamboo
is out of control, the hedges have not been pruned in this decade,
and a 3-foot snake—a copperhead with an attitude—suns himself at
the corner of the house and retreats into a crack in the foundation
when he sees me coming with a shovel. If I am barehanded, he just
looks at me. I swear he knows. There is a raggedy swimming pool
in the back, and I like to float there and listen to the wind in the
branches of the pecan trees, but there is a yellow jacket nest in the
ground close by and, no matter how many generations of them

I kill, they return every year to chase me out of the water and across the yard. I am told it is hilarious.

The point is, it is not a perfect house, but it is perfect for a man like me, a man who hates new things and pretends to be a carpenter. I have a real carpenter, a real electrician, and a real plumber, and that is fortunate. If I tried to plumb, to twist a wrench on a pipe, I would drown myself. If I tried to mess with wiring, I would become a human torch.

But carpentry? How much trouble can you get into driving a little-bitty nail?

I do not permit myself power tools, beyond a drill, so mostly I hunt for jobs that involve only hammering and prying, and occasional sawing. You have to work hard at it to maim yourself with a handsaw. You have to be dedicated to drill yourself to death. But I digress. One day, I got to lookin' at a chair rail that ran around the living room walls.

*That bothers me,* I thought.

It bothered me more, the more I looked at it.

After a week or so, I came to hate that chair rail.

*I can fix that,* I said inside my head.

*No, you can't,* another voice said, a voice that we will refer to as common sense.

But it is not a very clear voice and is easily ignored.

So, I got out my framing hammer, and started yanking. The man who put that chair rail up meant for it to last through The Rapture, but after yanking, pulling, cussing, and questioning that man's parentage, I had the chair rail boards on the floor ... and immediately saw why it was there in the first place. Every 3 feet, there was a hole, about 3 inches wide and 6 inches deep, in the painted wooden paneling. The holes had been cut for obsolete light switches, and instead of patching them, the way a master carpenter such as myself would have done, the man whose lineage I had questioned chose to hide them with the 6-inch-high chair rail.

*Well that's unfortunate,* I said in my head.

*You think?* Common sense said.

I told that voice to shut up.

I sat for a minute and stared at the holes.

*I can fix that.*

Common sense had left the building.

I got some wood putty, cut some patches out of thin scrap wood, and commenced. I knew I could not cut the patches precisely to fit the holes, which were irregular, odd shaped. So I planned to just place the patches inside the quarter-inch-thick paneling, glue them in place, and later fill the shallow depression, the quarter-inch, with wood putty, sand, and paint. The problem was, there was nothing, no stud, no beam, to fix the patches to. The logical step—at least inside my mind—was to angle the pieces, which had been cut slightly larger than the hole in the walls, inside the hole and bring them up flush against the inside of the paneled wall. I would first put glue around the edge of the patch, facing the inside of the wall, and pull it flush and let it dry. The problem was, there was nothing to hold to on the patch in order to secure it in place as it dried. But I am a genius. I put a small, thin screw into the center of the patch, safely away from where the glue would be, which gave me a little handle to manipulate the patch into place and a way to hold it flush as it dried. Once it had, I would carefully remove the screw, fill the now-shallow depression with the wood putty, which is the finest invention since onion rings, and sand.

What, as they say, could go wrong?

It actually worked, once, twice, three times. I got sure of myself. I was a carpenter, after all, the son and grandson of capable men.

I held the fourth patch in place till it was good and dry. I had seen in the first patches that the glue sometimes ran, but I was careful not to get any on me, and I thought I had done the same on the fourth patch. I really did think that.

When I tried to turn loose, I couldn't. A glob of glue had run unseen from the side and secured my hand not only to the screw I was using as a handle but to the patch of wood itself. I was glued to the patch, the patch was glued, apparently forever, to the wall, the wall was nailed to the iron-hard cypress of the house, the house was fixed to the brick foundation, and the foundation was dug into the earth. We were one.

*I can fix this.*

At first I just tried brute strength. I pulled, and twisted.

It hurt.

But it held.

That was my own damn fault. Some men would have carefully selected the glue they used on such a delicate operation, but when it comes to glue it seems to me that the job of glue is to stick and you ought to get the kind that sticks the most and the best. No one ever walks up to the counter in the local hardware store and says,

"Excuse me, but do you have any glue that just sticks a little bit?"
I had perused the glue aisle, which is a whole lot more complicated than you'd think, and settled on Gorilla Glue.

I can tell you now, those people make a fine product.

I decided there was no need to panic. I would figure something out. I would get my toolbox, and use a screwdriver to remove the small screw, though that presented some problems because my whole body would have to turn with the screw and I am not Spiderman. As a last resort, I could use a hammer or small pry bar to carefully pull it free. The glue that was fixed by fingers to the wood itself, I would scrape or shave away with a scraper or knife, all things I had in my toolbox ... the toolbox that sat on the floor, across the room.

I searched my brain. Whenever a cowboy was locked in the hoosegow on television, he always took off his belt and, using the belt buckle as a kind of grappling hook, swung it over to the sheriff's desk and dragged the keys across the floor and through the bars. I could have done that, but I hate belts—they just seem unnecessary—and refuse to wear them; and, my belt would have needed to be 15 feet long, anyway, to reach my bag. I moved to Plan B, but that one was hard. I would swallow my pride, and call for help.

Which would have been plausible if I had worn a belt. But because I do not wear a belt it means my pants are always slipping down, and the surest way to get them to slip all the way down in the buffet line at the Chinese restaurant is to walk around with a heavy smartphone in your pocket, so I had to choose between having a belt and a phone or having neither. It had seemed a happy choice, till now.

Well, I thought, somebody will come. But that meant it would be some random somebody, and not someone I could rely on to keep a really good secret. I had nothing but time, and my imagination ran amok.

I imagined headlines.
In the local papers:
*Author Glues Self to Wall*

In the tabloids:
*Author Finds Elvis*
*Living in Wall*
*With Aliens*

On the Internet:

*Dude, like, there was this wall, and this, like, guy who writes stuff, like, GLUED himself to the wall, bro'... It was AWESOME...*

I imagined the evening news.

*"...but other than a slight case of dehydration, the pride of northern Calhoun County, Alabama, seems none the worse for wear from his ordeal. Now please text your answer to our Channel 6 poll: What would you do, if your son or daughter were glued to the wall? Back to you, Chuck."*

On talk radio:

*Host: "And now let's hear from Big Sexy from Slapout. Mr. Sexy...*
*(Long pause, static)*
*Guest: "...am I on? Hello? Am I on the radio? Helloooooo... I just want to say that that feller, that'un what got glued to that wall? Well he must be an Auburn man. Roll Tide."*

And on Fox News:

*"...And it is rumored that President Obama is to blame for the tragic gluing incident..."*

I had nothing but time.

I would like to say, as the hours seemed to drag by, that I had time to assess my life, to prepare my soul. Mostly I just stood, ashamed.

I was the grandson of a master carpenter.

How could that man's blood be so helpless, so inept?

Maybe it would be better if I did perish here, if, someday, a team of archaeologists unearthed a skeleton of my rough dimensions still fixed to that wall—I'm telling you, that Gorilla Glue lasts—with only a short missive scratched out on the floor.

TELL PAWPAW I'M SORRY

and

SHOULD HAVE GOT ELMER'S

Time dragged.

The whole day, it seemed, came and went. My mouth and throat went dry. My legs grew weak. I could not really sink to the floor and rest, as I was glued awkwardly, too awkwardly for that. My back began to hurt, as the hours dragged by.

Actually, it was only about *an* hour. But you try standing next to a wall for an hour and see how you by God like it.

After a while it occurred to me that I had only run the screw into the wood the tiniest fraction of an inch, just enough to hold the patch in place, and I began to work the screw back and forth, just the tiniest bit, which was all I could do with two fingers glued to the wood. It was hard, unpleasant, but not really painful, and after a while it came free—still glued to my fingers, which were still glued to the patch, which was still glued to the wall.

But I was hopeful now. I decided to try the "it's better to rip a bandage off fast and hard than a little bit at a time" method, and just closed my eyes and yanked, hard.

The paneling bowed out, and made a nice loud crack, but I was still captive.

I never saw my grandfather, the carpenter. He died the spring before I was born. I have only stories of his toughness, his skills. It would be romantic to say I pictured him there, but this was not such a dramatic moment, only a ridiculous one. In fact, I was glad he could not see me like this.

I braced my feet against the baseboards on the wall and let myself fall back.

I left some skin, but no blood to speak of, and I was free. It took a while to scrub and peel the glue partway off, and I wore a lot of it around for a long time, before it finally wore off.

The real carpenter, when he came to redo my work, told me, kindly, that it was not bad work, really, though he would have to smooth it out some, and I did not tell him I was held prisoner by the wall, though I guess that proverbial cat is out of the metaphorical bag now. But it's funny. I am not really ashamed, being the grandson of a carpenter, that I glued myself to the wall. I think he would have grinned at that. I am ashamed my work had to be redone.

I told my big brother Sam about it.

The joy it gave him outweighed my embarrassment.

"Hey, it happens with that new glue," he said, kindly.

"Did it ever happen to you?" I asked.

"Of course not," he said.

## PART 5

# SPIRIT

# DOWN HERE

*ESPN The Magazine*, August 2012

W
e believe some things, down here. Some of them, I have lived long enough to question.

We believe that if a snapping turtle bites you, it will not turn loose until it hears thunder, but since I have seen a snapping turtle as big as a turkey roaster bite a broomstick in two, I believe it will turn loose any time it damn well wants. We believe snakes have mystical powers and will charm you if you look into their eyes. When I retire, I plan to test that theory on water moccasins at my stock pond, and if they have not charmed me in four or five seconds, I will shoot them. Then, in times of drought, I will hang them in a tree. That, we believe, will make it rain. My grandmother, God rest her soul, told me so, so it must be true.

And we believe—well, maybe all but the Unitarians—that God himself favors our football teams. On Friday nights and Saturday afternoons, our coaches, some of them blasphemers and backsliders and not exactly praying men the other six days of the week, tell their players to hit a knee and ask his favor at the same exact instant the other team is also asking his favor, which I have always taken to mean that God, all things being equal, favors the team with the surest holder on long field goals.

It is gospel—the gospel according to Bear. After a rare Alabama loss in the Bryant era, Bear's sidekick on his weekly television show told him: "The Lord just wasn't with us, Coach."

"The Lord," growled Bryant, "expects you to block and tackle."

The point is, and we talk real slow down here, so it may take awhile to get to it, that we believe some things regardless of science and sometimes common sense. And what we mostly believe in, across racial, political, religious, and economic lines—is football. We believe absolutely in our supremacy over all pretenders, upstarts, and false prophets from the North, East, West, and some heathen parts of Florida that are too sissy to mix it up with the real men of the SEC. We have been fed that belief since we were infants. That, and an unhealthy amount of Coca-Cola in our baby bottles.

But for years and years, we have even had the science of the BCS on our side and have grown accustomed to the pretty way that crystal trophy catches the light; for three years it has not even exited the state of Alabama. We are sure of this pre-eminence, so sure that we view all the years when the South was not dominant in college football as a surreal space-and-time fluctuation, like the dancing hot dog and bun they used to show at intermission at the Bama Drive-in theater on Highway 21 north of Anniston, Ala., which we watched through a blur of Boone's Farm. It was just temporary, just intermission, 'til the real show resumed.

We felt no disappointment in January, when two SEC teams played in a rematch for the national championship in New Orleans. We have long known that the real battle was in playing each other anyway. South Carolina's Steve Spurrier, who was nicknamed the Evil Genius when he was the head coach at Florida, said recently that it is harder to win an SEC championship than a national one. "Ask Nick Saban," he said, though he might have just been trying to be a smart aleck.

My uncle John Couch, who made tires for 20 years at the Goodyear plant in Gadsden, Ala., is a Crimson Tide fan. Years ago, in the era of Bear Bryant and Shug Jordan, he suffered through a brief Auburn resurgence, in years he cannot precisely recall, nor cares to. But he remembers seeing a co-worker strutting around the plant in an old Auburn jacket. He remembers how he walked up to the man, leaned in close to him and sniffed.

"I thought so," he said.

"What?" the man asked.

"Mothballs," he said.

Somewhere, right now, an Auburn man is telling that same

story, the other way around.

We know the true big games. We might not even be able to tell you whom we played in a bowl game long ago, probably against a Yankee team that would melt like Crisco in the furnace of a Southern summer, but we remember how we did against Florida or Tennessee or Georgia. We know that if our teams survive the outright savagery of an SEC regular season, their regional rivalries, they can beat anyone.

There will always be the occasional Utah or rare Boise State in down years, but they are an aberration, like heat lightning. "Somebody else might win a championship," says my uncle John, "sneaking out through the back door." Don't get him started on Notre Dame.

We know deep in our guts that it is not truly a birthright. We know that it takes blood and sweat to win in college football. We know that dominant programs are built by smart and relentless taskmasters like Saban, who is so serious about the process— the science of it—that when he allowed himself a big smile after winning a second national championship in three years, it kind of scared me, as if Billy Graham had done a handstand.

When Spurrier went to South Carolina seven seasons ago, he was disheartened when he heard fans applaud the team after a close loss. "Please don't clap," he told them, "when we lose a game."

I, personally, think we're a little wack-a-doodle but usually in a good way. Before the hate mail begins to flood in, or people start leaching bile into a chat room, they should know that this story— half of it, anyway—is written in fun, because that is how I view this game.

I had Alabama season tickets once, but it's hard to take anything too seriously when you're up around Neptune and can barely discern actual human beings. Situated somewhere above the catfish concession, I came home smelling like French-fried taters.

And while it is a joy to watch real Southern football, from any seat, my self-worth has never been bound to this game, though there have been times in our history as a region when it seemed it was all we had. For Southerners, to say we do not care is to invite suspicion. We must *know* football to *be* Southern.

"At LSU, for instance, everybody knows what Les Miles *should* have done," says George C. Rable, the Charles G. Summersell chair in Southern history at Alabama, whose football heart belongs mostly to his grad school alma mater, LSU. That means last season he was 1-1... in a purely mathematical sense. A friend at LSU tells him that since the championship game, "one of the big donors has refused to wear any LSU attire... he is not wearing his hat." How mad do you have to be to not wear your hat?

An award-winning author of books on Southern history, Rable is not a native Southerner but grew up in another football incubator, in Lima, Ohio, in the swirl of Ohio State-Michigan, rooting for the Buckeyes. He came down here to see real obsession. He once exited Tiger Stadium as the faithful chanted: "Go to hell, Ole Miss, go to hell."

"And," he says, "we weren't playing Ole Miss."

We do not care so much about professional football here because it is a new phenomenon and has had only 40 or 50 years to catch on. Whereas college football has been an antidote to an often dark history for as long as even our oldest people can recall. We are of long memory here. I gave a talk once in Mobile, Ala., and mentioned that the Southern aristocracy had been on the wrong and losing side in two great conflicts: the Civil War and the Civil Rights movement, prompting one older gentleman to rise from his seat, huffing that I did not know what I was talking about, and leave the room. Later, I said I was surprised that mentioning the turbulent 1960s would anger anyone so, after so much time. A nice gentleman told me, no, that wasn't it. "He's still mad," the nice man said, "about the war."

Wayne Flynt, professor emeritus of history at Auburn, says the South's devotion to college football probably reaches that far, to a time before there even was any football, to defeats at Gettysburg and Vicksburg, "to a whole lot of times when we just got the hell beat out of us, as a culture."

Reconstruction starved us. Then, the Ku Klux Klan swept candidates into pretty much every elected office in the state of Alabama and burned crosses on the skyline across the South. The rest of the nation, not that it was without sin, looked down in disdain. Then, just after Christmas 1925, the Alabama football team boarded a train for California, for the 1926 Rose Bowl, and fought back against that derision, even if the players did not know they were doing so at the time. Those young men drew, Flynt explains, "on a long history of not being afraid," of the hottest days of endless rows of cotton or a million bales of hay. "It's not like you're unprepared for a little physical suffering," he says, and next to the pain of just living down here, football was, well, like playing games.

Not knowing any of this, the rest of the nation gave Alabama no chance against its Rose Bowl opponent, the vaunted University of Washington, but Southerners knew there was too much at stake to lose. "Even the president of Auburn sent a telegram," says Flynt, "telling them, 'You are defending the honor of the South, and God's not gonna let you lose this game.' " Halfback Johnny Mack Brown ran, as one writer described, like a "slippery eel," and the South won something of great value, at last.

Years later, as the apparatus of Southern politics threw itself violently into the shameful oppression of civil rights, white Southern players again won national championships and acclaim on the gridiron, as front-page headlines belittled and ridiculed the region for its backwardness. College football was not a cure, not a tonic for what was wrong in the South, merely a balm.

Then, as black athletes finally made their way into predominantly white universities, they fought their own battles on those Southern fields, "for something else," says Flynt, for a place not only of acceptance in the greater society and therefore a heroic place in the national history, but also a place in that shining legacy of championships, until the color line in college football finally faded away. Most of us cannot even imagine a team of any other character. And through it all, the winning continued 'til it became expectation.

Other parts of the country would try to condemn us for the South's very success, which made about as much sense, Flynt says, as our condemning someone else for being good at math. Our climate, culture, and history made us supreme at this thing. "Why should you put us down," he says, "because we are?"

Elsewhere, fans still grumble that Southern colleges are dominant at football for reasons that are, amusingly, no different from what makes their own programs successful from time to time. They say we have better athletes because we have lower academic standards, but that notion has become a glass house in which other colleges in other regions no longer wish to throw stones. Because history has shown that all programs have intelligent young men, some who possess the potential of Rhodes Scholars, and other young men who think you spell that r-o-a-d-s. But region has little to do with which teams have more of the latter. Alabama's graduation ranking, as Saban points out, was third among BCS schools last season, behind Penn State and Stanford.

A recruiting scandal has also proved to have no geographical bias, as much as other programs would like to pretend it only happens, down here. USC, for instance, the place where Reggie Bush's Heisman once sat, could not be farther from the South unless it was floating in the Pacific on a barge. Intolerance for losing has no geography either—losing coaches are fired, even in places with ice fishing. The people who say "They're football-crazy down there" probably play on something called Smurf Turf, or wear blocks of foam-rubber cheese on their heads. The people who say "Football is religion down there" should be reminded that we did not invent Touchdown Jesus.

And the greatest scandal of college football, the greatest darkness, did not descend on the South but in Happy Valley, a tragedy beyond comprehension for another storied program, one that would rewrite a legend. The entire history of Southern football, in all its fanaticism, with all its lust for winning, has nothing to compare. But like SEC commissioner Mike Slive said, there is a warning in that lesson for everyone, including us.

We do lose, of course. We feel the air grow thick when we do. Our limbs grow heavy. I have stood on the beautiful campuses of Southern universities and seen what, I swear, was a kind of graying of the landscape, as if losing had bleached out the beautiful red of the bricks and green of the lawns. It cannot be true, of course, but it feels true, and it lingers for days. Books are read, papers written, problems solved. But it feels a little like the day after Christmas.

"It's absolutely spiritual; there is no tomorrow," says Mike Foley, master lecturer and Hugh Cunningham professor in Journalism Excellence at Florida, who has a Gator tattooed on his right shoulder. He got it in a fit of youthful exuberance and impetuousness. He was 40-something. Somewhere in this steamy landscape—Ole Miss, perhaps, or Vanderbilt—a regular-season loss is not the end of the world, and there are such things as moral victories and good college tries.

Not Tuscaloosa. Not Baton Rouge. Not Auburn. Not Athens. Not Fayetteville, where they wear rubber pigs on their heads and yell "Soooooooieeeeeeee." Judges do that.

Deacons. Florists. Presidents.

"It's a pretty damn hard league," said Texas A&M coach Kevin Sumlin, when asked by reporters about playing his first SEC West schedule. As my grandmother, God rest her soul, would say, he might need prayer. Yet the supremacy will someday end—probably on a bad call. "This, surely, can't last forever," says Rable, the Alabama professor from Ohio. "Texas will be back. USC will be back."

Says Foley: "God, that would be horrible. Lane Kiffin..." Tennessee people still hope to catch him in a crosswalk for what he did to them.

Says Rable: "I was in Ohio and they already had T-shirts in the malls that read 'Urban Nation.'"

I wish, often, that we cared as deeply about other things here in my native South as we do football. "It has become," Rable says, "what's important," sometimes to exclusion. But we are going to be football crazy anyway, my wife once told me, so we might as well beat everyone else. The fact is, it lifts our hearts. It always has.

In the winter of 1993, in an attic apartment in Cambridge, Mass., I sat homesick and watched Alabama beat the trash-talkin' Hurricanes—I mean beat them like they *stole somethin'*—to win its first national championship since Bear died. Late that night I walked through a deserted Harvard Yard, through snow and bitter cold, and I thought I might yell "Roll Tide," though no one else would hear. I did it anyway.

# FOR THE LOVE OF THE GAME

*Southern Living*, Southern Journal: September 2011

———

I know why I love it. It goes back to nights in Paul Snow Stadium, where the Fighting Gamecocks of Jacksonville State whipped Troy, or Tennessee-Martin, or Delta State. In my memory we always won, as, in dreams, you never hit bottom when you fall. My uncles, good men, took me there as a boy in the 1970s and bought me hot dogs wrapped in aluminum foil. We always sat up high, so I could see the stadium fill with people I knew: the insurance man, the lady from the Five-and-Dime, and every pretty girl in five counties.

The JSU school colors were red and white but might as well have been dark blue, from all the company jackets from U.S. Pipe or Goodyear. If it rained we hid under Caterpillar caps and programs, but not umbrellas. We did not believe in umbrellas. On occasion, one would unfurl in the seats in front of us, and my uncles would grumble that "We'd see some football, if it wasn't for all these parasols." Our heroes were Ralph Brock—he could throw a football from here to Edwardsville—and Boyce Callahan, who ran for his life. He's a chiropractor now. He was like lightning, then.

We never looked away at halftime. With a great pounding of drums and sounding of brass, the Marching Southerners, in perfect step, would sweep onto the grass. They played music from our history, and, if you listened close, you might hear a tuba player sing: *In the sky the bright stars glittered/ On the bank the pale moon shone/ And twas from Aunt Dinah's quilting party/ I was seeing Nellie home.*

And the beautiful Marching Ballerinas, in red velvet, kicked their white boots high in the air. Why do we love football? How could we not?

I teach now in the shade of the great stadium at The University of Alabama, and though my joy of football has hardened in middle age it has not faded. On Sundays, after a rare loss, the air goes stale. It seems harder to move. I have friends who say it is the same in Auburn, Athens, anyplace people live and die on a holding call, and joke that their new state flower is a satellite dish with high definition.

When Chris Roberts, an Alabama professor, explains our fascination "to the infidels," he describes his route to work: "Past the Bryant Bank on the left, then over the Bryant Bridge. Eventually, I turn onto Bryant Drive, home of the Bryant Museum and Bryant Conference Center. I park near the northwest end zone of Bryant-Denny Stadium. Then I walk past the Bryant statue. If they're not convinced, I show my ATM card—the one with Bear Bryant on it."

I do not know if I would love it as much if I had discovered it at an age of chat rooms, of anonymous bad-mouthing. I learned to love it in an age of newspapers, of fat Sunday sports pages filled with the lore of the game, all but lost in a time when every quarterback's tweet from behind a velvet rope sends ESPN all atremble.

Would I? Probably. "How could a game be better?" said Alabama fan Ken Fowler, who, for seven decades, has suffered and exulted through Saturday afternoons. "People united in common interest, in the outdoors, against one enemy. And, it reminds us that all in this world is not hurricanes and volcanoes."

I hope your teams, at least in distant memory, always win. Unless they are playing one of mine.

# ALL SAINTS' DAY

*Southern Living*, Southern Journal: October 2011

––––––––

**M**aybe it is why this city is so hard to kill, even when drowned. New Orleans is too comfortable with death to be consumed by it.

In most American cities, this is the season of the witch, though the witch may decide at the last minute to be a ballerina, or a fairy princess, or a Hannah Montana, though I am not altogether certain what that is, and am almost surely three years behind on what the cool kids are wearing. It is the same in New Orleans, where real witches, vampires, and such are said to convene, and not just on Halloween, but on Saint Patrick's Day, Boxing Day, the third Monday in January, and whatever that odd, tacked-on day is in a leap year.

October 31 is a wild night in the Crescent City, where voodoo priests in tall, black top hats glare from behind white greasepaint, and zombies wail and stagger along Bourbon Street, though that might have been just a bunch of frat boys on the way back from Pat O'Brien's. I once saw a young woman dressed as a New York City taxicab, wearing mostly just a license plate. I blushed and looked away... eventually.

But what makes New Orleans special to me this time of year is not the howling of October 31 but the traditions that unfold, peacefully, quietly, in her cemeteries the morning after. Much like

Ash Wednesday settles, usually, calmly and quietly after the insanity of Mardi Gras, the day after Halloween reveals one of the sweetest traditions I have seen in my rapidly changing South.

All Saints' Day in New Orleans is a day to honor and visit the dead, not in some philosophical way by thinking about them while on the living room sofa or in line for café au lait at Café Du Monde, but by traveling to the place of their interment and sitting with them. Perhaps the oldest holiday on the Western calendar, it dates back to 837, when Roman Catholics began honoring all saints, known and unknown, on the first day of November.

I am not saying there are caravans of people thronging through the Cities of the Dead, backed up six deep at a crypt, but if you pass by these old cemeteries you will see people, one or two or whole families, sprucing up the crypts—the water table requires that most New Orleans residents who can afford it be laid to rest in stone or concrete crypts above ground—and just generally being close to the loved ones who have gone on.

I will never forget, years ago, driving through the city one November 1 and seeing a family, dressed as if for church, filing through a cemetery gate with what appeared to be a picnic basket and an Igloo cooler. Later, I saw people eating oyster po'boys and drinking root beer in the shade of a crypt. I saw fathers and sons toast grandfathers and great-grandfathers with a clink of Abita bottles.

As I walked between the rows of stained granite and crumbling brick, trying not to look like a ghoul or an armed robber, I smelled something on the breeze that seemed odd here in such a holy place, a smell harsh and sweet at the same time. Only one thing smells like that. "Bourbon," I said. I watched two middle-aged men, brothers, I guessed, take a drink from a pint bottle of brown liquor, pour a swallow into the grass and dust, and shuffle away, not drunk, but apparently feeling better than when they shuffled in.

What a lovely notion, I remember thinking, that no matter what your faith, you really do live on and on, as long as someone, anyone, is willing to come see you.

One fall I went to Holt Cemetery, a resting place for the poor, where generations are buried not in stately crypts but in this almost liquid earth, and watched old men get down on their knees and smooth the dirt the best they could in a place of wooden crosses and tinfoil angels. One old man could not remember the name of the little daughter he had buried there, but came to see her, anyway.

# WHEN FIREWORKS GO SOUTH

*Southern Living,* Southern Journal: July 2014

S outherners, I believe, should not be trusted with fireworks. It is not in our blood. The North had most of the artillery. The South, which does not always think things through, entered The War believing its officer class could merely hurl mint juleps at the encroaching Yankees and glare insolently. The Gallant John Pelham, Robert E. Lee's vaunted cannoneer, may have been the last Southerner to be truly trusted with a lit fuse. Since him, there has been a long line of Southerners who light bottle rockets with a Camel Non-filter and shoot for the moon, only to see the projectiles blaze ankle-high through the Johnson-grass, scorching cats and burning worms.

I love my people, but you know there is truth in this. Even when we are sober, bad things happen. Even when we do everything right, things can still go wrong.

Take the case of poor Rob Roy, a suicidal, wirehaired Jack Russell terrier in Valley Head, Alabama. He had a short tail. On the Fourth of July about 10 years ago, it got some shorter.

"Mammaw named all her dogs Rob Roy," said Elizabeth Manning, a graduate student at the University of Alabama. "I'm guessing this was Rob Roy number two..."

This Fourth began, like most, with the lighting of short fuses.

"At dusk, all the women would sit up on the porch, and all the men would go into the field in front of the house and shoot off fireworks. My Uncle Jeff was firing off one of the prettiest ones, and he had it lit and they backed off. Rob Roy, who had a reputation for biting wheels on cars, ran to it, and it shot off right before he got there."

A spark got caught in his tail, which began to smoke. Rob Roy ran in wild circles, as Jack Russells are bred to do, so fast that the flock of grandkids on his tail could not catch him to put it out.

"He finally just sat down and dragged his butt through the grass," Elizabeth recalled.

"Mammaw just watched."

She is 88.

"Well, goosey gander, goosey gone," she likes to say.

I, myself, am careful when it comes to fireworks. Before inserting an M-80 into a bed of fire ants, I follow careful safety protocols.

1. Twist together two M-80s, for more "Holy smokes!" potential.

2. Giggle.

3. Run.

I am qualified to opine on fireworks because The Gallant Pelham, killed by the Yankees as he tried to rally his troops, is buried in my hometown of Jacksonville, Alabama. His statue gazes down upon us—and on the loading dock of the old TG&Y. I have always believed the Fourth—because of all the booming that goes on—is also a celebration of his life, though he was fighting to dissolve the Union and all. But every year, as the sky fills with fire, I wonder what he is thinking.

Probably:

"Duck."

I know fireworks safety is a serious matter. That is why I now leave the shooting of them to professionals. In my hometown, we go to the field beside State 204, set our lawn chairs up in the back of my brother's pickup and watch the falling dusk transform through the miracle of gunpowder. Or, if I am on the Gulf, we watch the colors rain into Mobile Bay.

I think, some years, I would like to shoot one last bottle rocket into the dark, though I am too old to run away.

But at least if my tail were to set on fire, I would be easy to catch and put out.

# O CHRISTMAS TREE

*Southern Living*, Southern Journal: December 2011

———

The Southern landscape, let's face it, is not intended for Christmas, at least not the storybook Christmas we cut out of red and green construction paper and taped to the windows at Roy Webb Elementary School. Most of the snowflakes I saw, until I left home, were frozen in place on a cardboard sky with Elmer's glue.

I do not love snow—I lived in Boston and New York and came to regard snow as a hard-packed, car-obscuring, finger-numbing, gray and dirty substance—but it was nice at Christmas till the snowplow came along and shoved it over the top of your Subaru. Down here, I ride the highways and gaze out on the grass that has finally, grudgingly gone dormant, as the voices on the radio—Bing, Elvis, and them—try to assure me that it is indeed a time of white Christmas, and roasting chestnuts, and sleighs. And then a big ol' boy in a tank top and a Santy hat waves at me from his mailbox, and I am more confused.

That's when I see it, there at the side of the road: a single, perfectly shaped cedar or pine, not too short, not too tall, and I think, for just a second, that I wish I had a saw. And I know that, for me and mine, it is truly Christmas, after all.

There is no nice way to say it. We are Christmas tree thieves, or used to be (though I am not ruling it out if I see just the right one outside a rest stop near Tupelo). I know that larceny has no place during Yuletide, and before you think badly of me, let me explain. It is not like we were rustling sheep from the manger scene in front of the city auditorium, or absconding with the Three Wise Men, which I think would be hard to pawn anyway. It was just trees. And in that we had scruples. We were not skulking through the lot at The Home Depot at three o'clock in the morning, or robbing a Douglas fir from the Knights of Columbus. It was just that we were less than particular about property lines.

When I was a child, we never bought a tree. We got an ax, or a handsaw, and went into the woods. It would have been a scene straight off a Christmas card, if we had actually gone hunting for one on our own land, which we did not have. I guess it was poaching in a way, but it seemed harmless. In the deep woods, it was more like we were just thinning the herd, rather than stealing.

And, I doubt if a landowner ever walked up to a stump and said, "I'll see them Bragg boys swing for this." But we knew, my brothers and I, that there was something wrong about it. So we decided to steal them from the State of Alabama. We would cruise the bigger roads and highways until we saw one on the state right-of-way. Sliding to a halt in the loose gravel, car tires smoking, I would leap from the truck with my ax. Three to six whacks would do it, unless I saw a car coming. Then I froze, trying to look innocent—with an ax in my hands.

That was a long time ago. I have not stolen a tree, from Alabama or anywhere else, for 35 years. We buy our trees now, and pay what feels like $900 for a tree cut last Fourth of July, a tree I am afraid to shake too hard, lest it look like something Charlie Brown would have. You got a much better quality of tree, when it was stole.

But I am too old and stiff now, too fat to jump a ditch or climb a bank. The police would get me, sure. Still, I see the trees there, at the side of the road in that balmy air, and it makes me happy.

I guess, to be truthful, those stuck-on paper snowflakes did, too.

# WHEELS OF TIME

*Southern Living,* Southern Journal: June 2014

---

T he Pontiac, *ragged, dented, rust-flecked, means it was '74, since cars*
*are the way working-class people of the Deep South truly mark time.*
*Listen to them, when they are groping for a memory, and they will*
*find it beside a yellow Oldsmobile, or baby-blue Malibu...*
    —From *The Prince of Frogtown*

Ever since I was 16, I have kept track of my life in an almanac
welded from tail fins, fender skirts, and chrome. I think many
people do. The other day, as my mother and aunts sat trying to
remember the date of some trivial thing, Aunt Juanita finally
asserted she knew, exactly, because it was the year Uncle Ed
"got that red truck." Her sisters nodded yes, it was. It seemed to
me they were all red, his trucks, but I do not argue with women
who were around when the Italians hanged Mussolini.

They recall the Depression, how their family left a rented house
in early morning dark, sneaking out on the landlord. A pig they
were trying to load up panicked and ran head first into the tailgate
of their Ford, and fell dead. That was '39, maybe '40; the Depression
lingered long down here. They do not recall the pig, much, but
the Ford was a cut-down Model A, black, bad to rust.

My daddy's whole life passed to the hiss of turning tires. He
worked the chain gang in '54, and it almost killed him, watching

cars pass him by. He courted Mother in '55, in a black-and-pearl
'49 Mercury. It burned a lot of oil, as she recalls. He went AWOL
from the Marines soon after; drove off in a '54 Hudson Hornet,
the law close behind. He wrecked it in Georgia, steered it off the
asphalt into much of the adjoining countryside, in '56. Even when
he was sitting still, he was in a car, listening to the radio in the
shade of a cedar tree. It was a gray Chevy, so it was '65. I was in
first grade.

My brother Sam broke his leg in the fall of '73; hit a tree in a
powder blue Willys. I won the Calhoun County 4-H Club speech
championship that year. I spent the day rubbing pinesap off a
white '66 Corvair, hoping it might get me a date someday because
being an award-winning public speaker did not. In summer '75,
Uncle John bid $540 at auction on a '69 Mustang he could have
gotten for $400 if I had not been jumping up and down, hollering
"Git it!" But I hit a guardrail and warped the front end, and took
my driver's test in my Aunt Sue's car, in fall '75. I borrowed it again
for prom. I wore a white tuxedo and my date dumped me, but I
rode home, stylin', in a green '75 Monte Carlo. It was May '77.

The first time I truly flew was in a '69 Camaro; wrecked it in
August '76, a week before senior year. It was 92 degrees in the
dark. I moved on to a '70 MGB, but no one knew how to work on
it so it sat under a tree. My buddy Mike Ponder finally wedged a
transmission in place with a 2 by 4, and we motored. We were big
boys; people said we looked like circus clowns riding around in
that tiny car.

We buried Mike last year, but every time I see one of those cars
I think of June '77, my friend, and British racing green.

# THE GIFT OF LOAFERING

*Southern Living*, Southern Journal: June 2012

———————

O ld women call it loafering, and I've always loved that word. I guess it is just how we say the word "loafing," but the way we say it makes you think of loafers, of wearing out your shoe leather for no good purpose. Old women like to sniff and use it as a condemnation. "He ain't here. He's off loafering." It means you are shirking work and responsibility. To the men who loafer, it means they are free, free to waste time, to count mailboxes, and wave at other old men who, as the rear bumper vanishes in the distance, wish they were loafering, too....The one thing you cannot do is loafer with a heavy heart...Bill Joe rolls down his window and just drives, sometimes as far as the Georgia line. The mountains and hills are at their prettiest now...the hardwoods, the pines, even the weeds take on a luminescence that will shimmer into summer, till the heat itself makes the landscape fade. But for now it all just shines. His heart is light. His conscience is clear.

—From *The Prince of Frogtown*

I am only 52 years old but have been badly used and poorly maintained. I have worked since I was 11, digging in dirt, heaving hay bales around, loading pulpwood. Now I mostly stack paragraphs on top of each other, which I claim to be work, though no one believes me. Anyway, I have at best a few more raggedy pages left in me. So, I have decided to retire early.

I used to say I planned to fish, but that is a bigger lie than I now have the energy to tell. The fact is, I am the worst fisherman in my family line. My grandfather came home from the Coosa too drunk to stand, coat pockets stuffed with fish. I couldn't catch a fish standing over a washtub sober with a stick of dynamite.

But I can loafer.

I can walk to my truck, turn the key, and ride. I will dodge everything worrisome—my wife, traffic, the uncollected garbage under the sink—find a country road that leads no place in particular, and let it take me there. I can lie and say I am going to exercise or pick up a gallon of hateful skim milk, say anything to slip the surly bonds of home, and roam, till the wanderlust subsides.

You may not be familiar with the word if you were born north of Fort Payne or in a bloodline that thinks a bad day is a flat tire on the million-dollar motor home. I come from a long line of loaferers, from semi-sorry men who vanished for days, if not years, in the highlands and deltas of the Deep South, sometimes with nothing more than two dollars and a Zippo lighter, men of beautiful, restless spirit and less-than-rigid adherence to jobs and spouses and other constricting things.

I had two bachelor great-uncles who loafered a lifetime, from Tampa to Chattanooga, high-steppin' alongside an accelerating freight train, a guitar case in one hand as they reached, reached for freedom with the fingers of the other. My great-uncle Fred reappeared just before his death in a college bar in Jacksonville, Alabama, dressed in a checked sport coat and brown-and-white wingtip shoes. He finished a beer, took a roll of money off some college boys at the pool table, and disappeared forever into the night. It may be he never left very deep footprints in the sands of this society, but by God he left a lot of them.

I'd get too homesick to be like him, truly. Most of us loafer only in an afternoon. The descending sun sends us home to a woman's worried face, or sometimes wrath. It may even be we were not greatly missed while we were gone. But at least, occasionally, someone will lie and say we were.

# HOLIDAY LIES

*Southern Living*, Southern Journal: December 2012

---

I'm dreaming of a Christmas free of the harmless fibs, gentle untruths, and little white lies that pile up like (fake) snow.

The holiday season officially begins when they take down the Halloween decorations in the drugstore and start foisting off the fruitcake and the crème drops. It is what we have instead of snow. My brother Sam likes fruitcake; it is the only thing about him that troubles me. My mother told me she liked it, too, but that turned out to be a lie, a lie she told for 45 years to keep from hurting my feelings, dating back to the first fruitcake I gave her when I was a boy. I found out she foisted that one and every fruitcake that followed off on Sam, who, now that I think about it, may not truly like fruitcake either but may just be forcing it down, gob after candied, gelatinous gob, so as not to hurt her feelings. Either way, I guess, it is a lovely lie, in a season of lovely lies. How would we get through Christmas without them?

Think about it, about the lies we have to tell—or just let drift along from year to year—just so we can have peace on Earth. In my family, you had better not dare tell an ugly truth for fear of eliciting the dreaded: "You have ruint my Christmas!"

Invariably, it was because someone was caught in a truth.

But I am done. I am out of holiday lies.

We shall start with the weather folks. I am done pretending the

blip on your radar on Christmas Eve is Santa. I am not saying
Santy ain't coming; I'm saying that blip over Fort Smith, Arkansas,
ain't him.

Everyone knows the real Santa has magic powers that prevent
us from seeing him, and if Santa can steer Donner and Blitzen
across the December sky unseen by every child on Earth, I doubt
your Doppler can track him. Maybe I can pretend, just one more
year, if he brings me a fly rod.

I am through being nice to carolers. I have, for years, been
one of the designated shut-ins on my street the carolers come to
serenade. I do not sing well with others, and besides, it involves
a great deal of walking. So I am left at home where I can cheerfully
open the door and smile like a Stepford wife while everyone
else on the street sings to me. Last year, I opened the door to
be greeted by:

"You're a mean one, Mr. Grinch…"

I'll show them Grinch. We'll see how jolly they are dodging
rocks through Glendale Gardens. I wonder if Santa would hold it
against me if I went upside their heads with a fruitcake.

I usually do not have to spin any untruths when unwrapping
presents. My people are wonderful gift buyers. They get me
Carhartt shirts and good, thick socks and wrenches and screw-
drivers and jeans that fit and 36 pairs of white undies from Fruit
of the Loom, whom we have forgiven, apparently, for shutting
down the plant and laying off the entire extended family. But I
will NOT pretend to like a purple velour pullover with a V-neck
collar, three sizes too small. I put it on and looked like a 300-pound
grape. Don't do that to me no more.

And I am through pretending that my one, special Christmas
wish will come true. I am a low-tech man, but have begged for an
iPod loaded with the Allman Brothers Band, The Amazing Rhythm
Aces ("Third rate romance/Low rent rendezvous"), and some Jerry
Lee Lewis. The iPod did arrive under the tree, two years ago.
Empty. Silent. Christmases and birthdays and Father's Days have
come and gone and it is still silent as a box of saltine crackers,
because my family members who actually know how to insert
music into the magical device do not love me enough to do so.

Well I am through. From now on, during Christmas, I will
celebrate in the warm light of truth.

Guess I'll go see what's on the radio.

# O CHRISTMAS SOCK

*Southern Living*, Southern Journal: December 2013

I wondered, until I was about 21, why they called them "stockings." They were not stockings. Stockings were something women wore to church or when they were "going out." They came in a kind of nondescript tan, or, if you had completely forfeited your immortal soul, fishnet. I often wondered why they were called that too, because even a fool could see they were useless for fishing. Maybe in queen size.

Anyway, what we hung by our chimney with care were not stockings. (Actually, we did not have a chimney, so Santa had to be let in at the front door.) What we hung on our wall, to the left of the cedar tree that we'd liberated from the state highway right-of-way, were socks. White. Knee-high. Three stripes at the top. Of the classification known as "tube." Now, children call them "old-school."

They came from the Cloth Barn in Hokes Bluff, Alabama, for $3 a packet, and a packet had, like, 400 pairs. But back then you could also get a wheelbarrow of underwear for $5 and a Green Stamp. My point—and it has taken me much longer to arrive here than it should have—is that in my childhood you could not have Christmas morning without a tube sock swaying on a tenpenny nail driven into the Sheetrock. Imagine Christmas without fruitcake, or firearms, or tube socks. See? You can't.

My mother explained that the vast importance of the Christmas sock goes back to the Great Depression. It used to be all there was. Well, first, of course, came the baby Jesus.

Let us explain further.

The sock was the depository for Christmas cheer. If my grandfather had found carpentry work in the mountain South—or at least if he had been unmolested by the federal men long enough to run off some selling liquor—my mother and her siblings would find their socks bulging with an apple, an orange, Brazil nuts, walnuts, and a piece of peppermint candy. (This was, of course, an age before tube socks, but the wool socks of the age did fine.) To my mother and her sisters, it was all they could have wished, dreamed, or prayed for.

Me, I arrived about the same time as the tube sock, one size fits all, and it was bottomless. It held an orchard of tangerines, three chocolate Santys, 1,000 peppermints, and 4,236 walnuts, which was a little like giving a child a hunk of iron to open. The only way to do it was with a 9-pound hammer, otherwise used in railroad construction. I do not ever remember eating one piece of walnut, just looking forlornly at a smashed patty of obliterated shell and walnut paste. But I digress.

Sometimes my mother even fit a small toy in there, like a plastic Indian chief on a rearing stallion. My point is, it would stretch to hold anything, stretch to hold the whole world, though they would stretch about 4 feet straight down until they brushed the floor.

Sometimes inside the Christmas sock would be a new pair of socks, which caused me momentary consternation though I still cannot quite explain why. It must be how you feel when you slice into a turducken.

We have stockings now. They have garland, ribbon, and sparkles, and come from town. You cannot wear them. I am not ungrateful. I love my stockings. But they will not stretch a lick.

# COWBOYS ARE HER WEAKNESS

*Southern Living,* Southern Journal: January 2015

———————

N ow wait a minute, Shep. We don't want to kill us no ol' ladies, 'cause I
like ol' ladies.
　　　—The actor Dennis Hopper, just before shooting the train
conductor

My mother is not a panicky woman; she is a Southern one. She
was born in the cold heart of the Depression and has survived
things most people encounter only in the pages of Faulkner. She
has propped up more than one sorry man, and lived through a
real-world heart attack and the demise of *General Hospital.* When
*As the World Turns* stopped spinning, she did not miss a step—
though it almost killed Aunt Juanita. But there was panic in her
voice, one bleak day, as she stabbed the remote control, searching.

"I can't find my Virginian," is all she said.

"Oh, Lord," I said, and meant it.

My mother loves *The Virginian.* She is, I believe, sweet on him—
not on the actor who plays him in the classic television Western
but on the tall man in the black leather vest who looked good on
a horse.

"I saw him the other day on the Western Channel, that Jim
Drury, and he was *old,*" she said.

They have been riding off into the re-run sunset, him and her, every day for as long as I can remember, usually after he shoots somebody. My mother does not like guns, but guns in the Westerns are not real; she knows this because a man who gets gunned down on *Gunsmoke* will be resurrected a week later on *Cheyenne*, killed again, reappear on *Wyatt Earp*, and killed again. Dennis Hopper was killed 5,000 times before his actual death, and still gets shot down twice a month in black and white; Ken Curtis was bush-wacked and buried on a *Gunsmoke* cattle drive and reincarnated a week later, as Festus.

But I digress. *The Virginian* was gone, cancelled, leaving my mother with a sorry choice between Bat Masterson and the hundredth replay of the *Gunsmoke* where Miss Kitty gets kidnapped. But even a sub-par Western is better than none, for us. Some people go south in the cold, the shut-in days. My mother, little brother, and I, we go west. The gray afternoons are a good excuse to do nothing, once the stock is fed and wood toted in for the fire. We sit down with a cup of coffee or some tea and unwrap a Little Debbie, and ...

'*Have Gun, will Travel*' *reads the card of a man*
*A knight without armor in a savage land*

My mother loves the scenery, of the Plains, and Monument Valley. I love the horses. We know they are not historically accurate. There is no bullet wound that cannot be healed by putting the man's arm in a sling. The Indians always, always ride in a circle around the wagons, to provide a better target. "I pull for 'em," my little brother said, and I do, too.

I am addicted now. I like them because they make me feel young again, especially when I hear a line from my childhood. "If whiskey cured something," Miss Kitty told Marshal Dillon, "I could save the world."

My mother is, once again, at peace. She found *The Virginian*, a few months ago, on the Inspiration Channel.

"*My* Virginian," she said.

# A CAST OF CHARACTERS

*Best Life*,  September 2005

I hunted for her the last time in a hot, wet, sticky gloom, mosquitoes needling the back of my neck. We had been blessed with blackberry winter well into May, cool and dry, but almost overnight the Alabama summer had smothered Bean Flat Mountain. The yellow pollen that had swirled on the springtime breeze now filmed the surface of the pond and caked the wet leather of my high-top work boots.

As a boy, I had run barefoot and buck wild through pastures like this, chasing fireflies with a minnow net and a mayonnaise jar, unafraid of what hid in the waist-high grass. But now I armored my shins in leather, and I moved old-man-slow and easy around the pond, listening for the rasp of belly scales on the dead stems of last year's weeds. The cottonmouths are surly things that will bite you out of simple meanness—no matter what the nitwit snake handlers on the nature channels say. Mature snakes had little to fear here in the Appalachian foothills except the big owls, the hawks, and of course, her. She would come at them from below as they glided across the surface of the pond, open her maw to the size of a Quaker Oats container, and suck them in. Only the biggest bass take a grown snake that way, and she was as big—for her kind— as I have ever seen.

I raked at the mosquitoes with one sweaty hand, slid my index finger under the line of my spinning rig, and lofted a steel-gray rubber worm into a pond I could no longer see. Some people would have called it fishing, but fishing is a random thing—you fling a hook into space and wait for something dumb enough or hungry enough to bite. This was more specific than that. I hunted one fish, as I had for a year, going on two. I cast over and over well into the night, the mosquitoes humming in my ears, fluttering up my nose. I twitched the rod up to make the worm dance from the bottom, then cranked it in, slow, slower.

Then again and again and... until it seemed like someone was tightening a crescent wrench onto the nerves between my shoulder blades.

She is bigger now, I thought, than the last time she was caught, when my big brother, Sam, the consummate, patient fisherman, set the hook hard and watched a brand-new rod bend double under her weight. I remember the surprised look on his face as he tried to reel and wound up having to tap-dance along the rim of the pond, wearing her down. I remember how this man who has caught untold thousands of fish hooked his thumb inside her lip, hefted her, and caught his breath.

"Lord," he said. "What a fish."

I ran one finger down her green scales, a little boy again. Six pounds and more—from a stock pond.

The eye I looked into, as he showed her off, was as big as mine, cold and blank.

You have to read your own story into an eye like that, because it gives nothing away.

In it, I saw my own failure.

I have never caught a fish like her. In this place I was born, a place cut by rivers, drowned by massive man-made lakes, and dimpled by ponds, if you're not a fisherman, you're not much of a man.

But I could set it right if I could catch that one fish, that amazing fish. It didn't matter that she had already been caught. That only proved that she was real, not just another hopeful lie told over a creek-bank banquet of beans and weenies and saltine crackers.

You, I thought, staring at the yellow-scrummed surface of the pond, are my redemption.

I remember that first time, how Sam had to reach his whole hand into your jaws to work loose the hook, how he reverently eased you into the shallows, and even rocked you back and forth a little, like a baby, filling your gills. You scraped silt off the bottom with your thrashing tail and vanished. Sam straightened the rubber worm on the hook and flicked it back into the water, and as soon as he took the slack out of the line, a smaller bass took it. As he cranked it in, the rod shattered into three pieces, and he stood for a minute, wondering.

"The big 'un ruint it," he said. The fiberglass had cracked like a spiderwebbed windshield, and then shattered, a moment later, when the little fish thumped it.

––––––––

I learned to fish with a cane pole in baby-size hands, staring at the red-and-white plastic bobber. I graduated to a Zebco 202 closed-face reel by the time I was old enough to read. On any given Saturday, my people caught enough crappie from the Coosa backwater to fill a washtub, and I can still see my Aunt Edna mixing cornmeal with diced green onion and commodity cheese, then dropping them into iron skillets for the best hush puppies I have ever had.

Fishing was our birthright. My grandfather Charlie Bundrum, a folkloric figure, hunted for the giant catfish below the Guntersville dam with a massive snag hook screwed into the end of a pool cue. He simply stood on the rocks, waiting for the turbines to churn to life, bringing the big cats to the surface. And then he would swing the cue down, hard, and sink the barbs into the fish's head. There wasn't a whole lot of sport in it, maybe. But you could feed a lot of people with a fish as long as a love seat. His boat was made from two car hoods welded together, and he never wet a line sober. But when he came from the river and took a nap, his wife, Ava, would find fish in his coat pockets. My own gentle Mama, with a cane pole and a snuff can full of cow manure and red wigglers, is a bream-catching machine.

There was not a bad fisherman in the whole damn bloodline, male or female, until me. I could cast beautifully into open water, but if there was a tree to snap up in, I would find it. And once I cast, I cranked too fast and jerked the rod tip too high, and made the fish work to catch the lure.

A patient man named Joe Romeo took me fishing for trout on the flats of Tampa Bay, and I caught a cormorant. You haven't lived until you've tried to remove a hook from a live bird. I don't drink much, hardly at all, but on a trip to Destin, Florida, as a young man, I got knee-walking drunk and waded out into the bay with a saltwater rig and a bowl of boiled shrimp. The Coast Guard was not amused.

Once, fishing a small lake with my brother, I hung my crankbait up on power lines that crossed the water.

"Just reel it up to about a foot shy of the line," Sam told me, "and flip it over."

I did as I was told and flipped it too hard—and into the high branches of a live oak tree.

Sam just stared.

"I do believe," he said, "that's the first time I ever seen that happen."

It is still up there, shining in the sun.

———

The path to my redemption—or what I hope will be so—can be traced back to the fall of 2002, when I used the money from a book contract to buy my mother 40 acres of pasture and mountain land on the ridge where my grandfather, the expert fisherman Charlie Bundrum, had made whiskey 75 years before. Near the blacktop, just inside the cow pasture, is the pond, and the one fish.

It is a beautiful place, sandwiched between two ridges of hardwoods, alive with deer and wild turkey and rumors of bears. The pond is shallow and clear on one end, where the bream form a moonscape of round beds in the spring of the year, and deep and green on the other, where the big bass hang suspended in the murk. A snapping turtle the size of a 14-inch tire lurks here, and I have my orders from my Mama to shoot it if I can, because she is afraid it will eat her ducklings. There ain't much glory in shooting a turtle, so I hope it stays hid until one of us dies of natural causes. Her mature ducks dodge my casts, and her two miniature donkeys, just pets, come down to drink and snort. They have never seen a real donkey, and believe they are normal size.

The place is so green it looks painted on. The live oaks dip their limbs into the water, and the grass is waist high except where Sam has used the tractor to cut a trail for my mother to walk. The path blossomed with tiny yellow flowers. "Ever'where Mama walks is flowers," he said, and it struck me, for the thousandth time, how beautiful the language of my people can be.

It is paradise, this country, give or take a few billion ticks and red wasps and fire ants, but the pond is all I really see anymore.

I have fished it since the day we bought it, and, almost from that day, I have known she was here. It happened when my mother and I walked the rim of the pond, checking to see if her duck was on its nest. In the deep end, the fish hovered.

"What is that?" Mama said.

"Bass," I said.

"It ain't," she said.

"Well," I said, "what is it?"

"Sea monster," she said, and walked to the house.

We got our first good look at her when she was on the bed. She had laid her eggs on the gravel bottom, then floated above, watching. I teased topwater baits across the very end of her nose and trickled worms past her lower lip—being careful not to drag the bait through the bed itself—and she either ignored them or followed them for a few feet before circling back to the bed.

I hooked her, I am sure, in the late spring.

I never really believed in the science of fishing—I always thought there was more luck in it than most people allowed—but I always paid attention when Sam lectured me on the mechanics. When a fish hits, he said, don't worry about popping the line in two or snatching the bait out of the fish's mouth.

"Break 'er jaw," he said. Set the hook hard and quick. Not only will it hold, but it will also keep the fish from taking that second gulp that will often pull the hook deeper into her guts.

When I felt the tug on the tip of the rod, I broke 'er jaw.

The fish—it had to be her—broke water, well and truly caught, but as I began to reel, I felt the line go slack and my stomach go sick.

It was her.

It had to be her.

I am 45 years old. I guess I must face the fact that catching one fish would not truly cure me, would not alter my legacy as the worst fisherman in my bloodline. It is too late, I suppose. I would just be the bad fisherman who got lucky, once.

Still, as the dusk creeps over the ridgeline, I carry my rods and tackle to the edge of the pond. The day, another day, will end in disappointment.

But sometimes it also ends in fireflies.

# NICK OF TIME

*Sports Illustrated,* August 2007

———

They say college football is religion in the Deep South, but it's not. Only religion is religion. Anyone who has seen an old man rise from his baptism, his soul all on fire, knows as much, though it is easy to see how people might get confused. But if football were a faith anywhere, it would be here on the Black Warrior River in Tuscaloosa, Alabama. And now has come a great revival.

———

The stadium strained with expectation. The people who could not find a seat stood on the ramps or squatted in the aisles, as if it were Auburn down there, or Tennessee, and when the crowd roared, the sound really did roll like thunder across the sky. A few blocks away 73-year-old Ken Fowler climbed to his second-story terrace so he could hear it better and stood in the sunlight as that lovely roar fell all around him. He believes in the goodness and rightness of the Crimson Tide the way people who handle snakes believe in the power of God, but in his long lifetime of unconditional love, of Rose Bowl trains, Bobby Marlow up the middle and the Goal Line Stand, he never heard anything like this. His Alabama was playing before the largest football crowd in state history, and playing only itself. "We had 92,000," he said, "for a scrimmage." It felt good. It felt like it used to feel.

They came from Sand Mountain, the Wiregrass, the Black Belt, the Gulf Coast, and just wide places in the road. They came in motor homes, private jets, $30,000 pickup trucks, $400 cars, and dime-store flip-flops to see Nick Saban walk the sideline of Bryant-Denny Stadium in April.

They have welcomed him as Caesar, as pharaoh, and paid him enough money to burn a wet dog. Now he will take them forward by taking them back to the glory of their past—the 21 Southeastern Conference championships, the 12 national championships, the Team of the 20th Century (as *The Wall Street Journal* called the Crimson Tide in 2000).

Saban has not promised them so much—"I don't believe in predictions," he says—but they believe. It may take two years, three, more, to be in the discussion again when people talk about the best teams in college football. But they know he will take them home.

"I've been on this roller coaster for a long time," says Fowler, a self-made businessman who could live a lot of places but settled on a house so close to the campus that he can all but see his reflection in the go-go boots of the Crimsonettes as they strut down University Boulevard before the homecoming game. "In the '50s, under coach J.B. (Ears) Whitworth, we went 14 games without a win, and I watched grown men cry. People said then there would never be another coach here as good as Wallace Wade [who won national championships in 1925, '26 and '30] or Frank Thomas [1934, '41]. They said it was over.

"Then in '58 we hired a coach who could do the things we needed to put us in a position to win SEC championships again and national championships again. People used to stare at him as he stood on the sideline, too, like he was about to turn a stick into a snake."

His name was Paul Bryant, and he was popular here. They named an animal after him.

How people loved that man. But it is time, past time, to love again.

"There is never anything wrong with remembering the past, but you can't live in it," says Mal Moore, the Alabama athletic director who was all but dragged through saw briars when it appeared that Saban and other marquee names—most notably West Virginia coach Rich Rodriguez—were passing Alabama by. Then on Jan. 3 he brought Saban home with him on the school jet from Miami, where Saban had been coaching the Dolphins. People who had been calling for Moore's resignation praised his leadership.

There is no nice way to say it: The Alabama faithful are done with waiting, with mediocrity, and with disappointment. They are sick of Auburn, which has beaten them five years in a row; bone weary of NCAA investigations and probations reaching back to 1993; and finished with coaches who cannot gut out the expectations here, or who might have done well, someday, with more time or a railroad car full of luck.

"We wanted a man who had won a championship, and Nick Saban is that and more," says Moore. "Saban brings a sense of command, a sense of toughness and discipline."

Saban is no rainmaker, no snake oil salesman. The way to his mountaintop is hard and paved with woe. "We can be part of something, build something all these people can be proud of and excited about again," says the 55-year-old coach, who can look intense even when he is not mad and probably looks that way holding a kitten. "I got on our guys in a team meeting. I said, 'I'm tired of hearing all this talk about a national championship when you guys don't know how to get in out of the rain, don't know what to do in the classroom.' It's like you've got little kids in the backseat, saying, 'Are we there yet?'

"The journey itself is important, not just the destination. You have to follow direction. Discipline, off-season recruiting, conditioning, practice, more recruiting, player development, classroom development. I'm not interested in what should be, could be, was. I'm interested in what is, what we control. And when we lose—and we will, one game, two, or more—we have to have a trust that what we are doing will work, trust and belief in who we are. And you get where you're going, one mile marker at a time."

People here believe Saban is tough and smart and do not care that he can seem impatient, if not angry, when dealing with the media or hangers-on or just about anybody else, as if he has more important things to do. Like coaching football. In a state where some old men still test their truck's electrical system by grabbing hold of a hot coil wire, football coaches are not supposed to be in touch with their inner child. Saban won a national championship at LSU in 2003, out of a conference where every game can feel like a knife fight in a ditch. No one cares how he did in charm school.

One LSU fan told Alabama fan Sammy Maze that Saban could

be, well, a little difficult. "You know he's a son of a bitch?" the LSU fan said.

"Well," Maze said, "he's our son of a bitch now."

Never assume that Alabamans give a damn what others think. "People can write and say that this exemplifies a fanaticism that needs to be curbed," says Fowler, who would have gone to the Tide's intrasquad scrimmage himself if it had not been broadcast live on television. "All Alabama proved, with 92,000 people at a practice, is that nobody loves football better. I don't see how that somehow makes us subhuman. I mean, in some countries they kill soccer players, don't they?"

Saban has yet to coach a down for the Crimson Tide, but people are already naming their children for him. Tim and Hannah Witt of Hartselle, Ala., named their baby boy, born March 20, Saban Hardin Witt. They already had a son named Tyde. "At first I thought my husband was crazy," says Hannah, "but it grew on me."

In these parts you do not name a child for a coach you expect to go 8-5. The Witts had talked at first about naming their second son Bear.

Hank Williams once said he could throw his cowboy hat onto the stage of the Grand Ole Opry after he finished Lovesick Blues and it would get at least one curtain call. It has been that way for decades in Tuscaloosa, except the hat is houndstooth.

Will Nevin, a first-year law student, places an offering the night before every game at the feet of Bryant's statue in front of the football stadium. He and his friends leave a bag of Golden Flake potato chips and an old-fashioned glass bottle of Coca-Cola, the sponsors of Bryant's old TV show. Nevin, 21, never saw the show, never saw Bryant on the sideline. But the image of the Bear is alive in his mind's eye. He just knows how it must have been, like hearing someone tell you how sweet an old Mustang used to run, before it was put up on blocks in the barn and covered with a tarp. The most you can do is run your hand over the paint and imagine.

It seems like a dream now: From 1958 through 1982 there were six national championships, 13 SEC titles, a 232-46-9 overall record, a 19-6 mark against Auburn, and a stable of immortals that included Billy Neighbors, Lee Roy Jordan, Joe Namath, Kenny Stabler, John Hannah, Ozzie Newsome, many others. But the Bryant magic was about more than numbers, more than X's and O's and big ol' boys who would have blocked a pulpwood truck if he'd asked them to. It was about how he could draw every eye in the stadium to him as he leaned against that goalpost during warmups, a growling, mumbling golem glued together out of legend, gristle, and a little bit of mean. It was almost cheating, having him on the sideline, like filling your trunk full of cement blocks before a demolition derby.

After a quarter century of dominance Bryant retired after the 1982 season with a 21-15 win over Illinois at the Liberty Bowl in Memphis, in the freezing cold. Less than a month later he was dead, as if his life was hard-wired to the game. One paper sent reporters to interview the grave digger, and on Bryant's burial day people stood on the overpasses and the roadside, hands over their hearts, to watch a hearse take away one of the best parts of their history.

At any flea market in Dixie, you can still find Bryant commemorative plates. At every roadside bar, church basement rec room, or courthouse café, you can hear this joke:

Guy gets into heaven. Sees an old man in a houndstooth hat walking on water.

"Hey," he asks Saint Peter, "is that Bear Bryant?"

"Naw," Pete says, "that's God. He just thinks he's Bear Bryant."

Nevin will always love the idea of Bear and always honor his legend, but it is clear that praying to a memory, however fine, has not worked amid so many missing elements. "We want something to celebrate," says Nevin. "By God, it's our right."

In one of the most storied, demanding, and impatient programs in college football, the comparison with Bryant has smothered the coaches who've come after him. With the exception of his protégé, Gene Stallings, who delivered a national championship in '92, schooling trash-talking Miami 34-13 in the Sugar Bowl, men have perished in the shadow of Bear. It is his taped voice, God-like, that still booms across Bryant-Denny Stadium at the start of every home game: "I ain't never been nothin' but a winner."

But Saban totes his own national championship prestige into Tuscaloosa—the first Bryant successor to do so—and a résumé that Alabama was willing to spend a reported $32 million over eight years to procure. "I don't think Saban's afraid of the past," says Kirk McNair, founder and editor of 'Bama magazine, who has covered Crimson Tide football across five decades. "I don't think he cares."

Saban is 91-42-1 as a college coach, in stops at Toledo, Michigan State, and LSU—all rebuilding jobs. LSU had had only three winning seasons in 11 years when he took over in November 1999. Four years later he coached the Tigers to the pinnacle of college football. His 48 wins from 2000 through '04 ranked third among major college coaches over that span. The Tigers were SEC champs in '01 and again in '03, when they went on to beat Oklahoma 21-14 to win the BCS national title. Saban builds his teams methodically, on a backbone of conditioning, rigid discipline, and a swarming, ball-stealing defense.

He leads like a tough-minded CEO. Listening to him, you get the feeling you would not want him to decide your fate if your job production was down and your equipment obsolete. The lore of football, the poetry of it, does not complicate his language. But he knows that before the kickoff of Alabama's season opener with Western Carolina on Sept. 1, thousands of Crimson Tide fans, especially the ones who remember, will look to the goalpost and miss the coach who led them so grandly for so long. It should be that way.

"[Bryant] accomplished as much as anybody ever has," says Saban. "He is someone you respect, admire, and appreciate. He established the standard of excellence, him and the players who gave their blood, sweat, and tears.

"That, in itself, has no effect on the future," says Saban, who knows that no ghost, or alumnus, has ever thrown a halfback for a loss. "We have to do the work now."

Saban will not go into great detail about his team, any more than he will discuss his opponents. There is no profit in it. But it is clear that 2007 is a true rebuilding year, with a typically tough SEC schedule. Alabama goes against Vanderbilt, Arkansas, Georgia, and Ole Miss in the first half of its SEC schedule, then Tennessee, LSU, Mississippi State, and Auburn. A Sept. 29 game against Florida State in Jacksonville is not exactly a nonconference breather.

It may be a team unfamiliar to fans used to seeing the Tide carried by a talented defense. Alabama lost too many big, fast, scary people. "If you can't stop the run in the SEC, you're in trouble," says Mitch Dobbs, the assistant editor of 'Bama magazine, and a lot of the middle is just gone.

But instead of an offense that was too often effective only between the 20s, Alabama may show off a little with junior quarterback John Parker Wilson and a corps of game-breaking receivers. The offensive line, which bore criticism—well, let's face it, scorn—is expected to be less porous. And a redshirt freshman named Terry Grant, a former Mr. Football from Mississippi, runs like something bad is after him.

Concerns that Alabama's defense would be leaner this year materialized in summer practices, but the offense moved the ball smoothly in scrimmages on days when the temperature reached 106°F and 107°F. No matter how hot it got, however, Alabama players did not complain. Saban and his coaches would not allow their players to even use the word hot or heat in conversation.

Alabama's athletes could have made Saban's summer a little cooler if they had behaved better off the field. Simeon Castille, an all-SEC cornerback, was arrested early last Sunday in an entertainment district near campus and charged with disorderly conduct. The police were not talking about precisely what Castille had done, and Saban indicated that he will handle the matter internally. Three other players—defensive linemen Brandon Deaderick and Brandon Fanney and running back Roy Upchurch, all reserves—were charged after a disturbance in July.

Saban might not coach the Tide to improbable wins, say Alabama fans. But he will not lose the handle on the games that are winnable and leave Alabama at the ugly end of a soul-killing upset. That is what they want from him, at least right now. In any event, it is unlikely any booster will look into Saban's drill-bit eyes and tell him, "That ain't the way Bear did it."

From the moment Saban was hired, there has been an electricity, a high-stakes poker feel to his every move. In Miami and on the national talk-show circuit he was badmouthed and lambasted for adamantly denying, as the Dolphins' season wound to its 6-10 conclusion, that he would be the Alabama coach, then turning around and taking the job. He was called a liar, a snake, and other pleasantries. Of the firestorm he says, "We gave up a little bit to be here."

Then on April 21 Saban walked onto the field for the intrasquad game to that thunder, the pure and positive manifestation of the expectations at Alabama. "There is something special about this place," he says. It is the only time in almost an hour and a half of discussion about football that Saban does not talk about work ethic, goals, discipline. "It was ... emotional."

Saban is not surprised that Alabamans agree with his ideas on what it takes to win. He grew up in coal mining country in West Virginia, pumped gas and broke down tires at a filling station his father owned. "The worst I could ever do is go back to West

Virginia and pump gas again," he says. "Life's been pretty good to me."

He understands that in Alabama people believe you have to work for what you get. "The best thing about winning the championship at LSU was that it gave people hope, something to be proud of," he says. "I don't wear the ring. It wasn't a personal accomplishment. But I think the people of Alabama understand what it takes to be successful, understand persistence, overcoming adversity, mental and physical toughness."

Saban does not see himself as mean, brusque, or distant: "I think most people who get to know me don't have that feeling." His wife, Terry, told him there might be a slight gap between how he sees himself and how others see him. That, she told him, "is your blind spot. And it's as wide as the Grand Canyon."

"And she wasn't even mad at me," Saban says.

There is no gap between what he wants and what Alabama wants. While "the name of the stadium's not going to change," says McNair, smiling, he believes that Saban, one Saturday at a time, will realign the program with its rich past. "It's been a long, long time since I had this good a feeling."

To find the source of Alabama's hunger, you have to go back further than the Bear. You have to go by train.

It was always a tough room.

Alabama's first coach, E.B. Beaumont, went 2-2 in 1892. "We therefore got rid of him," says the 1894 school yearbook.

It was hard-nosed Wallace Wade who took Alabama to its first recognized national championship, in 1925, when his undefeated team beat Washington 20-19 in the Rose Bowl, the first time a Southern team had ever played in the game. Alabama won more national titles—and Rose Bowls—under Wade in '26 and '30. His successor, Frank Thomas, who had learned his football as a quarterback for Knute Rockne at Notre Dame, took Alabama to Pasadena three more times, won a widely recognized national title in '34—with Paul Bryant playing end—and a still-debated title in '41. Some fans say Thomas' best team was the undefeated Rose Bowl-winning squad in '45.

They were college boys in suits, but on the trips home from California, across Texas and the lower South, people stood beside the railroad tracks, waving and cheering. It was Faulkner's South, Huey P. Long's, and the Klan's. Night riders in sheets still enforced their doomed ideals, and mill workers spun cotton all week for pocket change. Writers from the North and the West would question if it was wise to open the nation's premier bowl game quite so often to the unsophisticated South.

"Columbia or Pennsylvania would make a much better game with the Pacific Coast Conference representative for the 1946 Rose Bowl than would Alabama and, in addition, such a game would have that intangible thing called 'class,' something it can never have with a southern club being one of the participants," wrote Dick Hyland in the *Los Angeles Times.* "Me, I'm kinda tired of hillbillies and swamp students in the Rose Bowl."

But from beside the tracks, people waved and waved. Reconstruction had faded into the Depression, and not much had changed. "It became our culture," says Doug Jones, the former U.S. attorney who successfully prosecuted two Klansmen for the infamous 1963 bombing of the 16th Street Baptist Church in Birmingham. "We were a poor state, with a great darkness in our history, but we took a team by train across the nation and played the best and beat the best."

From 1947 through '54 Harold (Red) Drew kept winning at Alabama, but it is a testament to the expectations here that a coach who went 45-28-7 with berths in the Sugar, Orange, and Cotton bowls would be considered subpar. Over the next three years, under J.B. Whitworth, it got much worse. He was a nice man, people said, but he was 4-24-2. They needed something else.

Bryant always said his impetus for winning was the fear that he'd have to go home to a plow in Fordyce, Ark. In December '57, after having coached at Maryland, Kentucky, and Texas A&M, he came to Alabama. "One year [my family and I] were in Miami, and Auburn happened to be playing the Hurricanes," says Fowler. "I walked out on the beach, and there were all these Auburn people. It was terrible. I looked up as one of these little planes went by pulling a banner, EAT AT JOE'S STONE CRABS, or something, and I got to thinking. The next day the Auburn people were still there, and a plane flies over, and it says ATTENTION AUBURN, THE BEAR LIVES. I don't remember what it cost, but it was pittance for what I got for it."

There was a swagger then. "I had an Auburn friend, Spiro Gregory (Speedy) Mastoras," Fowler says. "He would tell me, after another Auburn loss [to Alabama], 'Wait till year after next.' He knew that next year was out of reach."

What a shame it couldn't last forever.

Except for Stallings, no coach after Bryant lasted more than four years. Bear's successor was Ray Perkins, a wideout on the 1964 and '65 national championship teams, who went 32-15-1 and forever angered fans when he pulled down the tower from which Bryant would watch practice. It went back up after Perkins left. Bill Curry went 26-10 and was never beloved. (An 0-3 record against Auburn didn't help.) Stallings won his title and 70 games, but the record book reads 62-25 after the NCAA stripped eight wins and a tie from the '93 season, when a player was found to have had improper dealings with an agent.

Then came everything but locusts. Mike Dubose, mired in a harassment scandal that the university would settle, went 24-23 as the NCAA investigated booster Logan Young's involvement in the recruitment of a Memphis tackle named Albert Means. Dubose resigned under pressure after he lost homecoming to Central Florida.

Dennis Franchione fled after two years (17-8) as NCAA sanctions became a crippling reality. He left for Texas A&M, and one Alabama fan, Morgan Plott, felt so betrayed that he went to Norman, Okla., to see A&M get whipped 77-0 by the Sooners in 2003. "I wanted to see Coach Fran get beat," says Plott, "but I didn't know it would be that good." Alabama brought in Mike Price, who forgot he was in the Bible Belt and was let go after a visit to a topless bar, having never coached a game for the Tide. Then, in a hurry, Mike Shula was hired.

People liked Shula, who had won a lot of games as a Tide quarterback in the '80s. But, again, this is no business for a nice young man. Hamstrung by probation that was an earlier regime's doing, Shula went 26-23 in four years. He was fired last November, after his fourth straight loss to Auburn. As it became clear that the program was losing ground, fans grew weary of players who talked big and did not do much, talked about realizing their potential and showcasing their talents, and then got beat on the line of scrimmage by Mississippi State.

The expectations are cemented into the architecture. Four bronze giants watch over the promenade in front of Bryant-Denny Stadium. Here stand Wade, Thomas, Stallings, and, of course, Bryant. But because this is Alabama, there is space left for a fifth pedestal. "How could it not be?" says Moore.

Fans expect Saban to take that place. "The brick masons are probably already getting started," says Jim Fuller, who won two national titles as an offensive lineman for Bryant and another as an assistant under Stallings. He has never seen the Alabama legions hungrier or more unified. Why else would 92,000 attend a glorified practice?

"Just so long as he knows that 91,000 of them will be kicking his ass" if things go wrong, Fuller says.

Does he really believe there are 1,000 benevolent Alabama fans? "Naw, I was being gracious."

They say college football is a matter of life and death down here, but it's not. Winning only makes life sweeter, and, once in a blue moon, losing can too. Last winter Will Nevin and his father, Randy, who was dying of cancer, took a road trip to Shreveport, La., to see Alabama play Oklahoma State in the Independence Bowl. "He got cold, and he coughed some, and we lost," Nevin says. "It didn't matter. It was one of the best times we ever had." Randy Nevin died on March 28. At his funeral it was noted that he loved deer hunting, his family, Moundville Nazarene Church, and one football team.

# 109 YARDS RETURNED, TWO POINTS DENIED, AND ONE TWIST LEFT IN THE ROAD

*ESPN The Magazine*, January 2014

---

W hen I can, I watch the Alabama-Auburn game with my brother and sister-in-law, in the blue-collar foothills of Calhoun County, not far from the Georgia line. We do not scream at the television; we would not flint a Cheetos across the room. Our mama raised us right. We love football, but we have gotten old together in a place where padlocks and logging chains seal the doors to the mills and factories where people used to work. Football is not the world, merely our escape from it, and we are blessed to live in a place where dusty history and the here-and-now have both been kind to us, and rich for the University of Alabama. I would have liked to have watched the storied rivalry there, in their snug wood-frame house, for the rest of my days, wood smoke curling up through the pines, the sound of halftime drifting faintly out into the yard as we look over his beautiful hunting dogs. It is what I have done, off and on, since the days of the Bear, and now through the twilight of the BCS era. I would like to do that, but I know I am not welcome here anymore, even if I showed up with a 21-piece bucket and three-dozen Krispy Kremes.

I am banned, for life. The past two times Auburn beat us, I was sitting in their house. First it was 2010, when Mark Ingram fumbled what seemed a certain touchdown and the ball rolled dead straight for what seemed like 50 yards, feet from the sideline, and through the end zone. "A football," my brother Sam said, "ain't even *designed* to roll straight. Try to roll one. Just *try* it." And I was there again over Thanksgiving weekend, the last big weekend of the BCS, when God proved He is a vengeful God and smote Alabama with a 109-yard return of a missed 57-yard field goal. Considering how poorly executed our response was, when the impossible happened, I guess I should be glad He did not just turn us all into salt.

Others will remember the two-point try in the Big House, at the end of the Ohio State-Michigan, or Oregon's last-minute defeat of Oregon State, or that South Carolina and the Evil Genius whipped Clemson, again, or Georgia's OT win over Tech, or Stanford over Notre Dame. But for me the last gasp of the final BCS weekend will always be the one stuck in my throat, as I watched a young man in orange and blue gather in the missed field goal and streak up the sideline with no one to catch him but some lumbering behemoths and a little-bitty kicker, beating us in a way no team has ever beaten another in the history of college football. Such a thing does not happen in the natural world. It made me wonder if that old nursery rhyme, the one every AU child hears, might be true.

*God must be a Tiger, too*
*'Cause the sun is orange*
*And the sky is blue*

Only divine intervention brings a people so low when they are just trying to have some time off. So I am unlucky. I made God mad at us, probably for whacking my brother in the head with a bucket while he was caught up in barbed wire fence in the summer of '64; that, or some kind of coveting. Anyway, my brother did not even have to say it. I banned my own self.

I know I said we were not crazed, drooling football fans. But I also pointed out, early on in this, that we live on *this* side of the Georgia line. We can take no chances. Roll tide. When this story gets out, I will be lucky if I am not banned from some parts of the Great State of Alabama altogether, and do not wind up listening to next year's game on a taped-together transistor radio from inside a refrigerator box under the interstate. I have been banned before. I am also unwelcome at one auto parts store and at least one cellular phone franchise, for scaring clerks.

But that's what made the BCS era grand, in my eyes. Every

weekend was life and death for those fortunate enough to be in the title hunt, and here in Alabama, if you can't have the whole hog, why settle for a chitlin'? I worry, when the high sheriffs of the playoff era clamp their objective hands around our football, will every week of the season still be quite so dramatic, grim, wild. I guess it will make teams that don't play defense—or play anybody—feel good, and I am all for making others feel good about themselves. I just wish I could have had a better, final image in my head, to remember it all by.

Alabama student Elizabeth Manning comes from an Auburn household in Valley Head. Her father, Alan, graduated from AU, but stood helpless as his only daughter and only son left for Tuscaloosa. On the last big weekend of the BCS, father and daughter tried to be civil and watch the game together. "That lasted two and a half minutes," Elizabeth said. He watched upstairs in the den. Elizabeth watched downstairs in the kitchen. "I was a lady, the entire game," she said, not once screeching up the stairs as Alabama pulled ahead. But after Auburn's miracle, her father ran down the stairs, flung a Tiger hat and T-shirt in her face, and crowed:

"Get to wearin'."

Her last memory of the BCS is little better than mine.

At least she can go home if she wants to.

# LONG TIME COMING

*Sports Illustrated,* April 2004

---

H istory really was made here, in the college town of Starkville, Miss., not far from the Alabama line. One of the last unwritten taboos in college sports really was busted here, amid the dark pine barrens and clear-cut timber and nowhere roads, when Sylvester Croom became the first man of his color hired as a head football coach in the storied Southeastern Conference. Yet four months later if you ask players, fans, or university officials whether history has been made, they tend to say much the same thing, at first: Mississippi State hired a coach, not a color.

"We have never once mentioned in a press release that he is the first black coach in the SEC," says Mike Nemeth, the school's associate director for media relations. People at the school say that Croom's race had nothing to do with his hiring, where the respected longtime college and professional assistant coach is being asked to snatch up a sliding program—one that may slip deeper still, as the NCAA mulls punishment for alleged recruiting violations under former coach Jackie Sherrill—and shake it into something people can be proud of again. The university's president and its athletic director, praised for their courage, almost shrug. "The university could not have bought this publicity for a million dollars," says the president, J. Charles Lee. But, "That courage issue was never a significant factor for me."

It is the same in the community. "Well, I asked my boyfriend, Buster, about him, and Buster said, 'He's going to be a good one,' " says Louise Ming, who is 78. Croom can win, people are saying. Too much time has passed to yammer on about color. Mississippi State has an A-plus football man, they say, and by God, that is all that matters.

"Same thing as if he was white," agrees Howard (Buster) Hood, who is retired from the dairy business and food industry and already has paid for his season tickets. "We give him a chance. He can't do the job, we don't need him."

But something odd happens the more you let people talk, the more you ask them who they are, where they are from, what they remember about life before integration—or, if they're very young, what they were told about that time—and it becomes clear, as a Mississippi writer once said, that the past is not dead here, nor even past. Croom himself, sitting in a spacious office with still-bare shelves, first swears that maroon and white, not black and white, are the colors of this football team, the only colors that concern him now.

Then the 49-year-old coach drifts back in his mind to the people who bled and died in a struggle he remembers mostly through the eyes of a child and teenage boy—people who absorbed genuine hatred, who changed his society and made it possible for him to play his way onto the Alabama football team in 1971, the second year that Paul (Bear) Bryant allowed black players on his squad. And he begins to cry.

His father, in the late 1940s, feared being lynched. Croom himself attended a newly integrated junior high school where students refused to talk to him or even look at him, where a spit wad spattered on his face the first day of classes.

But none of that is worth crying over, for Croom. It is the memory of a white woman that is causing him to break down, a 39-year-old homemaker and mother of five from Detroit who volunteered to drive protesters during the historic Selma-to-Montgomery voting rights march in 1965. Three Ku Klux Klansmen pulled up beside her as she drove down a stretch of road, a black man in the seat beside her. It was more than the Klansmen could stand.

"Viola Liuzzo," says Croom, and he takes off his glasses and wipes his eyes. It looks a little strange, to see hands that big wiping at tears. "When she got shot ... all that lady was trying to do was help someone. Just plain ol' people, trying to do the right thing, and they killed her."

That was perhaps the first time the young Sylvester Croom realized the awful cost of the change that was taking place around him. And suddenly it very much matters that a black man is the head coach at a school in the conference of the Bear, the Big Orange, Death Valley, and the Loveliest Village on the Plain. Because if it doesn't matter, then what was all that suffering for?

"It was coming, sooner or later," says Ming, who is white, a few days after she approached Croom in a Starkville diner and asked him for his autograph, for Buster. She even had her picture taken with him. Not too long ago, this would have been scandalous. Now the autograph—a black man's name—is in a frame, a thing of value. Southerners get where they need to go, Ming says sweetly, "but we don't like to be pushed."

Nearly 40 years have passed since the first black scholarship athlete took the field in the SEC. And a lifetime, it seems, has passed since Sylvester Croom kicked a field goal over the clothes-line in his yard in Tuscaloosa and dreamed about being swept up into glory on the Crimson Tide. But even as he entered high school, the only players wearing Alabama jerseys were white. "No way I should be sitting here," he says from his MSU office, his mind hung up—for just a moment—on that clothesline.

Then, that quickly, he is standing before a team of SEC athletes—his boys—in the Mississippi State field house. He's one of only five black head football coaches in Division I-A, five out of 117. His players sit straight and tense, and you get the feeling that if he told them to jump off a roof, they would balk only long enough to write notes to their mamas.

"We're kind of tickled with him," says Jimmy Cowan, class of 1959, a retired engineer who lives in Aberdeen, Miss., and drives his recreational vehicle to all the Bulldogs' home and away games and—like most white Mississippians of his generation—went to all-white schools.

"It was a chance to do the right thing," Douglas Brinkley, historian, author, and director of the Eisenhower Center for American Studies in New Orleans, says of Croom's hiring. But, because of the coach's credentials, "it was also a safe thing."

Head football coach of a state school in the South is a position whose prestige rivals, and in some places exceeds, that of the governor. In the increasingly conservative, increasingly Republican

South, the first black coach in the SEC had to be someone too solid to question, too deserving to deny. "We have to be able to say we were looking for the best football coach, not to cure the ills of our state," Brinkley says of the Southern mind-set.

Croom wishes, of course, that his father had lived to see this. The Reverend Sylvester Croom Sr. passed in January 2000, but not before he saw many of the barriers that he once peered through knocked to the ground. His sons, Kelvin and Sylvester Jr., both played for the Bear, and Croom Sr. became the Alabama football team's chaplain, invoking God on behalf of whites and blacks (but rarely Auburn). He died too soon to see his older son take over an SEC program. But Kelvin, the baby brother, knows what their father probably would have done. He would have placed a hand on Sylvester's shoulder and, in a voice that always seemed to be dropping down from a mountain, told him something you had to know Croom Sr. to understand: "Son, you had the best ice cream."

In the glow of the stage lights, in a community theater in Tuscaloosa, a wrongly accused black man stood trial for his life. It was only theater, only another local interpretation of the classic *To Kill a Mockingbird*, but in the pitch dark of the auditorium, sweat beaded on the Reverend Dr. Kelvin Croom's face. In his mind he did not see an actor, a stage, or the curtain that could drop and cover the ugliness of the story with thick, soft velvet. "In my mind," he says, "I saw my father."

He saw the same South, the same story, but this one unfolded in Holt, Ala., not Harper Lee's Maycomb, in the mid-1940s. A white woman had been raped and had told authorities that three black men had done it. Justice had to be swift, for the sake of society. It did not need to be accurate.

Sylvester Croom Sr. had been out rabbit hunting with two of his brothers. They had blood and hair on their clothes when police went for them, acting on a tip from a black woman who said she had seen the Croom boys splashed with red.

Police arrested them and put them in jail, even as local clergymen tried to convince authorities that the boys were innocent. A short time later, fearing for the safety of their prisoners, officials spirited the boys out of the local jail and took them to a Birmingham lockup.

All this happened before Kelvin and Sylvester Jr. were born, and the story would be told and retold, sharpened every time, an old razor that still draws blood. How close, Kelvin would always think.

How close his father had come to being another victim of a doomed, hateful way of life. "It was hard to sit through that play," Kelvin says.

The elder Croom's arrest might have cowed some men, might have made some men walk with their eyes glued to the tops of their shoes. Sylvester Croom Sr. straightened up tall in the service of God and took to wearing a cowboy hat. "You can't keep a good man down," he would boom from his pulpit at Beautiful Zion A.M.E. Zion Church in southwest Tuscaloosa, "and you can't keep a bad man up."

He was 6'4", 290 pounds, and on the football field at all-black Alabama A&M he had hit like a pickup truck. The stories he told and the ones told about him made his boys want to be him. "Against South Carolina State, in about 1950, he picked up a ball on the one or two and ran it all the way back for a touchdown," says Sylvester Jr. "I'd always liked that story, and in my head I always saw myself doing that."

In the pulpit Sylvester Sr. was demanding, unbending. If he saw his sons acting a fool or just not paying attention, he would point one big finger at them, silently passing sentence, and it augered right into their hearts. "You didn't enjoy any of the rest of that sermon," Kelvin says. "You knew what was coming when you got home."

As the Civil Rights movement took hold of Alabama, Sylvester Sr. lived the nonviolence that the Reverend Dr. Martin Luther King Jr. preached, but in the afternoons he would stand at the practice field fence and stare at the vaunted all-white Alabama football team, and dream. His sons stood with him, dreaming too.

To work beside a man or share a lunch counter with him or sit with him on a bus, that meant something. But to line up across from him in full pads and slam into him with all the power in your body, without any consequence beyond the outcome of a play, a game? When was a man more free than that?

Tuscaloosa, like the rest of Alabama, was rigidly segregated, with an insidious Klan presence. The Alabama campus was off-limits—Sylvester Croom Jr. never strolled across it, or even walked past it. He saw it from the windows of cars.

Once, in the midst of the Civil Rights movement, an ice-cream vendor came to Croom Sr. for counsel. "He was having difficulty," Kelvin says. It was a matter of conscience. The vendor was known to have the best ice cream in Tuscaloosa, and people—blacks and whites—lined up for it. He served whites through the front door and blacks through the back door. His business thrived, within the conventions of society. But it was a time to question convention, and the vendor, who was white, wanted to do something revolutionary. He wanted to serve blacks and whites through one door.

"He knew what was right, but he needed someone to lean on," Kelvin says.

"You do have the best ice cream in town," Croom Sr. told the vendor. The people would have to decide if it was worth standing beside someone of another color to get some. "Serve it from one door," he told the vendor, and make it about flavor, not about color.

There is a Southern tradition of lamentation when it comes to daddies. Men have been known to drink too much and talk and cry all night, remembering. But a sober man sings the best songs of praise.

"I guess the best sermon he preached was the one he lived," Kelvin says. "If anybody did without in our house, it was him. It was important to him what Mom, me, and Sly thought of him. He always told us to love people, to never hold grudges." It would have been just words if Kelvin and Sylvester Jr. had not known that their father had a reason to hate.

"He always said, 'You got to do right every day,'" Sylvester Jr. says.

"Work within the system when you can," Kelvin says.

"Fight by the rules," Sylvester Jr. says.

"And," Kelvin says, "have the best ice cream."

The spit wad caught him square in the face. It was his welcome to the overwhelmingly white junior high school in Tuscaloosa that he and, later, his brother attended.

He did not do a thing except wipe it off. "I look around, and I'm ticked, and I see who did it," Sylvester Croom Jr. says.

"Follow Dr. King's teachings, no matter what happens," his father had said.

Later that day, at football practice, Sylvester Jr. saw the boy who had thrown the spit wad—across the line from him in pads. "I hit him as hard as I could," Croom says, and he laughs out loud. It was a bone-numbing hit. "I would find a way to hit him ... every day."

But is that in keeping with Dr. King's teachings? "Sometimes," Kelvin says, "you slip."

White students refused to be Sylvester Jr.'s study partners, to share a locker with him, to let him into groups formed for class projects. He was not so much mistreated as ignored. The thing he hated most was the silence, which he endured even in a hallway that rang with voices and pounding feet and banging lockers. "The biggest fear I had was just being isolated," he says. For all the interaction he had with students in some classes, "I might as well have been a tree."

But kindnesses, and courage, filled the silence. The practice field was three miles from the school, and the ninth-grade football players had to get there as best they could. The handful of black players did not have a ride, and it took time to walk three miles. They would have to miss part of practice. But the first week of football a car pulled up, and a white player, a quarterback named Stan Bradford, motioned the black players over. There was not room enough for all of them to sit in the backseat, so a couple of them squeezed into the front, beside Bradford's mother.

Every one of them knew that this was taboo, that people had been killed for less. "You just didn't sit with no white lady," Croom says. "It seems like a little thing, but that lady did something that wasn't supposed to be done in that time, and it changed my world."

Another challenge to convention came from the Tuscaloosa High football coach, Billy Henderson. Other Alabama coaches had black players, but they left them at home or on the bench when they played in racially charged places such as Montgomery—or across the state line in Mississippi. But no one was going to tell Henderson who could start on his football team. "It took courage, but he believed in us," says Kelvin. "He was some man."

Sylvester Jr. played practically every position—even did some kicking. He was big, strong, 5'11" and 195 pounds, and while his team won only about six games his whole high school career, he caught the attention of colleges. One day a recruiter from Alabama stood at the Crooms' door.

Sylvester Jr. had believed that Alabama was for dreaming, and that A&M was for playing. But Wilbur Jackson had broken the color line as the Crimson Tide's first black recruit, in 1970, and Croom followed him there the next year. He remembers his first day of college. White players, knowing he was from Tuscaloosa, asked him how to find this place or that on campus.

"How would I know?" he said. "I never been here."

"I wanted one thing," Croom says. "I was sick of losing. I wanted to win." At that time all Alabama did was win. "And I wanted to

stand there at the foot of Denny Chimes as the captain of the
football team." His teammates, predominantly white, made him
that in 1974.

As a center in the wishbone Croom won honors—he was on
Kodak's All-America team and voted the best offensive lineman in
the SEC—and signed with the New Orleans Saints, for whom he
would play one game. But coaching would be Croom's football
future, and he was an assistant for 10 years at Alabama before
moving on to the pros where he was an assistant coach at Tampa
Bay, Indianapolis, San Diego, Detroit, and finally Green Bay. Then,
last May, Alabama fired coach Mike Price. Mama called, as Bryant
liked to say, but the door closed in Croom's face before he could
step inside.

"At one point I thought I had the job," Croom says, and Alabama—
by all accounts—strongly considered him before settling on former
Tide quarterback Mike Shula, who was nearly 11 years younger
than Croom, and that much less experienced.

Croom loves Alabama. His brother, who took over their father's
place in the pulpit at Tuscaloosa's College Hill Baptist Church,
leads the devotion before every Crimson Tide home basketball
game. Not getting the Tide football job hurt Sylvester, says Kelvin.
"He had been successful at every juncture. He was All-America.
Why not bring him back?"

But Sylvester would no more bad-mouth Alabama than he
would his family. Asked about not getting the job, he thinks a
minute. Then he says, "I just remember something Coach Bryant
said: 'Go where they want you.'

"The interest Alabama showed probably opened this door for
me," he says of Mississippi State. "They wanted me. Not a black
coach. They wanted me."

The MSU athletic director, Larry Templeton, is not worried that
Croom will leave for Alabama if things go badly for Shula and
Mama calls again. "Not the least bit," he says. "Mississippi State
gave him the opportunity, and he will remember that."

He will have every chance to succeed and will not be penalized
for transgressions that may have been committed by his predecessors.
His new contract would be extended for each year the school
might be on probation. "If there are NCAA sanctions, his four
years will begin when those sanctions are over," Templeton says.

Any backlash to the hiring of a black coach has been minuscule,
says Lee, the MSU president. "We got mail from Ole Miss graduates"

praising MSU—and some from Alabama, expressing regret that Alabama didn't get him. The response "reaffirms that [people] just accepted that it is time. Private giving for athletics has increased. We're quite happy."

Mississippi State, at least for now, has more pressing problems than its place in civil rights history. "The program has to be above reproach," Lee says. He felt Croom would guarantee that. But then, of course, he also has to win in the SEC. Recruiting has gone better than expected for a team under an NCAA cloud, but the players will have to line up against faster, stronger, more talented teams, such as LSU, and bleed. They need a reason to do that. They say they will do it for Bulldog pride and a place in history. Everyone says color doesn't matter, at first. Then you ask them who they are, where they are from, and....

Deljuan Robinson's mama mopped floors and drove a school bus and worked every other job she could find to give her four sons a chance. "She raised us by herself," said Robinson, a 6'4", 295-pound defensive lineman from Hernando, Miss. "She made us finish school. Wasn't nothin' easy about that." If growing up poor and black wasn't a deep enough hole, the 19-year-old Robinson found out two years ago that he had a leaky heart valve. A scar from open-heart surgery bisects his chest. Now a black man will succeed or fail as a head coach in the SEC based in part on how Robinson performs. "I'll be proud to take on a role like that," Robinson says. "She'll be proud too," he says of his mom.

Quarterback Omarr Conner's father is on dialysis, and his mother used to work at a chicken plant and now works at a fish plant in Macon, Miss., about 30 minutes southeast of Starkville. College football was supposed to be a ticket to something better. Conner watched his first season, under former Bulldogs coach Jackie Sherrill, collapse into a 2-10 agony.

Conner will never forget the first team meeting under Croom. "I thought, God has sent us someone to save us. I am fixing to play for Coach Croom, and Coach Croom played under Bear Bryant. And I can tell my child, 'I was part of history. I made history with the first black coach in the SEC.'"

Croom knows how hard it is to keep believing when the things you want seem so far away. He is uncomfortable being a symbol. But there is no denying it, really.

Somewhere, in a backyard in Alabama or Mississippi, a boy is kicking field goals over the clothesline and throwing touchdown passes to himself, lobbing the ball so high that he can be quarterback and receiver all in one.

"He needs to know," Croom says, "that things do change."

# BORN TOO LATE

*Southern Living,* Southern Journal: January 2013

T he house is a century old. It towers into the treetops from its corner lot in Tuscaloosa, two massive stories of yellow brick with a porch so wide and deep I have watched little boys play football across it. The house is built around a massive staircase, the kind you see only in the movies. You expect to see an elegant woman descend it in her evening gown—I imagine Lauren Bacall. A ghost walks its upper rooms, people say. I was a guest here for months and never saw her. Still, something dwells in that house, something from another age.

The couple who welcomed me inside, Ken and Jessie Fowler, are true friends. They are almost a generation older than me, a generation of grace and civility. Their house has more rooms than a Marriott, but mostly we lived in the kitchen, talking about the places they had seen and the times they had lived, of Manhattan in an age of miniskirts, and Miami Beach when Gleason and Sinatra played, and glorious football teams that traveled by train.

It was there, beside a refrigerator filled with limitless pie, I realized I was a man lost in time. I had always been most comfortable in the past. But I had never really wrapped my mind around it till then, staring at a forkful of lemon icebox, talking about how, in a bad wreck, you really can't beat a Lincoln.

I do not want to turn back time. Too many people want to do

that already. Too much good, too much justice has come to be, out of the darkness of our past. But I felt a comfort in that room, and in that company, I have seldom known. Maybe that is because by taking me into their past, they took me back to my own.

The past we spoke of had music that did not make you want to murder the radio. It poured sweetly, static and all, from big console sets and Art Deco Bakelites, flew as if on a magic carpet from the orchestras in the Blue Room in New Orleans. Hank Williams played the VFW then, and rode a big Cadillac a thousand miles to an American Legion to do it again. I would have liked to have seen that. Now, country music sounds like pop music in a bad cowboy hat from Stuckey's. The radio seems mostly to consist of men hollering about how people do not belong. When I was a boy, we listened to Swap Shop, hoping someone was unloading a hubcap for a '66 Corvair, and heard Merle Haggard sing, "That's the Way Love Goes."

I used to love television. We had two channels—three if the antenna was turned toward Anniston—but there was always something on. Now I flip through banality till my thumb is sore. Used to be, the worst thing on TV was wrestling. Now they tell me I can watch every football game being played on this planet on my phone. I do not want to watch a football game on my phone. How silly would I look, hollering at my own palm?

I used to love cars. I loved tail fins, loved the sculpture of Detroit steel. My first Mustang cost $542. Last summer, my car's catalytic converter went out and it cost me $2,500.

Sometimes it seems I do not like anything anymore. I do not like outsourcing, or multitasking, or fusion restaurants.

But I remember a night when I stayed in that house. I came in very late, and eased quietly through the big rooms, every ancient board creaking underfoot. As I started up the stairs, I heard the faint sound of music. Big Band, maybe? Glenn Miller? And as I eased up the stairs I heard, I believe, the sound of two people dancing.

I liked that.

# AFTERWORD

I spent a large part of my life writing about places far from here. I once banged out a story in Peshawar, Pakistan, while eating a chicken salad sandwich, as demonstrators shouted their displeasure of all things American in the glow of burning flags and some steel-belted radials.

I was told, by well-meaning people, that I should tell the angry crowds that I was, in fact, Canadian.

I just looked at them.

How in the world do you pretend to be from Calgary, when you talk like me?

I thought, briefly, I would say I was from Alabama, and hope they did not know exactly where that was, but I am pretty sure that, if I had, someone would have answered back:

"Roll Tide!"

I am a Southern man, for better or worse. It is not a suit of clothes I can change when I feel like it.

I wish, at times, we were different. I wish we cared more about the working poor. I wish we acted on logic more than passion. I wish we were more open-minded, at least just a little bit. I wish that.

But you can't go ripping off pieces of that suit. You would be naked in time. It is a sometimes ragged, ill-fitting suit, but it really is the only one I have.

I was honored to do this book, which is a kind of love story to the South, and I hope you liked it. I have loved writing about our food, our ways, our proclivities. It is the softer side of my writing life, the side my own people seem to love more than anything else. I once did a story about Japanese junk bonds. That pretty much passed unnoticed in Calhoun County, Alabama.

But you write a story about a good pan of cornbread dressing, or a good dog, or football of any kind, well, you have got what we here in the business call a reader.

Loving this part of the world requires a sense of humor, and if you made it this far, you obviously are equipped with one.

It takes a sense of humor, too, to put up with me for any time at all.

I have been writing for a living since 1977. Many of you have been with me that long.

I can only assume that the 100 percent humidity, and the clouds of mosquitos, and the relentless heat of too many dog days of summer have affected your judgment.

# INDEX

# ACKNOWLEDGMENTS

I'd like to begin by thanking family, because without them there would be no foundation, nothing to hold up the world of stories that have given me my writing life. First, let me thank Dianne and Jake, who not only gave me that support but provided me with inspiration and kindness and sometimes even some much needed criticism. For a decade, you have been in so many sentences, as inspiration or ideas, or in spirit. In that same light, I would like to thank the members of my Calhoun County family, both the living and those who have done gone on. I still don't know if I believe in ghosts, but I believe in memories and I think it amounts to the same thing.

But to want to tell a story and to get to tell a story are sometimes two very different things, and for that I would like to thank the people of *Southern Living* and Oxmoor House: Sid Evans, Lindsay Bierman, Katherine Cobbs, Jennifer Cole, Kim Cross, Nellah McGough, Susan Alison, Maribeth Jones, Anja Schmidt, Margot Schupf, Lacie Pinyan, Sarah Waller, Erica Sanders-Foege, Diane Rose Keener, Carol Pittard, Bryan Christian, and Courtney Greenhalgh.

For the same reasons I want to thank Amanda Urban and Liz Farrell and the other kind people at ICM. If it were not for y'all, I'd probably still be on the end of a shovel handle.

There are so many other people who have helped prop up my writing life—friends and sometimes strangers—who had a tale to tell me, or just helped pry something loose in my memory. Y'all know who you are.

And I guess I need to pay my respects to the place itself...to the brown mules knee deep in the yellow broom sage, the black cats suffering in the heat, and that sifting sound in the pines. I would miss this place if I were ever taken from it.